Psychoanalysis and the Love of Arabic

Psychoanalysis and the Love of Arabic
Hall of Mirrors

Nadia Bou Ali

EDINBURGH
University Press

Edinburgh University Press is one of the leading university presses in the UK. We publish academic books and journals in our selected subject areas across the humanities and social sciences, combining cutting-edge scholarship with high editorial and production values to produce academic works of lasting importance. For more information visit our website: edinburghuniversitypress.com

© Nadia Bou Ali, 2020, 2021

Edinburgh University Press Ltd
The Tun – Holyrood Road
12 (2f) Jackson's Entry
Edinburgh EH8 8PJ

First published in hardback by Edinburgh University Press 2020

Typeset in 11/15 Times New Roman by
Manila Typesetting Company

Croydon, CR0 4YY

A CIP record for this book is available from the British Library

ISBN 978 1 4744 0984 1 (hardback)
ISBN 978 1 4744 9174 7 (paperback)
ISBN 978 1 4744 0985 8 (webready PDF)
ISBN 978 1 4744 0986 5 (epub)

The right of Nadia Bou Ali to be identified as author of this work has been asserted in accordance with the Copyright, Designs and Patents Act 1988 and the Copyright and Related Rights Regulations 2003 (SI No. 2498).

Contents

Acknowledgements — vii

Introduction: The Mirror of Language — 1

1 Literature as a Ruthless Excavator of Culture: From the Literary Mode of Being to *Lituratterre* — 19

2 ~~Why is There *Lalangue* Rather than Nothing?~~ Love of *Lugha* and *Lalangue* — 70

3 Piercing the Bull's Eye: The Sexual (Non-)Relation — 98

4 A Liberal Psycho-theology — 137

Conclusion: The Abstractions of *Homo Economicus*: Now a Stomach, Now an Anus — 161

Notes — 184

Index — 226

Acknowledgements

This book is dedicated to Layla who thinks that 'history is a nothing that cannot be ruined' and to Ray for all the love despite the nothing we have to give.

I would like to thank St Antony's College, Oxford University and Eugene Rogan for hosting me during the completion of this book. The project started in Oxford years ago and came to completion there after many long but necessary detours. Thanks are due to the Andrew W. Mellon Foundation for the Early Career Scholars Program team grant which gave me the time to write this book. Thanks also to the few but precious interlocutors I have had over the past years, in particular Faisal Devji, Mladen Dolar, Lisa Wedeen, Rohit Goel, Angela Harutyunyan, Samo Tomsic, Ahmad al-Dailami and Sami Khatib.

Arabists, get lost! Zayd Struck 'Amr' will ne'er set bread on the table.
— Ahmad Faris al-Shidyaq, *Leg Over Leg*

al-lugha mir' at al-umma
[Language is the mirror of the nation.]
— Ibrahim al-Yaziji, *Al-Tabib*

Saying remains forgotten behind what is said.
— Jacques Lacan, *L'étourdit*

Introduction: The Mirror of Language

In *Why Are the Arabs Not Free?* Mustapha Safouan claims that the existing schism between spoken and written Arabic instils a mode of domination that commands a 'voluntary servitude' to a master signifier: a signifier literally incarnated in the figure of the leader. Safouan argues that this state of servitude arises from within Arabic-speaking societies in modernity, and that domination gets generated 'internally' rather than through the external forces of colonisation alone. In Safouan's account, the separation of written from spoken Arabic disrupts the creation of 'culture' or the symbolic sphere of society, which is always fundamentally mediated by language. The co-optation of speech by the apparatuses of the State relies upon robbing people of the possibilities through which acts of freedom become possible. Safouan thus maintains, contra Edward Said, that speaking truth to power is not adequate as a strategy for liberation, but rather functions like a fantasy, precisely because 'power entails deafness to such speech'.[1] The condition of unfreedom in the Arabic-speaking world is premised on three factors: the isolation of people from the realm of thought through the confinement of writing to a classical language; the religious nature of the State's authority which, like God, commands the sole right of interpretation; and the subjection to an imaginary father or patriarch – in the figure of the monarch or the supreme leader – which places authority outside intersubjective relations, thereby rendering it unquestionable to its subjects.[2]

Absolute authority is analogous to the name-of-the-father who is removed from circulation, from the profane world of exchange, frozen as an imaginary image with which subjects identify.

In 1992, Safouan translated Étienne de La Boétie's *Discourse on Voluntary Servitude* (c. 1549/1576) into Arabic in an attempt to engage with the unquestioning faith in the figure of the unifying leader of masses in the Arab world (Gamel Abdel Nasser in particular). In a psychoanalytic vein, Safouan posits that there is a fundamental link between language and law. Despotism does not work simply through coercive force, but by instituting a transcendental master signifier, a One, who commands a 'voluntary' form of servitude. According to La Boétie, the love of liberty is unnatural to the human animal. Humans instead seem to be adaptable to servitude, even gaining satisfaction from the loss of freedom. Furthermore, 'the monarch can survive only as long as he takes every precaution to prevent the transformation of his authority from being an object of faith to being an object of thought'.[3] This is precisely why the politics of writing, or the State's control over the written, is crucial for hindering freedom. The monopoly over the written, and the strict separation of the spoken from the written, produces a narcissistic linguistic community that is captured in a hall of mirrors and imaginary identifications. This procedure fundamentally obstructs the emergence of a culture that has an actuality (in the Hegelian sense); it confines culture to a transcendental circle by which the conditions of possibility of meaning are likewise the conditions of possibility of experience.[4] The actuality of culture, whereby culture is understood as the 'world of self-alienated spirit', implies both its destructive and formative potencies. For subjectivity to emerge and for freedom to be possible in the modern sense, a break from the phenomenal world of experience is necessary, i.e. culture is an enabling and constraining force. It is only by recognising the private constraints of community, culture and the stated moral law, that the subject can be free. The recognition of constraint, however, is only the first step in this direction, as anxiety expresses this path of the unfolding of self-consciousness. The cognising subject cannot be reduced to experience: experience is not simply to be accumulated and synthesised, rather it must be undone, unlearned, in the search for universals.[5]

For the scope of this book, I heed Safouan's argument that the politics of writing Arabic, and the particular tendency to identify truth in the written word, is deeply interwoven with the question of authority. Safouan's general claims about Arabic are prescriptive: i.e. his goal can be seen as promoting an ideal of moral consciousness whose determination or vocation would be to impose a culture upon the world, to become the concrete deduction of the law against the abstract determinations of the law, which rule Arabic-speaking societies. The validity of Safouan's claims about the politics of writing notwithstanding, I argue that the act of *reading* modern Arabic texts is equally important and also has serious implications.

This book proposes that there is an unconscious subject that writes itself in modern Arabic through a symptomatic explosion of anxiety about language and culture beginning in the nineteenth-century intellectual movement known as the *nahda*. An unconscious subject writes, but it cannot read what it writes; it is a subject that has no self-knowledge. Thus, I develop a symptomatic reading of two formative Arab linguists and grammarians of the *nahda*: Ahmad Faris al-Shidyaq (1805–87) and Butrus al-Bustani (1819–83).

Ahmad Faris al-Shidyaq was born as Faris al-Shidyaq to a Maronite family from Ashkut in Mount Lebanon, and he led a life that took him from Beirut to Malta, Tunis, England, France and finally to Istanbul. His burial as Ahmad Faris al-Shidyaq in 1887 created a serious confusion: Christian and Muslim communities were uncertain as to where to place his body. A scribe by training, lineage and circumstance (caused by the early death of his father in a failed political rebellion against an Emir and the need to make use of the vast library he inherited), Shidyaq established in later stages of his life one of the leading Arabic printing presses in Istanbul, *al-Jawa'ib* press. It printed and published hundreds of titles in language, philology, philosophy, Islamic thought, jurisprudence, Ottoman law and fiction. The press published a political newspaper edited by Shidyaq, that also carried the name *al-Jawa'ib* (1860–84)). Shidyaq fled Mount Lebanon after his brother As'ad was placed in solitary confinement by the Maronite Patriarch in Qanubyn for his conversion to and preaching of Protestantism. As'ad's death in isolation infuriated Faris in his exile. He wrote harsh denunciations of the clergy and the Maronite Church of

Mount Lebanon. Shidyaq's life reveals the events that would make for a great novel, arguably one that he has already written: his renowned libertine novel *al-Saq 'ala al-saq* (*Leg Over Leg*) (1855). Upon leaving Mount Lebanon in 1834, he began his exilic life that took him to Malta where he established the teaching of Arabic and translated numerous texts for the Protestant Missionaries. Shidyaq went to Cambridge in 1848 where he worked with the philologist Samuel Lee on producing a translation of the Bible into Arabic. He also visited Paris and London about which he wrote his *Kashf al-mukhaba 'an tamaddun urupa wa-al-wasita fi ma 'rifat ahwal malta* (*The Unveiling of European Civilisation's Secrets and the Means of Knowing the Conditions of Malta*) (1881).

Regardless of the reasons for his conversion to Islam, Shidyaq gained for himself an access into Istanbul soon after he had converted. His relationships with the Porte cannot simply be attributed to his conversion. However, it is safe to say that his conversion hastened the expansion of his reputation among networks of intellectuals in the Empire. This is also largely due to the poems of praise that he wrote for the Ottoman Porte, an example of which is one that he wrote during the Ottoman–Prussian War in 1854. The Ottoman Sultan invited Shidyaq to work in the Porte's Translation Council (*Diwan al-tarjama al-sultany*). By 1859 Shidyaq had left Tunis for Istanbul where he remained until his death in 1887, his library was burned in a fire and most of his books were lost. Shidyaq's major works are: *al-Saq 'ala al-Saq* (*Leg Over Leg*) (1855), *al-Jasus 'ala al-qamus* (*The Spy on the Dictionary*) (1882) and the *Kashf al-mukhaba 'an funun urupa* (*The Unveiling of European Civilisation's Secrets*) (1881). I also examine a collection of essays and articles he wrote in his *al-Jawa'ib* journal between 1861 and 1890, on topics ranging from politics to the workings of the human imagination.

Butrus al-Bustani was born in 1819 in Iqlim al Kharub (an area in Mount Lebanon close to the Shuf Mountains). Having excelled at the local seminary and being prolific in Syriac and Arabic, he was accepted into the 'Ain Waraqa Maronite School. In 1840 Bustani met Eli Smith, a Protestant missionary who had settled in the city in 1833. Soon after this Bustani converted to Protestantism and established a National School in 'Abey for which he wrote a number of pedagogic texts on grammar and history.

He produced the first modern Arabic encyclopaedia, *Da'irat al ma'arif* (*The Circumference of Knowledge*) (1867–82). He was also intensely involved in journalism. He began publishing *al-Jinan*, a political, scientific and historical journal in 1870, which was circulated twice a month. In addition, he worked with his son on publishing *al-Janna*, 'a trade and literary weekly periodical' from 1870 until 1883. In 1871, Bustani and his son also edited and published a political and economic newspaper *al-Junayna* (*The Garden*) (with the intonation of a heaven on earth, Bustani uses *al-Jinan*, *al-Junayna* and *al-Janna* interchangeably to describe the Edenic state of a progressive civilisation fuelled by scientific progress and knowledge), which was circulated four times a week. One of the foremost modernisers of Arabic in the nineteenth century, Bustani produced a significant number of pedagogic texts on grammar and history. His books on Arabic grammar included *Musbah al-talib fi bahth al-matalib* (*The Learner's Beacon*) (1854), *Muftah al-musbah* (*The Key to the Beacon*) (1868), *Bulugh al-arb fi nahuw al-'arab* (*Advancing the Heart's Quest in the Nahuw of the Arabs*) (1887) and *Sharh diwan al-mutanabi* (*A Commentary on al-Mutanabi's Diwan*) (1860). He composed a dictionary in two volumes: *Muhit al-muhit* (*The Expanse of the Ocean*) (1870), and a summarised version of it, *Qatr al-muhit* (*The Circumference of the Ocean*) (1870). He also wrote two books on calculus: *Kashf al-hijab fi 'ilm al-hisab* (*Unveiling the Secrets of the Science of Calculus*) (first published in 1848 and in its ninth edition by 1885), and *Mask al-dafatir* (*On Accounting*). Bustani's public speeches at the Syrian Society have also been published whether in his own journals or in others like *al-Muqtataf*. The most prominent of these are '*Ta'lim al-nisa'* (The Education of Women) (1849), *al-Hay'a al-ijtima'iya, w-al-muqabala bayn al-'awa'id al-'arabiya w-al-ifranjiya* (On Social Organisation and the Comparison between Arab and European Cultures) (1849), and *Khutba fi adab al-Arab* (Speech on Arab Culture) (1859). Bustani's most celebrated work remains *Da'irat al-ma'arif*, the first Arabic encyclopaedia, of which he compiled and published the first seven volumes before his death. Bustani was also one of the founders of the Syrian Society (1847–52), and initiated an Arabic translation of the Bible with Eli Smith in 1847, which was completed by Cornelius Van Dyck and Nasif al-Yaziji (1800–71) in 1864.[6]

It would not be an exaggeration to say that Bustani and Shidyaq produced most of the major pedagogic, lexicographic and encyclopaedic works for Arabic in the nineteenth century. Between them we find an extensive archive of modern Arabic thought and to their neological work is owed much of the modern conceptual content of terms such as: ʿaada (habit), *adab* (culture), *ajala* (wheel), *al-dawla al-qanuniya* (state), *dababa* (tank), *ishtirakiya* (socialism), *jumhuriya* (republicanism), *mathaf* (museum), *mustashfa* (hospital), *safinat al-nar* (steam-ship) and *watan* (nation).[7] In many respects, the 'mirror of language' was the lifelong preoccupation of Shidyaq and Bustani.

The printed press flourished in the nineteenth-century Arabic-speaking parts of the Ottoman Empire and was established under the presumption that its products were 'mirrors of truth' in which readers could observe their world as an image. Language had to have not only the words and meanings adequate for the representation of reality but also a body of regulators and legislators to organise and fix the means by which words could be made and used correctly. For Shidyaq, *naht* – the grammatical function through which the creation of compound neologisms occurs – and the obsessive pursuit of mistakes in dictionaries were the only ways for language and thought to progress in history. Similarly, for Bustani, encyclopaedic and lexicographic methods held the promise of true progress and civilisation. Both men could only envision true civilisation through the refinement of Arabic into a language of knowledge and science because a language actively shapes the true nature of those who speak it. Arabic for them was a *Gestalt*: always an object of desire, it carried within it more than the sum total of its words and meanings.

A mirror, as we know, reflects an image of a double. Intuitively, doubled images might suggest to us a certain internal homogeneity or replicable sameness at work in the world. I posit that they are evidence, in fact, of a heterogeneous reality. A mirror image establishes the relationship between a subject and his image as that between an imaginary and a real. The mirror image gives the subject a sense of fixity, of an *I*. It reflects the mental state of the onlooker more than it does his body and the multifarious processes going on within it. As such it functions as a mediating object between the subject and reality. Most importantly it serves as what Jacques Lacan calls the 'drama whose internal thrust is precipitated from insufficiency to anticipation'[8] and thus manufactures a series of fantasies. A mirror image marks the subject with an alienating identity right at the moment of self-identification. The alienation is not limited to the subject's own self-perception but is implicit in the entire process of mirroring as a cognitive process, which implies some form of totality, of homogeneity between the subject and its reflection.

Lacan proposed that the specular image is crucial for the formation of subjectivity: in the mirror stage, the subject enters into the symbolic and begins to mediate itself through an Other. The illusion of autonomy however is kept up through the mirror representation of the subject. Lacan described this illusion as an originary neurosis that is at the core of the formation of selfhood. The captivation with a specular image is an inert passion. We can only recall how Narcissus's reflected image of his self revealed a tragic truth of irreconcilable love. In Ovid's myth, Narcissus was cursed to love and failed to command what he loved after he had scorned all those who loved him. He was cursed to thirst after his own image in a still water pond and to love a bodiless dream. Narcissus unknowingly came to desire himself: he would plunge his hands into the deceptive pool trying to embrace his self, but all that he could catch was water. Like a fool, he attempted in vain to catch a fleeting image that was nowhere to be found. He wondered in disbelief how he could be kept apart from his true love only by a little water.

The mirror of Arabic captures a similar moment of narcissistic identification. It is thus not surprising that mirrors and mirror images took on central roles as metaphors for understanding society and selfhood during the nineteenth century at the same time that the idea of an 'Arab nation' began to ossify into a historical form. Due to the increasing metaphorical and practical use of mirrors, the word *Mir'at* (mirror) even required a definition from Ibrahim al-Yaziji in 1884.[9] In an article in his *Al-tabib* magazine, Yaziji described the mirror as a sign of the civilisation of society: i.e. the ability to capture a reflection of the self is fundamental for civilisation to be possible. Yaziji even used a mirror to draw his own first self-portrait.[10]

The split subject that forms in the mirror stage at the intersection of nature and culture might as well be the only subject imaginable in modern civilised society. This book is interested in elucidating the 'imaginary knot of servitude'[11] that ties the subject to its image. But it maintains that servitude is not all that results from being captured by a specular image: there is also an excess element that emerges from the dialectic of identification, something that cannot be incorporated into the fundamental misrecognition that occurs between subject and other. This excess element is flagged by an anxiety that cannot be sublated into recognition. Far from providing a resolute self-identification, a happy ending of unity between the self and its image, the specular image in Jacques Lacan's formulation allows for the subject's entry into language, into the symbolic register, which is organised around desire. What the subject receives back from the mirror is an image that divides the subject, one that divides it with the problem of desire: the image reflected back is an Other, an object, with which the subject identifies. The subject seeks recognition from an Other only to receive back a misrecognised image of itself: an image of the Other's desire. This Other is not consciousness, but an unconsciousness whose recognition of 'me' implies that it lacks something without knowing it and that in the place of this lack I come to be as a subject. The specular image introduces a formative problem of subjectivity: the desire for the desire of an Other, the desire to be an object of the desire of an Other. Thus, the dialectic of identification with a specular image renders the subject an object affected by desire.

There is no neat mimetic correspondence with a mirror image without a third element, an excess remainder that has the status of an object-cause-of-desire: 'I identify you [the image in the mirror, the one to whom I am speaking] with the object that you lack'.[12] The curious identification with Arabic renders Arabic an object-cause-of-desire, the pursuit of which generates a state of anxiety. After all, can one imagine seeing their tongue speaking to them from an elsewhere? Surely this is an impossible sight, close to the scene of Oedipus facing his very own eyes lying on the ground before him after he has gouged them out. This scene is pivotal for modern Arabic thought but not particular to it; it is a symptom of subjectivity in modernity and calls for a particular kind of reading.

The symptomatic reading that I propose in this book is not simply an act of interpretation, another form of reflexive mirroring; it seeks to produce a new knowledge. It is a reading that identifies an invisible gap that presents itself in the written text. There is an element in Bustani's and Shidyaq's texts that can only be made present by recognising its absence. But this is not a deconstructionist reading in the Derridean mode, by which a text's *aporias* enable its decomposition into mutually incompatible narratives or contradictory arguments – a manoeuvre that is satisfying to perform but ends typically at an impasse, always oscillating between blindness and insight. This symptomatic reading proceeds in a different manner. Just as the symptom implies a fall (Latin *symptōma*, from Greek σύμπτωμα: chance, accident, mis-chance, disease; συμπίπτειν: to fall together, fall upon),[13] it is a falling upon something that is there but strikes as invisible. It is not about capturing a missing letter but about capturing that which is there but cannot be seen. It is about searching for 'those unsuccessful (i.e. inadequate) modes of expression that exemplify symptomatic procedures of misrecognition'.[14] The act of reading that Bustani's and Shidyaq's texts call forth is not simply reading as a form of listening-to the meanings intended by the author – but reading as a form of knowing, the elaboration of a new discourse from the articulation of a silence.

In this sense, the knowledge that can be garnered from the written is not about the rediscovery of a meaning that is already there, but a chance for the emergence of thought.[15] The knowledge that is rendered possible in this sense is one of distancing and separation, an act of circumscribing the difference within the work and 'demonstrating that it is other than it is'.[16] Reading a literary text then becomes the task of identifying *how* the specific form of knowledge it carries has been already produced; it is a tracing of the very principle that is a condition of production of a mode of writing, without which the object of this knowledge would not have been possible.

From the end of the nineteenth century and throughout the twentieth, the spectre of *lugha* has haunted the Arabic-speaking world. Countless odes, poems and prose pieces have been penned in praise of the *lugha* mother tongue. Shidyaq described *lugha* as an oceanic expanse that in concealing its depth reveals the plight of the modern subject:[17] 'My greatest ambition has been to dive deep into the sea of this language, to make sense of its seemingly contradictory meanings, bring them closer to the eye, and explain them through evidence'.[18] The task of the linguist, one that Shidyaq uneasily inhabited, was to tease out language's 'aesthetic secrets, its wisdom, and the artistry of its making and bring them out of concealment'.[19] However, the suitor can only remain at its shoreline, at the 'stainearth'[20] of deletion where the sea of language both reveals its presence and conceals its content. This passion for language or the love of language arises at the moment of standardisation and lexicographical work – dictionary and encyclopaedia making – during the nineteenth century. It is a passion that is unleashed coincidentally to the transformation of language into a pedagogical object of linguistic study.

Historians and literary theorists alike have defined modernity in the Arabic-speaking world as a 'literary modernity'.[21] Indeed the intellectual history of modern Arabic thought in the past few decades has taken a cultural and literary turn in which *nahda*, the modern intellectual movement, has been erroneously defined as a singularity. As a singularity, *nahda* is seen as having its own immanent logic: a linguistic and translation project unfolding under the aegis of philology. The focus on reading modern Arabic thought through the paradigm of a 'literary modernity' is premised on the depiction of thinking as a mere unfolding of the deconstructionist impulses of language – on rule-breaking and the appropriation of signs – and it is directed as a critique of 'colonial epistemologies' that are seen to be the sole import of modernity upon non-European societies the world over.[22] By maintaining that thinking is language, which implies a process of signification, and that Arabic is a community of discourse, this recent paradigm of Arabic intellectual history assumes that the sole function of language (or discourse) is the reproduction of community. Countering colonial epistemologies leads to affirming Arabic as a specific 'community of discourse'[23] while claiming to maintain the universality of the question of language. In this logic, a linguistic community is used to replace national belonging. But what are the assumptions upon which a linguistic community is defined if not national ones? In socio-linguistics, a discourse community is a community with a shared goal or purpose, and it uses communication for the achievement of these goals. A discourse community is distinguished from a speech community: where the latter functions according to the principle of inheritance (language and blood), the former recruits members by persuasion or an agreed-upon set of codes. A discourse community is meant to agree upon a shared *lexis* or lexicon; in other words, language serves the organic function of maintaining the genus of a group or a community. The notion of a 'literary modernity' explains literary difference through cultural or national identities. This principally assumes that non-Western literature is radically different and singular because it is allegorical, because it is overtly and consciously political and libidinal, and because, most importantly, it doesn't have an unconscious.[24] This assumed homogeneity between thought and language in its best version would assume communicative rationality as its horizon, but recent historians of Arabic thought generally dismiss this modern dictum as a mind-centric colonial epistemology. However, we cannot ignore that the modern passion for language – Arabic in this case – is a linguistic one. Unlike philology, linguistics circumscribes the field that brings the position of the observer into question: even though signification in discourse is guarded by a master signifier, no one is the master of language or its lawgiver. Linguistics thereby introduces the difference between the synchronic and diachronic and subverts the philological identification of etymology with logic: it asks, 'for whom are they the same?'[25]

Thus, it is not enough to affirm an imaginary linguistic community of Arabic in the course of refuting liberal and national identification. This merely substitutes one allegory of belonging for another. Moreover, it assumes that an Arabic community of discourse – a category that I argue obfuscates modern thought in Arabic – is merely analogical to any other community of discourse, and that all communities of discourse are particulars of equal value that cannot and should not be subsumed under universals.

Alain Badiou deems this trend in thinking 'democratic materialism', which is grounded in the axiomatic statement, 'there are only bodies and languages'. There is an ideological procedure at play when capitalist modernity is translated into the language of cultural difference. This materialism for Badiou, is a 'bio-materialism', a 'materialism of life' of 'mortal bodies, suffering lives'. The equation on which this materialism rests is 'existence=individual=body':

> Communities and cultures, colours and pigments, religions and religious orders, uses and customs, disparate sexualities, public intimacies and the publicity of the intimate: everything and everyone deserves to be recognized and protected by the law. But democratic materialism does admit of a global halting point for its tolerance. A language that does not recognize the universal juridical and normative equality of languages does not deserve to gain from this equality. A language that claims to regulate all the others, to rule all bodies, will be called dictatorial and totalitarian. Then it is no longer a matter of tolerance, but of a 'right to intervention': legal, international, and, if necessary, military. Offensive actions serve to rectify the universalistic claims, as well as the linguistic sectarianism. Bodies will have to pay for their excesses of language.[26]

Badiou defines his own intervention in the terms of a materialist dialectic: there are bodies and languages but there also truths. Truth acts as a third term that is a gap between the first two, a parallax of their synthesis. Truths are 'generic multiplicities' that cannot be discerned according to the logic of linguistic predication or through propositional statements. Badiou singles out the subject as the point of truth. 'Generic multiplicity' here means that the universal does not possess any particular property or is indeed indifferent to particular determination. The universal *is for everyone* by being *indifferent* to social, national, sexual, or inheritance principles: 'with the amorous couple, which is universal because it produces an undivided truth about the difference between sexuated positions; with scientific theory, which is universal to the extent that it removes every trace of its provenance in its elaboration; or with artistic configurations whose subjects are works, and in which, [. . .] the particularity of the author has been abolished'.[27]

Universality is a truth procedure that can be located in thought, or in the subject-thought, whereby the subject emerges as the local point of relation in a procedure constituted by the dialectic between subject and truth. Further, the universal is one and the same with truth: the universal is an 'incalculable emergence', it emerges from an event that cannot be adduced in the existing system of predicative knowledge. The universal truth cannot be part of what everyone already knows about politics, culture, sex, or art; it is not part of encyclopaedic knowledge, which is premised on assuming a certain neutrality of knowledge. Universality in this sense punctures the existing order of knowledge. It cannot be the mere addition of multiplicities, particular bodies and languages, but it arises from a split in the particular position. Concrete universality is when a particular species does not fit its universal genus, or when a particular element negates the very universal features of its genus. A concrete universality is determined by the constant questioning of the ideological notions and real abstractions that define the 'content' of identity. Real abstractions are determinants of capitalist society (e.g. legal persons, commodity fetishism, value). And as abstract categories they function concretely, they come alive: the legal person, the state, the nation, are but a guise, a mask or an impersonation that presuppose a generic essence (which does not originally exist) in their masquerade. These real abstractions mediate social relations not by hiding or concealing some pre-existent genus but rather by staging a relation in the absence of one. Capital is a system of real abstractions that articulate a system of differences and reveal a 'Real' of abstraction, 'an absence of determinations, the fact that [capital] has no historical or cultural content per se'.[28]

The question of universality is fundamental to this book, for the claim that I wish to make is that there is an unconscious and universal truth in modern Arabic thought which cannot be discerned by discourses that maintain a relativistic account of knowledge or modernity. This unconscious truth defies any identity principle: it presents itself as an antagonism that cannot be resolved by the existing terms of a particular identity. I argue that this node of antagonism is particularly evident in the modern recognition of uncanny elements in the subject's 'own house'; there is a misrecognition of Arabic itself as the mother tongue, a misrecognition of habit and custom, and most importantly a misrecognition of the knowledge around sex, sexuality, and the feminine and masculine. This misrecognition, or self-relating disavowal ('this is not me') allows for the emergence of a subject effect: i.e. there is something in me that is more than the symbolic gestures and identifications provided by society. This subject-effect makes it appear as though there is a subject prior to external processes of interpellation; it is an ideological effect par excellence, but it occurs in tandem with a renunciation of the supposed secret treasure or *agalma* of the subject that precedes interpellation. This book treads through the dialectics of subjectivity in modernity beginning with the reclaiming of subjectivity beyond liberal interpellation; continuing with the subsequent retroactive misrecognition of subjectivity (Arabness, Arabic and the Arabs); culminating in an overwhelming anxiety around habit (are we only the result of unconscious mechanical functions?); and concluding with subjectivity's self-renunciation.

An anxiety is generated from the de-familiarisation of the familiar, from the appearance of symbolic and cultural identification as uncanny: it is an anxiety that emerges from the context of a liberalising Ottoman empire and an exposure to life in global cities like Cairo, Istanbul, London and Paris.[29] The emergence of Beirut itself as a *fin-de-siècle* city in the nineteenth century is pivotal and occurred in tandem with a formative event: the peasant uprisings against the feudal lords between 1858 and 1860. These uprisings turned into a sectarian conflict, or 'civil war' as Butrus al-Bustani deemed it, and became the moment of origin for conceiving the nation-form and a notion of citizenship shaped according to a liberal ideal of the social contract (as an exchange of rights and duties). Despite the lack of a clearly defined territorial state formation for Mount Lebanon, the discourse around the nation was markedly different from that of empire.

The difference consists in the fact that the nation came to be perceived as a spiritual substance: love of the nation is an act of faith, *hub al-watan min al-iman* as Butrus al-Bustani claimed. The nation, *al-watan*, would become the expression of the individual's essential nature and the basis of individual actions. The wealth of the nation would be the result of individual labour, the fruits of which are the enjoyment of all: we can only recall here Bustani's claim in *Nafir Surriya* that 'he who is of no use to an Other has no use of existence altogether'.[30] When an individual expends their labour for the wealth of the nation to increase, their self-existence becomes inherently universal. However, this participation in the universal is merely formal. Universality here is twofold, divided between the individual and the wealth of society. In the former it is a universality in-itself (labour) and in the latter it is explicitly for-itself (the wealth of society). The modern individual perceives this twofold distinction as external objects: the dominion over his activity and the wealth of society are perceived as objective conditions against which he can form an abstract judgement. Dominion, which requires obedience, is bad, while wealth is good. This implies that the morality of individual action cannot be judged outside the whole context of its possibility and that judging can be twofold; it divides the individual who must be at once 'good' and 'bad'.

A contradiction is posited by the modern general social order – which interestingly enough is the literal translation of the Arabic nineteenth-century concept of *al-hay'a al-ijtima'iya*. It requires the estrangement of individual conscious life and its renunciation for the social good, while instituting an abstract social order that is premised on a specific political and economic organisation that are not immediately intelligible.

There is no better place to discern the schism between duty and enjoyment, or law and desire, which irks the modern subject, than in language conceived as a mode of signification. Every mode of signification evolves around a traumatic kernel and speech emerges as a medium of intersubjective recognition of desire. However, speech is always interrupted by symptoms and blank points that resist historicisation. The diachronicity of speech indicates an automaticity to signification as a process to which the subject is *subjected*. But this subjection to the symbolic is never without a remainder, an excess element that cannot be subsumed under the order of signification. This remainder to the subject's interpellation into the symbolic order is not a synthesis of the two previous stages but persists and can be detected in the anxieties that emerge around identification. I argue that the anxiety around language (*lugha*) and habit (*'aada*) in particular express a non-symbolisable kernel that emerges in modernity. The concrete universality of capitalist modernisation is punctured by an excessive element that cannot be reduced to particular identities.

What the 'literary turn' in the study of modern Arabic thought subverts is the very object of the latter's expressed desire, or the object-cause of its desire. Nineteenth-century Arabic thought is defined by a linguistic passion for language experienced as a tragic love affair. How can Arabic, the mother tongue, come to be experienced as an object of desire that haunts the subject? How does that which is meant to be the most familiar, a second nature, come to be experienced as a strange intruder that unmoors any sense of unity? Further, how was the linguistic (and not literary) turn formulated as a reaction to the anxieties induced by modernity – the anxieties over culture – and what do these anxieties reveal? How does the passion for language become a modern shibboleth?

It is here we can discern the limits or breaking points of liberal interpellation during modernisation. The false universality of the liberal model ultimately assumes egoistic individuals who are formally free and can be governed by abstract, autonomous conventions (like language, social contracts, and so forth). But this freedom is merely formal. It depicts a fantasy, according to Marx's famous quip in *Capital* where he argues that capitalist society appears as an

> Eden of the innate rights of man. There alone rule Freedom, Equality, Property and Bentham . . . The only force that brings them together and puts them in relation with each other is the selfishness, the gain and the private interests of each. Each looks to himself only, and no one troubles himself about the rest, and just because they do so, do they all, in accordance with the pre-established harmony of things, or under the auspices of an all-shrewd providence, work together to their mutual advantage, for the common weal and in the interest of all.[31]

The liberal model assumes an autonomous ego while harbouring fantasies of others as cultural beings that are subservient to a despotic power of community; in other words, culturalism (as a capacity that 'others' have and are had by) is a fantasy generated from within liberalism itself. This fantasy functions through disavowal: we are free from culture in the public sphere and can enjoy it privately while others are bound by culture, heedlessly enjoying their bondage. Recent scholarship on liberalism in the age of empire suggests that culturalism and liberalism have constituted a 'moving contradiction' of capitalist modernity. Andrew Sartori argues that they are antinomical insofar as they constitutively split the practical activity of the subject: for the liberal subject, practical activity is defined through relations of exchange in the sphere of circulation, while for the cultural subject, practical activity creates use-values, transforms nature to social ends and 'achieves emancipation from natural determinations . . . and . . . a higher subjective unity with the social totality'.[32]

In this account, liberalism and culturalism emerge as antinomical from within the formal determinations of capitalist society: the exchange-value of practical activity, of labour as a commodity, is guarded by the social contract, while the use-value of practical activity generates needs that only culture can fulfil through the 'appropriation of nature'.

In pre-capitalist feudal society, culture was reserved for the ruling classes, a sight of privilege for those who are not consumed by labour. However, the social possibility of culture in capitalist society revolutionises the delimitation of culture to the privileges of estate society: now all social classes including the bourgeoisie are subjugated to the process of production.[33] This renders the concept of culture unthinkable outside the processes of commodification and valorisation: the validity of culture (as meaningful free activity) is determined by capital. Culture then is placed in a relationship of contradiction with individual freedom (as the freedom to exchange commodities) in bourgeois society. There can be no harmonious conjunction between 'ways of life' as *formal validities* and the means through which social reality is produced in bourgeois society.[34] However, we cannot simply assume that culture emerges as an ideological sphere that is completely subsumed by capitalist reification; for if we do, how are we to account for the malaise of culture, the discontents and anxieties that accompany it? How do we account for culture's 'too much-ness' – as Eric Santner puts it – its overpowering proximity, which unleashes anxiety? In the following chapters, I argue that far from being a synthesising function exerted by subjectivity, the modern problematic of culture carries within it a power of dissolution. Culture has an excessive function, a negativity that underlies the constitution of symbolic fictions. It is a space from which we can witness subjectivity's contraction, retreat, and a cutting of links with the *Umwelt*.

This 'too-much-ness' of culture resonates in the works of Butrus al-Bustani, the foremost moderniser of Arabic language and pedagogy. For Bustani, it is only the solitary Robinson Crusoe, the lone individual who escapes society and culture to become a figure of pure utility, who is the example, the metaphor, for self-cultivation through labour.[35] However, despite his attempts to escape culture, Crusoe is doomed to his parricidal impulses, anxieties of cannibalistic others and incestuous wishes. Crusoe's struggles against the name-of-the-father, risk-taking and his fantasies of cannibalism are but theatres of the problem of individuation that Bustani chose for the stated purpose of cultural and pedagogical instruction in post-war society.

Shidyaq's writing is haunted by something which resists language. Shidyaq attempts to invent a fiction that could later on be accepted as a true story; he literally turns himself into a book through a split double (masculine and feminine Fariyaq and Fariyaqa), an aesthete couple who set out to create a new revolutionary language and ideal reader. While Shidyaq is possessed by language, Bustani inhabits language. Bustani neurotically attempts to classify and order this makeshift 'house of being', shelving and displaying words, gleaning the surface of the mirror, collecting and cataloguing habits, cultural practices and frantically compiling an encyclopaedia that would be the 'book to replace all books'. In contrast to Bustani's obsessive compulsiveness, Shidyaq expresses a hysteric position, railing against the lack of a master signifier only to be haunted by the parasite of signification that he experiences as a problem of sexuality. His discourse asks, 'am I man or woman, can I procreate?' Bustani answers, neither man nor woman, but individual myth, solitary Robinsonades following traces and signs everywhere, all for the sake of an Other.[36]

Between these two contemporaneous linguists, we discern signs of a failed interpellation into liberalism, as well as the breaking point of a particular identity. Their works are not only to be read in terms of the malaise generated by modernity – wounded attachments, tragic losses and the like – but as signs of the emergence of the ego itself as a symptom of modern times.[37] With Bustani, we discern a Robinsonade ego whose concern is with propriety and instituting modes of inheritance, the return of the repressed of parricide. With Shidyaq, we have an ego that is a symptom of the modern destruction of guaranteed symbols of authority. Fariyaq is a radical subject who refuses to serve any cause other than his own, one driven by an anxiety over inheritance and procreation, and the desire to own all of discourse.

1

Literature as a Ruthless Excavator of Culture: From the Literary Mode of Being to *Lituratterre*

The term 'literary modernity', which has been widely used to describe modern Arabic thought, originates in Paul de Man's deconstructionist understanding of modernity as the paradoxical condition of a literary period – following Heidegger's notion of an epoch of beings – within 'which it discovers the impossibility of being modern'.[1] Modernity in de Man's formulation is a 'concept that, like all concepts that are in essence temporal' acquires a further complexity when 'made to refer to events that are in essence linguistic'.[2] For de Man, the way to restitute the presumed incongruous relationship between modernity and history is to affirm that the study of literature can only be historical or, more specifically, historicist (neither scientific nor structural).[3] The reason for insisting on historicism to understand literary modernity (which is what necessitates that modernity be reduced to a literary mode of being) is that literature is an entity that constantly puts its own ontological status into question. For de Man, the literary is itself a mode of being: 'there is a literary mode of being that as a form of language that knows itself to be mere repetition, mere fiction and allegory, forever unable to participate in the spontaneity of action or modernity'.[4] Further, this 'literary mode of being' is experienced as a compulsion; as soon as a literary act is posited as a breakaway from the past into the future, the present is itself not 'allowed to come into being'.[5] It is as though the present is forever halted or stunted in between two successive moments in time: 'literature is an entity that exists not as a single moment of self-denial, but as a plurality of moments that can, if one wishes, be represented, but this is a mere representation, as a succession of moments or a duration. In other words, literature can be represented as a movement and is, in essence, the fictional narration of this movement'.[6]

The definition of literature as a 'mode of being' is evidently beholden to Heidegger's reworking of the categories of substance and existence in *Being and Time*.[7] But for de Man, language is assumed as a substance; and history or historicality is its mode of existence, the result of a self-reflexive stance of the literary mode of being from which a 'linguistic existence' can be discerned. This is the logic through which de Man posits linguistic modernity as historical through and through: the historicity of literature is generated from the play of presence and absence made possible through the literary text.

De Man traces the relationship between modernity and history to Nietzsche and in particular to his attempt at affirming modernity in its utmost radicalness (break with tradition, break with the past, absolute forgetting). On de Man's account, the eternal return is a search for a true present that marks a new and entirely original departure at every instant. However, de Man maintains that it is in Nietzsche's attempts to escape from history that we can discern a deeply historical thrust 'in that it implies the necessary experience of any present as a passing experience that makes the past irrevocable and unforgettable because it is inseparable from any present or future'.[8] There is an inherent paradox in modernity's denial of history because modernity itself as a principle of origination has a 'generative power that is itself historical'.[9] Modernity and history are co-dependent, even linked together in a 'self-destroying union that threatens the survival of both'.[10] It is in this paradox that de Man locates literature as 'essentially modern'[11] because literature or writing is temporally split between being an act and an interpretative process that cannot coincide with the act.[12] As such, textuality in de Man's reading exists between the symbolic and the real.

The double movement of affirmation and denegation that constitutes the concept of literature, argues de Man, is a temporal movement that cannot be measured in time, but for which temporality is mere metaphor: literary modernity, or literature described through the concept of modernity, is a necessary result of a synchronic juxtaposition of literature as 'entity' and not event. The movements of 'flight, return, and the moment in which flight turns into return exist on the levels of meaning that are so intimately intertwined that they cannot be separated'.[13] De Man explains this repetition compulsion at the core of literature as an ontological problem. But he reverts to an idealism when explaining the movement of repetition: on his account, repetition is a necessity for the mode of being of language; it pertains to its nature, to its substance.

The historicity of 'linguistic existence', in de Man's version of literary studies, and the insistence on a historical study of language, aims fundamentally at debunking the structuralist and formalist approach to language: literary forms assume that there is an ontological stability to the literary entity, and 'therefore [structuralism] systematically bypasses the necessary component of literature for which the term "modernity" is not such a bad name after all'.[14] The necessary component, modernity, is then nothing but the movement of repetition, flight from the present, return and the discrepancy between the two moments. This is the paradigm through which de Man reads Baudelaire, Nietzsche and others: they resort to a non-literary meaning – flight – only to return to a literary mode of being. The repetition movement, which defines literariness, is then reduced to its mode of existence; it is a movement that is ultimately metaphorical. Although de Man's aim is to criticise the structuralist approach to language for getting stuck in its synchronic elements, his epistemology of metaphor merely offers an ontological claim about the substantive nature of literature.

Psychoanalysis, however, in contrast to de Man's understanding of literature and repetition, offers us a way out of the deadlocks of 'literary modernity' and gestures towards a scientific modernity that postmodern thinkers have not ceased to target. This is a scientific modernity that I suggest can be discerned only if we employ the psychoanalytic discourse to analyse the linguistic works and manifestations of *lalangue*, the language of the unconscious. Lacan elaborates his approach to the written text through his study of James Joyce; in his later seminars he called James Joyce a *sinthome*, an old word that Lacan reverts to (as a direct performance of an element of *lalangue*) in order to rearticulate his understanding of the symptom within the topology of the real, imaginary, and symbolic. The *sinthome* is posited by Lacan contra the symptom in his analysis of Joyce. The *sinthome* is writing as symptom: 'in which writing allows us bit by bit an entry into the Real'.[15] This is only because the letter does not in any way represent sensible nature but literally replaces it. The solidity of a literary work itself, its apparent wholeness, is soldered together by a certain form of neurosis. However, neurotics can eventually turn their ideological symptom into a non-psychotic *sinthome*, as Lacan argues in the case of Joyce. The written work is to be treated as a 'testimony given by an obsessional subject on the structure that determines her, by which sexual rapport appears impossible to formulate in discourse'.[16] In Lacan's reading, Joyce's literary text is the means through which Joyce remade the name-of-the-father that he lacked. Through writing, Joyce was able to make a name for himself, not as an individual but as a singular subject – a subject of the unconscious, in relation to whom Joyce is a symptom. What Lacan means by this is that Joyce's literary text makes present a subject of the unconscious as a subject of language. Whereas the ego is finite, language is an infinite system of signification and Joyce manages to expose the split generated in the subject by language. The subject of the unconscious is a singularity, while the ego is individual and an imaginary identification.[17] The ego resists the infinite system of language; it is the imaginary identification that emerges from a primal repression, from an inclusion within a symbolic order that the subject does not choose.

On Lacan's reading, Joyce reveals that the human subject is split between a conscious ego and an unconscious subject, always exceeded by language. Joyce is important because he was somehow able to create in language a new bridge between the symbolic and imaginary: his idiomatic use of language, of *lalanguage* as the writing that is already in speech, comes so close to mastering the idiosyncrasy of language, or the idiomaticity of the mother tongue, but only to fail in absolute mastery and reveal that there is something indeterminate and singular that is beyond language.

The repetition compulsion in literature (which the deconstructionist model falls short of understanding) cannot simply be reduced to a prescriptive ontological tendency that is assumed to be pre-given in the subject; rather, psychoanalysis maintains, it is the result of an encounter with the real (opposed to the symbolic and imaginary).[18] The unconscious, which is the locus of the repetition compulsion and the site of the return of the repressed, is not 'a subjective distortion of the objective world, it is first and foremost an indication of a fundamental inconsistency of the objective world itself, which – as such, that is as inconsistent – allows for and generates its own (subjective) distortions'.[19] In this sense, the unconscious is not a subjective distortion of 'something that is objectively otherwise'. Instead, for Freud and Lacan, the unconscious is a distortion 'at the place of something that *is not*'.[20] The unconscious slips, *paraplaxes* and symptoms are not distortions or fragments of reality that are already there, rather, they tell us that representation is itself already 'constitutively fractured, thrown "out of joint": while the distortions use fragments of reality, they correspond to (and are driven by) the inherent void, or gaps, of this reality'.[21]

Freud's 1925 text *Die Verneinung* [*Negation*] carries in it the kernel of the most fundamental claims of psychoanalysis with regards to the unconscious. In this text, Freud reveals the curious nature of repression as a mechanism of negation that persists despite the uncovering of the repressed content. Freud shows that the content of a repressed idea can only make its way into consciousness on condition that it is negated. Grammatical negation ('This is not my mother') brings forth an element of signification which functions like a drive. It is language or the symbolic that brings negation into the world; the symbolic that is only there as interlinked with the un-symbolisable, or the Real (expressing itself in the primordial *Id* for Freud). Freud treats the patient's exclamation, 'This is not my mother', as a negation, a sign of *Verdangung*, of repression. Affirmation and negation are placed together at the same level without affecting the repression.

In a sense, repression through *Verneinung* is itself a failure of negation: repression means that something is rejected/negated, but only at the price of its return. This is where the function of repetition enters into the equation. The concept of repression entails two further sub-concepts: *Verdichtung* (condensation) and *Verscheibung* (displacement), which are the basic mechanisms of the dreamwork. Freud argues that the dream, and therefore the unconscious, knows no 'No'. In the dream, as in the unconscious, negation does not exist in isolation but in a web of substitutions, displacements and condensations that ignores the 'No' and functions via homonyms, similarities, slips and so forth. The dream, in a sense, functions as the negation of negation: all dream elements are reversible – that is, until the analysand utters the 'no', the 'not my mother', the 'it is not that'. It is only with the symbolic that negation comes into the world.

Verdangung (repression) is the structure of neurosis, of the persistence of symptoms. In fact, Freud's interest in the analysis of dreams was premised on the interest in the analysis of neurosis: he wanted to use the problem of dreams to solve more difficult questions in the psychology of neurosis. The application of the method of interpretation to dreams was a continuation of the method applied to the study of symptoms: lying down, shutting the eyes, self-observing in a way whereby the critical faculty is suspended. The main function of the dreamwork is the production of a specific form – a form of the dream, which is a distortion; and the method through which the dreamwork carries out this labour is a condensation – a production of composite structures, which is not a work of censorship but one that obeys some other economical principle. In Freud's words, 'One cannot give the name of the dream to anything other than the product of the dream-work, that is to say, the form into which the latent thoughts have been transmuted by the dream-work'.[22] The second method through which the dreamwork acts is displacement, through which a latent thought is replaced by an allusion, a metaphor. Ultimately, the dreamwork 'reduces the content of the dream thought to its raw materials of objects and activities'.[23] The dreamwork, as Freud tells us, is archaic and it also functions in a regressive manner; if thoughts arise from sensory images to which words were attached, the dreamwork undoes this form of development: now images have to be developed into thoughts.[24]

We can see, then, through these processes of negation that the question of history and time and its relation to structure is posed by the unique structure of the unconscious. The unconscious has a historicity in which history is nothing but the history of structure. The historicity of the unconscious lies in the different thematic structural manifestations of an ahistorical kernel, which is the very condition of (im)possibility of history.[25] The unconscious is a dialectical intertwining of synchronicity and diachronicity, or what Freud calls displacement and condensation (metaphor and metonymy). The dreamwork shows that the unconscious is not to be understood as a structure that is rigid and ahistorical but one that is in fact located through the processes of condensation and displacement, which, although synchronic, require diachrony as their necessary condition.

The return of the repressed (in the dream and other unconscious manifestations) is symptomatic of a specific failure of repression incarnated by the symptom as a disruption in the symbolic, which in turn indexes an un-symbolisable Real. It is on this side of the symptom that Lacan places the literary work. In his later formulations, he maintained that the letter, or the written word, is not reducible to the work of the signifier[26] – which is located in the symbolic – but belongs to the Real: 'the written word is the limit or shoreline against which the Real breaks into the symbolic'.[27] What does not cease to write itself for Lacan is the sexual non-relation, or the non-existence of the sexual relationship. Thus here, writing is not to be reduced to the written text; it is tied to the element of the Real that resists symbolisation.

Lacan's claim about the written word must be understood in relation to his claim that the subject is the answer of the real (*la reponse du réel*) in the symbolic.[28] In his later obsession with Joyce as a 'literary saint', we can arguably find a condensed version of Lacan's theory of the subject: a subject that is split between knowledge and truth, or between *jouissance* and the symptom. Joyce in his literary works is seen to have introduced a new *symptome* – or the *sinthome* – that is a compulsive repetition, in as far as writing provides a 'linguistic discharge for the structural and inadmissible *jouissance* of the Other'.[29]

In Lacan's elaborations on the *sinthome*, literature (as a form of writing) is to be seen as a model of linguistic equivocation. Psychoanalysis, he maintained, forces literary criticism to measure up to it with 'the enigma remaining on the latter's side'.[30] What is the enigma that is on the side of psychoanalysis? As an artist, Joyce's *savoir-faire* reveals that 'there is something we cannot enjoy', that there is 'no other of the other to pass the final judgement': i.e. the enigma that Joyce reveals is that with writing, bit by bit, we cease to *imagine* and enter the Real, the Real of the sexual non-relation, of the body and the drives.[31] Ultimately, Joyce the *sinthome* calls into question the status of the Real, the possibility of non-ideological identification in the subject's assumption of the name-of-the-father, and the function of repetition in re-symbolising the lack in the symbolic: all of these will prove essential in the reading of literature that I propose in the following chapters. First, it is important to elucidate the terms of Lacan's engagement with Joyce in order to single out the distinctive components of a psychoanalytic approach to literary criticism.

If we read Lacan closely, Joyce reveals the 'virus of the signifier' or the ceaseless work of *jouissance* against which psychoanalysis must put together the pieces of the Real, here and there, and provide it with its lucubrations. There is in *jouissance* a resistance to the Real, and the discourse of psychoanalysis works to reveal the ideological work of enjoyment. The *sinthome*, or the symptom *tout court*, 'writes' what it cannot 'read' alone. That is why Joyce is more of an artist, for Lacan, than a poet, he does not realise he is making a *sinthome* but is 'a pure artificer [. . .] a man of know-how'.[32] Joyce is an artist because the master signifier has not managed to steal his know-how, his enjoyment, which gradually erodes mastery and gnaws away at it.[33]

The terms that Lacan uses for describing the function of writing, '*lituratterre*' and 'gullying', carry the meanings of passageways in a landscape: a shoreline, stream and shimmering course describe the cut into a landscape or stone instilled by the slow yet persistent work of water. The 'gullying of the signifier' is meant to be an interruption of the signifying chain or the repetitive automatism of the symbolic passageway through which the *sinthome* emerges; in other words, the *sinthome* is not caught up in intersubjectivity or in the symbolic. The written work is to be treated as the testimony given by an obsessional subject on the structure that determines her, by which the sexual relation appears impossible to formulate in discourse.

The littoral or the written is a shoreline, a border between centre and absence or between knowledge and *jouissance*. Furthermore, the void that is carved out by writing is distinct from *objet a*, because it is not always ready to welcome *jouissance*. Joyce cannot simply be the object of a psychoanalysis that seeks knowledge in the symptom and psychoanalysis cannot be conceived as a science of a nagging object, insofar as '*objet a* is not peaceful . . . it doesn't leave you in peace'.[34] The *sinthome*, or Joyce's literary act, is a pure know-how that does not know itself; it is the site wherein writing makes a name for itself, a site whereby literature approaches the status of science or the status of a 'littoral fact'. Language is only possible because of the impossibility of symbolising the sexual relation and the 'littoral fact', as Lacan argues in *Seminar XXIII*, is a fact because it does not feign the sexual relation but exposes it as a non-relation. The *sinthome* then is distinct because it approaches the truth of non-relation by being a 'defile' of knowledge.[35]

We can now understand how it is that literature ultimately exposes the 'illiteracy of the symbolic', as Daniel Nobus has put it.[36] The relationship then between psychoanalysis and literature is complicated: it is one of a measuring against each other. Lacan's replacement of *Litura* for *litterra* replaces writing with the notion of erasure, deletion and correction. Joyce's writing does something different to *Literature* for it makes a litter out of the letter: if the letter is a litter, then culture or 'civilization is a sewer'.[37] It is only by admitting this that Lacan says a position can be made from which 'to save the honour of literature'. Literature uses up the leftovers of society and in fact becomes a piece of trash: Joyce 'slips from *a letter* to *a litter*, from *a lettre* to a piece of trash'.[38] Psychoanalysis in its understanding of waste as surplus *jouissance* carries the key to discerning in literature what is more than the endless repetition of symptomatic compensations for the lack of knowledge. The endless cycle of repetition is halted only to be replaced by an acknowledgement of ignorance, of the ignorance of *savoir-faire*. This ignorance is nothing but the ignorance of *savoir faire* itself.

The task of psychoanalysis then is not simply to interpret the literary text but to insist on the 'weapon of equivocation' against the *sinthome*. As Lacan puts it in *Seminar XXIII*, 'it is uniquely by equivocation that interpretation works. There must be something in the signifier that resonates'.[39] Words have an effect, and drives are the echo in the body of the fact that there is speech. The letter always arrives at its destination without recourse to any content; it outlines a hole in the edge of knowledge; it isn't simply a frontier between the *Umwelt* and *Innenwelt*, but a limit, a point that exposes the two as non-reciprocal frontiers. In other words, writing is not an impression on the mystic writing pad, but functions in an economy of language by which *langue*, language, is affected. Writing, or what Lacan calls the *Littoral*, functions as an erasure of the symbolic; it produces a gap in which the subject is allowed to emerge.

However, erasure does not simply conjoin with a presence: it is 'as erasure of no trace whatsoever that constitutes the land, *terre*, of the *littoral*'.[40] For Lacan, the literal is pure *litura*: pure erasure, pure deletion. The written can only turn into the literal if in the rupture between knowledge and truth, between presence and absence, an expulsion of what may constitute *jouissance* is possible. Lacan insists that it is a turn that is possible at every moment for the subject. From knowledge in failure to a failure in knowledge – this is what psychoanalysis can make of literature:

> It is insofar as the unconscious knots itself into a *sinthome*, which is what there is singularly in each individual, that one can say that Joyce, as it is written somewhere, identifies with the individual. He has made himself privileged enough to have, at the extreme point, incarnated in himself the symptom, that by which he escapes any possible death, by reducing himself to a structure that is precisely that of LOM [l'homme, man], if you will permit me to write it quite simply as l.o.m.[41]

If the *sinthome* exposes the illiteracy of the symbolic order then the interpretation of literature is premised on reducing it to rubble, to the remainders of gullying that it really is. Literature acts as a violent intruder that takes away something from culture; it is 'a ruthless excavator'[42] that introduces a rupture or makes a hole in knowledge. This invasive function of literature does not puncture what was full before but introduces a rupture in knowledge that has the ability to continuously repeat only if allowed to retrospectively create the illusion of an absolute *jouissance* that has been lost. This is what we could call idiotic enjoyment – Joyce's enjoyment? – the *jouissance* of *objet a* is the fundamental fantasy that has to be traversed: it is ultimately an ideological function when considered from the standpoint of structure rather than from the standpoint of the subject failing to be interpolated by it.

In his *Seminar on the Purloined Letter*, Lacan argues that the signifier's *caput mortuum*, or worthless remains, takes effect through a repetition compulsion that departs from the Freudian understanding of the notion of existence as reminiscence. With regards to the question of repetition, Mladen Dolar has placed Lacan on the side of Kierkegaard in this debate, pitting repetition against memory and reminiscence.[43] Lacan does indeed move beyond Freud and reinterprets Freud's discussion of the child's *fort-da* game: the modulation of the alternation of presence and absence through syllables in the game is the direct manifestation of the determination that the subject receives from the symbolic order. It is not however a question of genesis for Lacan but of structure: 'it is at the moment of their essential conjunction [presence and absence] and, so to speak, at the zero point of desire that the human *object* comes under the sway of the grip which, cancelling out its natural property, submits it henceforth to the symbol's conditions'.[44]

The autonomy of the symbolic is evidenced in repetition, in the indestructible persistence of unconscious desire and not in some scholastic understanding of an imaginary inertia of free associations. Lacan argues that his own understanding of *insistence* as the essential characteristic of repetition is beholden to Freud's suggestion in *Beyond the Pleasure Principle* that it is 'prevital and transbiological' and not in any sense spiritualistic. Thus, if man comes to think about the symbolic order, it is because it is a forced choice that curtails his being. The illusion that he has formed this by his consciousness itself stems from a gap in his imaginary relationship which allowed his entrance into the symbolic only via the 'radical *defilé* of speech' that is not a moment of genesis (although it is a genetic moment in the child's entry into speech) but a structural determination: one that is 'reproduced each time the subject addresses the Other as absolute, as the Other who can annul him himself, just as he can act accordingly with the Other, that is by making himself into an object in order to deceive the Other'.[45]

Mladen Dolar argues with regards to this point that 'repetition is pitted against the law, regularity and causality, and it poses the problem of the impossibility of spelling out the identity of what is repeated. It appears in a discontinuity, a break in the causal chain'.[46] If so, then how does this structural determination link back to the *caput mortuum* of the signifier? Here it is important to consider Lacan's argument that literature is what makes a claim about the meaninglessness of the written and its destiny to function despite its meaninglessness:

> The essence of the latter [Purloined Letter] is that the letter was able to have its effects on the inside – on the tale's actors, including the narrator – just as much as on the outside – on us, its readers and also its author – without anyone having had to worry about what it meant. That is the usual fate of everything that is written.[47]

Everything that is written functions according to a limitation embedded within it. This limitation is what Lacan calls 'the role of the possibility of representation' that governs the relation between metaphor and metonymy: the former being in the field of condensation or *Verdichtung* (poetic), and the latter in the field of displacement or *Verschiebung* (the unconscious's method of foiling censorship). Again, here it is not genesis that is at issue: the limitation inherent in writing is not to be understood as a limitation of 'natural expression' or figurative semiology; rather, it is a limitation that is constitutive of writing itself.

Furthermore, the symptom is determined by the mechanism of metaphor – between the signifier of sexual trauma, sexual non-relation and the term that comes to replace it in the signifying chain – while desire is 'caught in the rails of metonymy eternally extending toward the *desire for something else*'. To recall Lacan's familiar formulation, 'it is the truth of what this desire has been in his history that the subject cries out through his symptom'.[48] But it is not a matter of giving the truth its rightful place; it is about taking up our place in the truth: the conflictual truth of social relations. And this is where Marx becomes Lacan's main reference as the inventor of the social symptom. The symptom is what manifests the incompatibility between truth and knowledge, and the *sinthome* is what produces a discourse that is not one of semblance, or of *objet a*.

The traversal of the fundamental fantasy is about *re-signifying* the symbolic by assuming temporarily the real of the symbolic: its constitutive lack or *jouissance*; in other words, it is the assumption of a new fantasy and not a remembrance. It is a repetition that cuts into continuity and installs a break that is irreducible to the continuity of memory; one that cannot be captured by symbols and signs.[49] It is in this sense that the unconscious is fundamentally an arche-writing (and not a meta-language); it is what predates both speech and writing, or what antedates *lalangue* but also poses the very question of the relationship between language and world.

Contra Freud, Lacan argues that the symptom does not simply emerge where there is a lacking signifier or a lacking representation, which upon repression becomes the grounds for repetition. Further to this, he posits the *sinthome* as a marker for a possibility of repetition that does not simply reinstill the symptom. And this is why *lituraterre* is a smearing of a surface, or rather a torsion in the surface, a negativity that is constitutive of the Real. Lacan resorts to Joyce to enlighten the enigmas of psychoanalysis: the letter in the case of Joyce no longer insists but becomes a breaking point, which is to say that Joyce introduces a limit of the Real. The *sinthome* in this sense is not a tragic repetition, but names the Real. Joyce the writer, the *sinthome*, is already separated from the symptom: writing allows the subject to be relocated in the meaning that he lacked. The *sinthome* shows that there is nothing opposite the Symbolic or that the Real is the support of the Symbolic:

> What is at stake in *jouissance*, the *jouissance* not of the Other [because there is no other of the other] is that there is nothing opposite the Symbolic [which is the locus of the Other as such]. And that there exists a hole within the symbolic itself based on the division of the symptom: into symptom and symbol – the sym that toms and the sym that bols. But this division of the symptom which puts the chain of signifiers into work, the shift from S1 to S2, is a false hole.[50]

The consistency of the Real, Symbolic and Imaginary as we know from Lacan's topological representations of Borromean knots, are like the consistency of a circle and a circle in its nature presupposes a hole. But the logic of the hole, or, one could venture to say, the void of the symptom, is that it is not simply a matter of turning around continuing, a return to a point of origin, to a repressed origin; rather, the hole of the symptom generates a new origin, a form of *ex nihilo* creation. The *sinthome* is introduced into the borromean knot as its fourth element: the written – or writing as a symptom – allows an entry into the Real only because the letter does not in any way represent sensible nature but literally replaces it.[51]

It is not simply that the written is pitted against the presence of a subject of enunciation, but that the written emerges as a remainder of the gap between nature and culture, or between the rock and the voice. As Dolar has argued, it is that dead letter which disrupts the living voice, the supplement which usurps its subsidiary place to tarnish presence. And ultimately, it is not writing in its positive and empirical appearance that is at stake, but more fundamentally the trace, the trace of alterity which has 'always-already' dislocated the origin.[52]

Writing as the stainearth, the border and *terre* instils a temporal thrust; the written text has a futurity to it insofar as nothing *really* happens in it. This dislocation of an origin that was not there to begin with is the function of writing as 'the stuffing of the signified by the signifier'. It is no coincidence that Lacan resorts to the example of stuffing to describe the function of the written in Joyce. For why would Joyce believe 'that there is a book of himself? What an idea to make oneself be a book! This could only come to a stunted poet, a pig of a poet!'[53]

It cannot be ignored that the saintly posture ascribed to Joyce is one of a modernist egoist, a 'radical individualism defined by a refusal to 'serve' any other cause than that of the subject's own [which] entails a rethinking of 'ownership' and a desire of owning . . . the entire world of discourse at least'.[54] Joyce seems to be at once a 'singular individual' or a 'littoral fact', on the one hand, and on the other, an incarnation of the ego as symptom. Is Joyce – the *sinthome* – then an answer to the Real insofar as he straddles the border between *lituraterre* as an erasure of the symbolic, and a *literalisation* of the imaginary? Is Joyce, the omniscient God, really a limit, and a breaking point?[55] Or does Joyce bear witness to the limits of the Lacanian subject, not as a lost cause, but as what emerges from the narrow passageways between the Real and the Symbolic?

We know well by now that Lacan wished to maintain a notion of the subject that is in line with Descartes and Hegel. The split subject of the unconscious cannot but be the correlate to the subject of science; that is, a subject that is not the result of ideological interpellation but a 'defile' of the rejection of all knowledge:

> I sustain that this rejection of all knowledge constitutes the subject of science in its definition, this latter term to be understood in the sense of a 'narrow doorway'. This light did not guide me in vain, for it led me . . . to formulate the experienced division of the subject as a division between knowledge and truth.[56]

The analytic discourse is not concerned with saving the truth (*salva veritate*)[57] for it addresses the *jouissance* of the subject by acting like its *dechet*, the *trashitas* of the subject of the unconscious (the analysand's desire here). Most importantly, the analytic discourse is only specified in writing: in the *objet a* (an object which is nevertheless a letter), in the S ($\bar{A}$) barred (the subject's assumption of the position of lack in the locus of the Other) and the phallus, signified by the letter Φ.[58] All that is produced in discourse, understood as the fantasy structure of the social link, is considered by Lacan to be an effect of the written. The written, here, is not simply to be understood in terms of the 'autonomy of the signifier' as it is posited by Saussurean linguistics. Rather, the dimension of the written has nothing to do with the voice but with the gaze, or 'What you hear is the signifier. The signified is the effect of the signifier (*la lecture de ce qu'on entend de significant*)'.[59] The analytic discourse then gives 'a different reading to the signifiers that are enunciated (*ce qui s'enonce de signifiant*) than what they signify'.[60] It has to assume that the 'subject of the unconscious knows how to read', or that it can be taught how to read. However, what the unconscious is taught to read in the analytic setting is on a different plane from what psychoanalysis as a discourse can write of it.

Lacan's reading of Joyce provides an account of the imaginary, which is lacking in de Man's deconstructionist reading of the literary. The deconstructionist account that de Man provides assumes that there is a literary mode of being, which precedes the relation between text and non-text. Lacan's analysis of Joyce introduces the category of the name-of-the-father, against which Joyce creates a name for himself, institutes a new symbolic, and thereby names the structure that constitutes him as a subject. Literature then does not remain stuck between the boundaries of presence and absence (which delimit De Man's understanding of the literary) because it introduces the problem of an origin that was not there to begin with.

Lacan's account of literature is crucial for the analysis of Shidyaq's *Leg Over Leg* in Chapter 2 of this volume. Despite preceding Joyce by many decades, Shidyaq sets out to carry out this precise literary act: the turning of oneself into a book. The question that psychoanalysis raises then with regards to literature and its relation to the symbolic is a question of reading: how to carry out a reading that is an act of separation between the signifier and signified, an isolation of the signifier in analytic discourse, a distancing between *jouissance* and the symptom?

Fantasy: The Tain of Modernity

Shidyaq, who was trained as a traditional scribe, is often characterised as an Ottoman reformer and loyal supporter of the Ottoman Porte. However, the scathing satire of modern society (both Ottoman and European) that he presents cannot be ignored. Can Shidyaq indeed be called Ottoman just because of the presence of the Ottoman world and its mentalities in *Leg Over Leg*? In fact, it would be fair to argue that Shidyaq's modernism[61] can be located in the 'stream of consciousness' style through which *Leg Over Leg* is written in the mode of an interior monologue (between Shidyaq, Fariyaq and Fariyaqa), with a constant sexual banter that generates a sense of irony. In chapter after chapter, there are constant encounters in different cities and towns in which there is an ongoing dialectic between characters who are given a certain freedom, but only to be controlled by the master puppeteer. The trivialities of everyday living, of household affairs, social engagements, customs, habits and practices, are orchestrated in a manner that generates epiphanies. Chapter by chapter, one *maqama* after another, is punctuated by a renewed commitment to an ideal of beauty (the beauty of language, the beauty of woman) against any commitment to ideological authority and religious conformity.

The only letter that Shidyaq accepts as the bearer of truth is that which he receives from the poor and downtrodden Fariyaq, not from a sultan or a king, and not from a priest or an emir. Shidyaq's fantasy is not centred on an identifiable master in social reality because masters are no longer masters, women no longer women, men no longer men. In this empty place appears a surplus-father figure split into two: the God of grammar and Fariyaq. God, or the big Other, is split into two: a God who has no interest in human affairs and their particular bodily functions but guarantees the eternal truths of grammar; and a God who is involved in their most private affairs, their bodies, bowel movements and dreams.[62]

The blind respect for the letter is a modern European fantasy of the despotic regime of power in the Ottoman Empire. Alain Grosrichard's reading of the fantasy of Oriental despotism – foremostly defined by this blind respect and submission to the letter – in modernity is crucial for understanding the fundamental role of fantasy in establishing the mechanisms of liberal political power. Fantasy is not simply a realm of representations, ideas that function outside of social reality; it is 'the mechanism of production and canalization of enjoyment and in this way it may hold the key to our status as subjects—both political subjects and subjects of desire—and to our practices'.[63] The fantasy of Oriental despotism in the works of Montesquieu and his contemporaries reveals the anxieties underlying Enlightenment democratic thought itself. The Oriental despot emerges as a phantasmatic Other that reveals a specific economy of enjoyment that 'accompanies modern structures of the social and the status of the subject'.[64] Particular to the fantasy of Oriental despotism, in Montesquieu, Baudier and Chardin's accounts, is that it exercises 'absolute power . . . by means of the graphic signifier'.[65] The king commands through the power of writing, always accompanied by a 'chief scribe' who makes sure that the letter always arrives at its destination.

What Grosrichard reveals in his analysis is that the supposed arbitrary power of the letter in despotic regimes is nothing but the logic of the signifier as it emerges in modernity. In the depictions of the Ottoman Sultan's absolute command through the power of the written word, 'it is as if the signifier itself flies, strikes, and kills by being materialised in the letter. It is at one time the sentence, axe, and the executioner'.[66] The whim of the master as such is embodied in the flight of the signifier that directly affects individuals under his rule; in the fantasy of despotism 'the only value that individuals have depends on how the seal of the master is marked upon them'.[67] Thus, rule is assumed to be instantiated by the very *name* of the king: 'This name is what allows the prince's will infallibly to produce its effect just one billiard ball hitting another must produce its effect'. It slips at lightning speed along the chain which, from despot to vizier and from vizier down to the lowest of subordinates, links the centre of the Empire to its periphery'.[68]

Grosrichard provides us with the flipside of European Enlightenment's liberal ethos: a fantasy of despotism that emerges when the Ottoman regime had already been in decline since the seventeenth century. Despotic power is the phantasmatic Other, the necessary screen on which are projected the anxieties of the modern liberal discourse of the state. This Enlightenment fantasy, Grosrichard argues, served to reinvent Aristotle's Asia of the classical age in the era of colonisation; it Gallicised Aristotle's statesmen, the efficient cause of power, into a mechanistic *pouvoir despotique*.

The analogy of Ottoman despotism is the result of repressing already existing perversions of European monarchical rule in the heart of Europe; the internal threats to which were disavowed by European writers only for them to return from the outside, in the external threat of the Ottoman Empire: 'As if, by learning to decipher the structures of an impossible power from the outside, Europeans were discovering that they had equipped themselves with the best key for interpreting their own present'.[69] This 'endoscopic fantasy' of the Ottoman seraglio, as a realm of perverse enjoyments of every kind (eunuchs, women, slaves, etc.) serves for the 'stripping bare (a nudity of dream and delirium) of what the whole century fears, and perhaps, secretly desires'.[70]

The structure of despotic fantasy is premised on a fetishistic disavowal that is similar to Marx's analysis of commodity fetishism as the act of exchange practiced despite the knowledge that commodities disguise relations between people under the mantle of relations between things. Just as the commodity is endowed with 'metaphysical subtleties and theological niceties', the Ottoman despot, perceived as an Other who commands unconditional subjection, is a fantasy for democratic societies: 'I know very well [that I live in a democracy], nevertheless I believe that power is despotic'.[71]

The modern fascination with subjects who debase themselves for the sultan, offer themselves to his enjoyment and are in a state of complete compliance, deindividuated and subject to the capriciousness and arbitrariness of his rule, is a fantasy that reveals a hidden kernel that underlies the very attrition of sovereignty in modernity. Kantorowicz had called into question the premise of medieval political authority and coined the phrase the 'king's two bodies' to describe the body politic as the other site wherein sovereignty is located. The political theology of the 'body politic' includes a 'mystical body' rooted in metaphysical understanding.[72]

Eric Santner elaborates on the modern shift of sovereignty, or the 'afterlife' of political theology, in his study of Daniel Schreber (1842–1911). Santner's psychoanalytically informed analysis focuses on Schreber's delusions, paranoia and psychotic symptoms as well as his preoccupations with bodily illness, specifically with 'decomposition and feminisation'. These are analysed as the manifestations of the excessive pressures of the biopolitical regime of capitalist modernity:

> these pressures pertain not only to questions concerning the foundation and constitution of political authority but also more generally to those concerning the patterns and procedures whereby human beings come to be vested with the authority of various 'offices' they occupy and the ways in which such procedures of investiture, such transferences of symbolic authority are ultimately legitimated.[73]

Santner argues that Schreber's illnesses only become comprehensible 'against the background of the issues and questions generated by the such political and institutional states of emergency provides'.[74] Schreber, who suffers from an intensification of bodily excitations and psychic pressures, is a symptom of the crisis of the social and symbolic guarantees to meaning.

This institutional crisis is experienced as an unbearable pressure, an inability of the subject to 'seize himself in his self-understanding'.[75] Schreber's rotten soul is itself 'the inner rottenness of every symbolic investiture insofar as it remains dependent on a dimension of performative force',[76] of compulsion and drive. This 'crisis of symbolic investiture',[77] as Santner calls it, is a crisis that afflicts the modern subject's relation to the law, which in modernity appears to demand enjoyment rather than restrict it. There is a specific disjuncture that is introduced by the discourse of the state in capitalist modernity (after the decomposition of feudal modes of kingship) one in which the moral pressure to abstain from pleasure becomes a pressure, a moral duty to enjoy. Schreber's madness expresses that there is something lacking in the symbolic – something rotten in the state of Denmark, as Marcellus puts it in *Hamlet* – which does not escape the modern subject and befalls them as an excessive demand.

Modern power, as we know from Foucault's *History of Sexuality*, is not repressive but functions through excitation, through a proliferation of discourses and a multiplicity of subject positions in relation to power (the criminal, the insane, the pervert). It can only multiply and spread through a power–knowledge nexus: practices of subjectivation are the modes through which epistemological power 'extracts from the individuals a knowledge [savoir]'.[78] *Épisteme* is the concept Foucault uses to denote the means by which power disperses, and the field in which the subject intervenes by reconstructing the historical processes through which we have been led to make certain distinctions (such as between madness and reason). Foucault emphasises the historicity at work in the production of knowledge by focusing on a structural analysis of discourse that asks: what are the determined positions that an individual must occupy if she is to be a subject at all?

Lacan, on the other hand, argues that the subject's intervention, insofar as we understand the subject as a subject of language, is always-already formed or structured in the Symbolic order. Moreover, the Symbolic forms within which discursive practices occur are themselves also always-already structured through the logic of fantasy. But for Lacan, a subject's formation happens in its *failure* to integrate into the symbolic structure; a failure evidenced in jokes, slips of the tongue, dreams, neuroses and psychosis. In these moments, the subject is revealed in persistently negative relation to existing orders: it is the subject of the unconscious.

The pivotal shift in modernity, which Lacan describes differently from Foucault, is a conjunction that is not simply the binding of power and enjoyment but the very impossibility of this alliance that suddenly comes to generate a 'surplus-enjoyment'.[79] The watershed of modernity is the eclipse of the master's discourse, the symbolic death of the king. While for Foucault this generates a multiplicity of heterogeneous disciplinary measures or biopower, for Lacan the onset of modern capitalist relations designates a shift in the structure of *jouissance* or enjoyment; a shift through which for the first time enjoyment itself becomes valorised.[80] The relationship between power and enjoyment clearly goes back to antiquity. However, it is only with capitalism that enjoyment comes to serve as a source of surplus-value; this surplus element is supported by a libidinal mode of production, a fantasy that is necessary to keep the discourse of the master alive after the theft of knowledge, i.e. for the modern slave to go to work a chain of signification needs to be put in place.

The work of fantasy in sustaining a discourse of power is specific to modernity, in which power has come to be organised not around brute control and repression, but through love, desire and enjoyment. La Boétie's *The Discourse on Voluntary Servitude* (1576) – first translated into Arabic by Safoun in 1990 – is a testimony to the unnaturalness of the love of liberty.[81] In modernity, the source of servitude is no longer to be deciphered in Aristotle's understanding of human nature: i.e. the master–slave relation is no longer about the simple theft of knowledge or *savoir-faire*, but has to do with putting the slave to work through a master signifier that commands a regime of enjoyment. The source of servility in modern political regimes is commanded by love of family, nation and state.

It is precisely in the context of this shift that the category of the modern subject of the unconscious comes to fore. This subject is not equal to a homeostatic liberal individual, a self-transparent ego. Rather, as Slavoj Žižek puts it:

> subjects are not the 'effective' presence of 'flesh-and-blood' agents that make use of language as part of their social practices, filling abstract language schemes with actual contents: 'subject' is, on the contrary, the very abyss that forever *separates* language from the substantial life process.[82]

In Shidyaq's magnum opus, *Leg Over Leg*, a modern epic, it becomes evident that it is from this historical shift, the break or rupture introduced by modernisation – during which the displacement of a pre-modern grammarian tradition with a modern science of language became necessary – that the problem of the subject and its distance from symbolic identification emerges. There is an anxiety over language, an anxiety over sexual difference (masculinity and femininity), habit, taste and culture (*'ada, dthawq* and *adab*), and the sources of legitimation of authority (*al-hukm, al-siyyasa*).

Far from being simply a self-Orientalising moment generated from a colonial encounter, this anxiety was symptomatic of the emergence of a universalism underlined by the contestation between reason and the unconscious: it is an anxiety that addresses core Enlightenment oppositions. Shidyaq claimed that believing in the ways of modernity, a performative practice of the rituals of modern society, was not enough for true modernity (*tamaddun haqiyqi*). Habits are embodied material forms that take shape in response to needs and desires, and that do so spontaneously, unconsciously and socially. Merely believing in modernity can easily give way to a form of superficial mimesis, one in which the essence of modernity goes unrealised – this essence being the transformation of habits, a subjective reconstitution that is necessitated by the modern drive for progress, an unquenchable pursuit that is in turn generated from the ongoing production of human needs.

It would not be an overstatement to say that modernity itself was experienced *tout-court* as uncanny, as a process within which all that is familiar comes to be experienced as strange and out of place: the Arab's moustache, the noble women's horned hats, the sheikh's thick turbans, the use of certain words, even eating habits. The self-consciousness about habit, or habit's self-consciousness, generated an impasse that is particularly modern: underneath the harmonious appearance of the subject as a creature of habit lies a mechanism for the splitting or erasure of subjectivity. With habit the internal world is essentially constructed on the outside, made to predict the external world and to be instantiated by it. When individual habit is shaped by accommodation to external forces, as an internal feature it becomes elevated into a disposition, the defining trait of an 'inner essence'. Thus, habits that are mandated by the external world become internal faculties that define individuals: i.e. what we witness in this juncture is subjectivity's emergence from its own disappearance. The anxiety about any resolute self-identification with Arabic posits etymology against the 'etymo-logos' and introduces the problem of the value of differences in language without a firm assumption of a positive substantial content for Arabic that would be trans-historical. Words do not have a memory as such; words are only possible in a system of differences that is relational and demands conceptualisation regardless of the place of articulation. We can no longer assume that the modern subject of enunciation is unitary.

The Subject and Ideology: The Ego's Hall of Mirrors

The epistemology of linguistics, a modern science, cannot be countered by a philological method that begins from disavowing the peculiar relationship of linguistic attachment to a mode of learning and its object of language, both inextricable components of the linguistic love for language. Modern (i.e. post-Saussurean) linguistics is defined by the shift away from a substantive to a relational mode of thinking that assumes a non-relation at the core of signification (the arbitrariness of the sign): this non-relation defines language itself and not singular languages like Arabic or English.

There is a logic that maintains that language *tout-court* is non-relational, but it reaches entirely different conclusions from the deconstructionist and philological models; it is the logic of structural linguistics and Lacan's reinvention of Freud's subject of the unconscious.[83] Freud argues that we obtain the concept of the unconscious from the theory of repression. He describes the unconscious as 'what we call a psychical process that we take to exist (inferred from its effects but that we know nothing of)', except its mechanism, its topological structure.[84] Thus, Freud's theory and technique poses a question about what exists and what doesn't exist: even if dreams are superfluous phenomena, they do exist, i.e., we can count something to exist even if it lacks any substantial content, or we can account something as existing although it bears traits of inexistence.

This inexistent object, the unsaid, lies in the discontinuities of 'consciousness', in the holes of what is said, its inconsistencies, and not behind them at some deeper level. In other words, Freud gives a twist to materialism as he does to rationalism: the matter of psychoanalysis is unmatter, or immaterial: dreams, slips of tongues are not objects like grandmothers and trees. It is immaterial or unmaterial, the *un* being the function of what Freud calls repression. This dynamic view of the unconscious perceives of mental processes through a topography that is both psychical and economic [anticathaxis, cathaxis]; a libidinal economy that is non-homeostatic and has nothing to do with anatomy or regions in the mental apparatus. The unconscious is not made up of feelings, of affects; rather, it is constituted through repressed ideas, and repression is about the suppression of the development of affects after which unconscious ideas continue to exist.

Moreover, the unconscious is irreducible to any biological mechanism or set of cultural determinants. In fact, it was Freud's major discovery that the physical and mental overlap and are inseparable: 'The object of psychoanalysis is the zone where the two overlap: biology/somatic is already cultural while culture springs from the impasses of the somatic'.[85] Culture tries to resolve these impasses but only to create new ones. The unconscious is the overlap and intersection that generates what appear to be distinct entities: body and mind. It is what Freud calls the architectonic principle of the mental apparatus that 'lies in a stratification, a building up of superimposed agencies', namely of superimposition.[86] Thus the unconscious doesn't intervene from some beyond; it is there all the time, revealing itself in the gaps and holes of what is actually willed, decided, said and done. This understanding of the unconscious implies that psychoanalysis is never really concerned with individual problems – the unconscious is not equivalent to an individual's problem – but in showing how what appear to be the most intimate and internal problems are in fact already inscribed from the very beginning in a socio-symbolic field: the field of the Other.[87]

Lacan further maintained that the 'unconscious is structured like language' and that 'there is no such thing as a metalanguage'.[88] For Lacan, there is no criterion that delineates the system of differences in language, which is determined primarily by the primacy of relations between signifiers. The autonomy of the signifier is thereby asserted over the relation between signifier and signified. The unconscious can only be realised in the locus of the Other: it disrupts the distinction between the inner and outer domain. Furthermore, the subject of the unconscious is an effect of the signifier, of the locus of the Other in the subject (the subject–object relation here is non-reciprocal but circular) and it is a subject divided by language; through the effects of speech, the subject seeks himself in the Other but only to receive back a distorted image. This relation between subject and other is non-reciprocal, a non-relation, but one premised on a lack from which desire is generated the subject seeks to secure a place for themselves in the desire of the Other and thereby desire is the desire of the Other.

This conception of the unconscious (as structured like language) does not see language as communicative and relational; i.e. language is not to be understood as an Aristotelian organon, a tool or instrument, but instead as a non-totalisable and effective sphere: 'One can speak of the unconscious only under the condition that language constitutes an autonomous register serving more than mere communication and having material consequences that cannot be reduced to cognitive and neurobiological processes'.[89] In the psychoanalytic model, unconscious manifestations have concrete linguistic autonomy (the unconscious is structured like language) and they are sites of production of both subjectivity and *jouissance*.[90] The signifier is an apparatus of *jouissance*: i.e. there are libidinal investments for the signifier that are fundamentally political in nature.

Lacan's conception of subjectivity stands in contrast to the structuralist dismissal of the subject at the time in which he was teaching. Althusser, for instance, broke with humanism and construed the subject as an effect of structure. The Althusserian-interpellated subject is one that is captured in imaginary identification and remains a subject of consciousness at the site(s) where both recognition and misrecognition occur. But what is omitted in Althusser's account of interpellation is the symbolic itself; while for Lacan, it is the symptom and fantasy (the barred subject and *objet a*) that are beyond interpellation, and connected through the notion of the symptom.[91] Lacan provides an account of the subject as that which emerges at the point of failure of interpellation, thereby recognising the loss that has to be incurred for entry into the symbolic. This view challenges Althusser's clear-cut distinction between materiality and subjectivity, in which the subject is only a result of the process of interpellation and materiality is what is asserted as the exterior of ideology.[92]

In contrast to this duality of materiality and subjectivity, Lacan's account posits the subject as the remainder of interpellation: 'the psychoanalytic point of departure is the remainder produced by the operation ... the clean cut is always unclean; it cannot produce the flawless interiority of an autonomous subject. The psychoanalytic subject is coextensive with that very flaw in the interior'.[93] The Lacanian subject is then one that 'emerges at the point of non-recognition: this is not me. I was not there'[94] – that is, there is an alien kernel to subjectivity, one of which the symptom is the most striking manifestation. In the dialectic of identification, or the confrontation between the subject and the other, the subject drops out of the picture and the subject's own disappearance, *aphanisis*, is the first step towards subjectivity. In Lacan's mirror stage, the ego as imaginary identification emerges to replace a non-existing subject, or the subject only retroactively emerges as an imaginary identification when faced with the other (the mirror image, other child, the Other).

Alienation is a process through which the subject appears precisely as a non-being or in the place of a lack in being. But there is no subject prior to the Other and the encounter with the Other affirms the subject as an 'empty set', or as what is out of place. If the subject is without being and only appears in the field of the Other, then what comes back to the subject in imaginary identification is not really his image, i.e., the imago is fundamentally (de)formative.[95] Rather, what comes back to the subject is a sign: the sign comes back to 'petrify the subject in the same movement by which it calls the subject to speak and function'.[96] The sign or the signifier here comes to represent the subject for another and the chain of signification is put into place: the subject is completely submerged by language or by 'empty speech', as Lacan calls everyday language, in contrast to the full speech of analysis. The lost object that is to be re-found is a signifier of a missing signifier, and the desire of the Other acts as a stand-in for a structurally missing representation, for representation in the unconscious is not whole, not-all.

The subject is thereby inscribed in the field of representation; it features as something represented, and not that for whom something is represented. This step was also crucial for Freud in his seminal text on negation, *Die Verneinung*, which proposes that we can detect the two-fold process of alienation in what Freud calls the form of intellectual judgement or 'reality testing', where the subject comes to be represented for something else.[97] Freud posits reality testing as the process by which 'whether something which is in the ego as a representation can now be rediscovered in perception, reality, as well'.[98] It is the process through which a foreign body – the ego – is formed as internal to the subject, as a foreign intruder through which external objective reality is then experienced. What is inaugurated in this process, or the first signifier as such, is the inaugural point of the Ego-Ideal [S1], what Lacan will call 'the unary trait', the trait of oneness, but this One-ness is only possible in relation to another [S2], through which the chain of signification is put into place. Separation in this sense is to be put in the world in the field of the Other, whereby the other is revealed as also lacking; it is a two-fold alienation through which subjectivity emerges. The example Lacan gives is of the child's question, 'Why are you telling me this?':

> The desire of the Other is apprehended by the subject in that which does not work, in the lacks of the discourse of the Other, the child's questioning, the why's of children, are about securing a place for themselves in the desire of the Other whereby the question posed is: can you lose me?[99]

The subject now devotes himself to the lack of the Other: desire is the desire of the Other; i.e., man's desire is for the Other to desire him. This is the (lost) 'cause' of his desire: the *objet a* emerges here precisely because the Other's desire is elusive; it is (always-already) lost and cannot be squared with the subject's desire – 'desire crawls, slips, escapes, like a ferret'.[100] For instance, the child cannot decipher the desire of the mother: there is something about her desire which escapes him. We can think of Hamlet here and his mother's desire, for which Ophelia acts as a stand in, as *objet a* or *O-phelia*.[101] Where the rift is introduced between the child (subject) and the mother's (other) desire, *objet a* emerges, and this is no longer the realm of the demand to be desired by the Other. Instead, the subject is now in desire proper: 'it is a repetition based on a lack engendered from the previous time that seems to reply to the lack raised by the following time'.[102] The subject's symptom or the 'silent point in the speaking subject' is a site of conflict in which *objet a* is kept alive, the lost object (*objet a*) is not really lost but 'constituted-as-lost'[103]: the *objet a* reveals that the object of the drive is independent of any other (real) object. The structure of any act of desire is a search for its object-cause, only to reconstitute it as a lost object. It is important to note here that *objet a* is neither an immanent *agalma* nor a transcendent Thing, but is premised on the modern discovery of the autonomy of the signifier. *Objet a*, as Samo Tomšič argues, is 'unthinkable outside modernity and is so to speak a modern invention, a consequence of the foundation of science on universal mathematisation and of the social relations on quantification and mass production'.[104]

The dual between desire and *objet a* then seems to be the stage set of modernity, of its symbolic and imaginary forms that seek to restitute the subject's place in structure and in relation to the Other. Culture's utility lies in this *purposive uselessness*, for there is no possible synthesis between desire and the drive, or between desire and *objet a*. Social relations are in this sense non-relational; there is a constitutive non-relation between subject and Other that is mediated by all kinds of fantasies and fetishisations. Modernity is primarily characterised by the retreat of the discourse of the master and the shift away from pre-capitalist social relations based on direct domination (king and his subject, the lord and the bondsman). Servitude or direct domination is a form of interrelation that assumes fetishised relations between people (a king is a king, a slave a slave by nature). It is only in capitalist society that abstract domination arises through commodity relations: fetishism is no longer inter-subjective but arises from a relation between things.[105] The fetishism of commodities is symptomatic, and it was none other than Lacan who claimed that Marx had invented the symptom: fetishism is the return of the repressed of pre-modern forms of domination; it is a sign of the haunting of capitalist modernity by ghosts and apparitions.

For Marx, Freud and Lacan, fetishism is not dealt with as a problem that simply arises from colonisation (or as a concept derived from a colonial relation), but as an internal problem of bourgeois thought. As a real abstraction that formally determines structural synchronic moments of social life, fetishism is not a primordial religious cult, or a form of survival, but a historically specific way of fixing an image (in capitalist society) that has been inverted in the symbolic process.[106] For psychoanalysis as for Marx, fetishism describes phenomena in which the observer is part of the object described: s/he is not an anthropologist, an observer from the outside, but one bringing forth unconscious processes that dictate his/hers and other's own activities. Thus, phenomena that are 'internal' to the observer are considered as if they originated from without. Moreover, this inversion is doubled: the imaginary reflection has a second layer of deformation, a second inversion, 'a symbolic torsion' in the imaginary reflection that can only be accounted for through the autonomy of the value-form in capitalist society:

> There are two moments in the inversion, the first moment concerns the process of restitution of the image of social characters of human labour, the second moment concerns the fact that the restituted image is modified in relation to the reality it reflects. It is very important to mark the distinction between the two moments, in order to avoid the simplification and misunderstanding, which very often make the inversion simply coincide with alienation.[107]

This double inversion in fetishist disavowal whereby an element is foreclosed only for it to return from without gives rise to the question of negativity in the psychoanalytic and Marxian framework. Or what has been discussed above as the 'constitutive alienation' of the subject that is disavowed in capital for commodification to be possible.[108]

The constitutively alienated subject is precisely the one that capital must reject only for it to re-appear in fetishist relations or 'constituted alienation'.[109] The constitutively alienated subject is defined in Lacan's mirror stage, or his recounting of the process of identification, where he argues that there is a deformative function of *imagos* through which the ego is generated in the subject. Lacan shows that the ego is an other that through imaginary identification resides as an external object in the subject – Freud's where it (id) was I (ego) shall be. There is a dual alienation or misrecognition that occurs in identification: the ego resides in the place of the other *and* it does not recognise itself as alienated.

Consequently, the image that institutes the subject as ego is at the same time what separates him from himself. In other words, the recognition of identity is always-already a recognition of difference: it is the identity of identity and difference. The mirror stage results in a double alienation: a constitutive one (production of the split ego) and a constituted one, an asymmetrical relation between the subject and the Other. Thus the psychoanalytic subject – which is not to be conflated with the ego – is fundamental for any engagement with the critique of liberal modernity precisely because it is not the substantive subject of a *weltanschauung* or a worldview: i.e. it is not a unified self-consciousness, a will to power, a self-transparent ego, or a human individual. The subject in this account is always-already out of joint; it is only located by exclusion from the order of things, from the positive order of entities. Just as the worker is a split subject who has no positive substantial being and has to sell his very 'substance' of being.

Who is the Other of Liberalism?

It is already a *fait accompli*, and a known fact, that the liberal revolutions of the eighteenth and nineteenth century, which Marx had called the 'political revolutions of civil society', did not bring emancipation to many social groups the world over. It would be naive to argue that the acquisition of (liberal) rights that were not previously recognised or enjoyed was not accompanied by a dis-emancipation, a deprivation of the rights whose recognition and enjoyment the excluded had won.[110] For example, one can hardly qualify the American Civil War as a war of political emancipation given the protracted nature of the racial question; in its aftermath, by 1877, racial segregation and lynching had already retracted any already acquired rights, within a society that proclaimed itself as liberal.

It often goes unnoticed how much the supposed rights acquired in liberal regimes are in fact won by influences from the most hated 'others' of liberal cultures (we can only recall the examples of the Haitian Revolution and the October Revolution for anti-racist struggles in the twentieth century). It is also an inconvenient truth that the gains of liberal societies have gone in tandem with the dis-emancipation of people under their rule in the colonies, through the imposition of forced labour on those perceived as immature or barbarian. Under the tyranny of the free market (free buyers and sellers of commodities), liberalism in the past century has grown through exclusion, terror and de-humanisation: slavery, deportation, the decimation of populations – these have all developed in close connection with the legacy of liberalism.

We know by now that the contemporary postcolonial and de-colonial critique of liberalism as the handmaiden of Eurocentrism focuses on its silencing of different particular cultures, lifeworlds and identities. The relegation of culture to a realm that is 'natural' and outside politics is one of the distinctive traits of liberalism, as its postcolonial critics argue. The split liberal subject is meant to maintain culture, religion, faith and all other 'idiosyncrasies' within the private realm where they belong, while the public is where the subject attains autonomy, freedom and independence. Even the harshest critics of liberalism resort to the argument of 'leave us our culture'. But what is missed in these analyses is a distinction between the false universality of capitalism, which pivots around four fundamental concepts enumerated by Marx (freedom, equality, property and 'Bentham'), and the universality of modernity. The false universality of liberalism functions as a negative force that purports to destroy particularity, yet in fact sustains it and essentialises its various forms around the globe – that is, it renders the distinction between the particular and universal *a merely formal one*. As capitalism subsumes various societies around the globe, conflict is increasingly presented in terms of differences between cultures and societies. However, the important site of difference that is often overlooked is that which is *within* culture and identity itself.

Despite the multiple critiques of liberalism for its cultureless universality, the relationship between culture and liberalism requires further elaboration, for they both seem to emerge as an antinomic pair of capitalist social forms.[111] And by 'antinomies', what is meant here is that they are not only subjective distortions, pertaining to equally valid thought processes or propositional content, but also expressions of the contradiction of the existing social relations of capitalism as an objective and concrete abstraction: 'discursive practices do have constitutive social effects; nevertheless, we cannot overlook the logically prior historical constitution of discourses in the specific historical context of global capitalism'.[112]

Thus, the aim ought to be to insist that a position of critique is necessary; but one which does not reduce itself to either positions, culture or liberalism; one that doesn't reduce itself to either the false universality of freedom of choice (which comes down to the freedom to sell one's labour, etc.), or to the purely relativist position of culturalism that assumes a singularity (Muslim, Arab, Indian, Jew) as a counter to the absolutes of universalism. The logic of singularity, which characterises the culturalist critique of liberalism, is one that ultimately assumes that knowledge can be affirmed only when it complies to specified social value, giving one a sense of being at home in the world and affirming a *Weltanschauung*. This relativism, although meant to protect the particular and oppressed from the powerful, renders the critique of the powerful impossible precisely because of the incommensurability it postulates between the singularity of, for example, Arabic thought and its Western Other. Ultimately, the question that I suggest needs to be addressed in considering modern Arabic thought is this: where do we locate the subject of politics? It is this site of politics (or site of the political) that remains to be determined. And in order to get there, we must be able to ascertain the retreat of politics, its scarcity in both liberalism and culturalism.

Although the concept of culture emerges from the context of Enlightenment Europe, in its modern instantiation, culture cannot simply be read as a 'Europeanisation' of the conceptual universe of societies the world over; but rather as what 'has served to de-Europeanise the concepts that constitute the now global thought forms of modernity'.[113] The object of cultural discourse 'is a historically determinate form of human subjectivity' that is ultimately 'grounded in structures of social practice' specific to capitalist society.[114] In a society that is organised around commodity production and exchange, the individual subject is split between two roles: one of practical activity (the liberal pursuit of private interests in civil society), the other of a different practical activity through which the individual strives to achieve a unity with the social totality (culture). This split liberal subjectivity is precisely the thing whose wholeness culture appears to be an attempt to restore; yet culture proves to be transgressive of economy, excessive, sacrificial, a source of malaise and discontent: its utility or value seems to lie in its precise functional uselessness. This excessiveness of culture, its 'too-muchness', cannot be grasped without resorting to the very epistemologies that the critics of liberalism wish to debunk: fundamentally, those of psychoanalysis and Marx.

The contemporary critique of liberalism seems to hinge on a non-dialectical logic: culture versus liberalism, liberalism versus culture; here we have a naive synthesis at best in this analysis, a culture of liberalism. Added to this synthesis we have a new level of confusion: we have arguments for the affirmation of organicist culture (conceived as liberalism's Other, a new nature) posited against liberal culture. It seems that what is emerging in the critiques of liberalism is a strange renewed opposition between nature and culture, and it is none other than Freudian psychoanalysis that is singled out as promulgating this oppressive distinction.

For Wendy Brown, the 'culturalisation of politics through the liberal discourse of tolerance', or the logic of 'we have a culture (of tolerance), while they are had by culture' hinges on 'an imaginary opposition between culture and individual moral autonomy, in which the former vanquishes the latter unless culture is subordinated to liberalism'.[115] This opposition between culture and liberalism perceives group practices (e.g. religious, cultural, ethnic) as 'sites of natural or native hostility'. The staged conflict is one between 'the binding force of the social contract and the binding force of culture or religion'. Thus, for Wendy Brown, liberalism regards multiculturalism as a problem that 'tolerance is summoned to solve'.[116]

The moves that Brown subsequently makes are as follows: the root problem is Enlightenment, which privileges deliberative rationality as opposed to 'the embodiment of cultural practices and beliefs'. And it is the Cartesian subject, defined as the 'splitting of the mind from embodied, historicised, cultured being', that is culpable for the anti-cultural prejudice of liberalism.[117] For Brown, the Cartesian subject is somehow endowed with Aristotelian qualities: it is fundamentally liberal because it is thought *to have* the freedom of choice as a capacity. There is a crucial distinction that is missed in this proposition. Descartes's faculty of thinking is not Aristotle's *theoria*: the latter unfolds in a finite cosmos while the former operates in a decentred infinite universe.[118] Descartes's decentring of subjectivity is crucial for the psychoanalytic concept of the unconscious. Lacan maintained that the task of modern philosophy was from the beginning an attempt to fend off madness: to separate transcendental philosophy from madness.[119] This is not to say however that the modern subject of reason is nothing but an illusion, but that the subject of the unconscious cannot exist outside the modern subject of reason. Like the *cogito*, the subject of the unconscious emerges from the reduction of all personal substantial content, from the exclusion of the subject from the positive order of things. The subject of the unconscious emerges from the split between the subject of the enunciation and the subject of the enunciated: it is an *extimate* kernel that emerges between the 'I think' and the 'I am'. The function of the 'I' is what Lacan interrogates in the mirror stage: the 'I', the ego, is itself the source of all fantasy formations. However, what is crucial in Lacan's formulation is that the I is not the subject: the I is on the side of the Imaginary and the subject on the side of the Symbolic. The subject emerges always in a relation of misrecognition, hence, the subject is not simply a product of structure, contrary to what structuralists maintained at the time (Foucault's death of man, Althusser's death of the subject, etc.).

Moreover, Lacan claimed that the *cogito* itself is a forced choice that depends on the signifier: if I stop thinking, then I cease to exist. Mladen Dolar's formulation is crucial here:

> Thought depends on the signifier, which turns the subject into the empty point of enunciation, instead of founding his/her being. In the place of the supposed certainty of the subject's being, there is just a void. *It is not the same subject that thinks and that is;* the one *that is* is not the one *that thinks*, even more, the one *that is* is ultimately not a subject at all.[120]

The forced choice of the *cogito* is precisely what curtails its obverse side, that of the unconscious.[121] If we accept Brown's dismissal of the *cogito* as the crux of liberal individualism, then we forego the unconscious itself as a category, which I will argue is irreducible to liberal individualism. In other words, we throw out the baby with the bathwater.

Brown also traces liberalism's autonomous individual to Kant. She construes his argument about intellectual maturity as presupposing an 'independence from authority in general, and the independence of reason itself'.[122] This is one possible (although prevalent) reading of Kant, but there are others that position Kant against the liberal legal and moralistic interpretation of his ethics.[123] Freedom and autonomy can only be achieved through a heteronomous act of recognising the law as what is external to the self; in other words, the categorical imperative is a recognition of a law or standard that is external to the self; it is precisely about relating negatively to oneself for the purpose of an openness to all others, such that the 'public use of reason' for Kant is essentially about accepting homelessness as a true fate.

The opposition that Brown posits is one between the Cartesian/Kantian liberal subject, in her reading, and their 'nonindividuated opposite who is so because of the underdevelopment of both rationality and will'.[124] The drama of liberalism as such is that individuation is pitted 'against culture and religion as forms of rule', which are to be 'dethroned, replaced by the self-rule of men'.[125] So the opposition that liberalism creates is as follows: culture as merely a way of life versus culture as power and rule, religion as a choice and source of comfort versus religion as a source of irrationality and violence. These ideological presuppositions of liberalism hinge on the notion of individual moral autonomy, and the liberalisation of the world hinges on the notion of tolerance, which in turn assumes the 'good of individual autonomy' above all cultural differences.

Brown is right to claim that liberalism assumes freedom of choice as a subjective capacity, but this is fundamentally an Aristotelian and not a Kantian position: freedom as a capacity we have, that we have to think we already have, precedes Kant's argument that a free act must go against private institutional/communal belonging, an act that goes against common sense. The Aristotelian understanding of freedom – which is Brown's real target – leads to the precise indifference of freedom, a deadening of freedom, for it reduces humans to animals and foregoes the radical import of freedom as an act that transforms the conditions of what is perceived as good in society.[126]

In the coming chapters, I provide evidence for the following claim: the anxiety around cultural practices, habits and customs, which characterises modern Arabic thought, is an anxiety that emerges from becoming conscious of the unconscious mechanical repetitions that come to inhabit the subject. In other words, this is a particularly modern consciousness insofar as it harbours from the beginning the anxiety of liberal tolerance. The choice that this form of anxiety poses, I argue, is a choice in habit: there is no escape from habit, but there must be an escape from the double-bind introduced by capitalist political economy that essentialises the identity of 'being and having'.[127] The mechanism of habit is the precondition of freedom. But what occurs under capitalist subsumption in modernity is the transformation of the preconditions of freedom into its actuality.[128] Marx and Hegel posed the following question: how can having a habit not become identical to being *had* by a habit? The worker's transformation into animality, her reduction to isolated bodily functions (which we can discern in Shidyaq's depictions of sensations as produced by disjointed bodily functions) is simultaneously a reduction and an abstraction. I will return to this issue in Chapter 5. But for the time being it is important to point out that under conditions of capitalist abstraction, the human, in the figure of the worker, is reduced to an animal: there is a 'capitalist nature' that is characterised by the transformation of abstract functions into ends.[129] It is against this capitalist nature that we must locate any discussion of nature/culture.

The Non-liberal Freud

Brown argues that Freud is a renewed field of contestation for critics of liberalism. There are two Freuds: one that can be enlisted as promoting a liberal ideology that assumes a 'progressive historical anthropological narrative, in which tolerant liberal orders represent the highest stage of "maturity" for man and are equated with civilisation'[130]; and another that understands the contingency of group formations 'and their basis in affect rather than essential traits'. The latter Freud can be employed to critique the 'ontologisation of blood and belonging at play in modern liberal theory and cultural tolerance'.[131] However, Brown maintains in her reading of Freud that the account of the progress of civilisation that he provides, vis-à-vis civilisation as what emerges from sublimation or repression, assumes a *telos* of progress from primary 'organicist identities – groups – to civilised individuals'.[132] Thus, the target of Brown's critique is the ego as the figure 'whose ontogeny captures phylogeny': the figure assumed by a discourse of tolerance premised on the distinction between those *who are had by culture and those who have it*.[133]

Freud's account of the ego's formation – according to Brown – risks falling into the liberal tolerance talk, which assumes that organicist societies are oppressive to the liberal individual. In Brown's reading, the egoic function – perceived as what defines the autonomous individual – ratifies tolerance as that which is only available to liberal subjects and confirms organicist orders 'as a natural limit of liberal tolerance and as intolerable in consequence of their own intolerance'.¹³⁴ Brown is claiming that Freud perceives organicist orders as 'not simply pre-civilised social relations and subject formations but de-civilised ones'.¹³⁵ The main liberal assertion that she singles out in Freud, across the spectrum of his works, is that of an 'analytical *a priori* individualism' and a colonial account of individualism: the lone savage and primitive tribalist.¹³⁶ In Brown's account, Freud appears to have confirmed the nature/culture dualism of liberal thought by turning the problem inwards: the ego is the site of conflict between primitive, instinctual, infantile forces on one hand, and individuation and rationality on the other.

> Regressed man, unindividuated man, isn't regressed *to* the group but *by* the group to a more instinctual psychic state. And his de-individuation derives not from his relation to others but from his own instincts. He is without the independence of will and deliberation yielded by a developed super-ego.¹³⁷

In this reading of Freud, the group is (paradoxically) thought of as an *internal* force of regression, which is simultaneously instinctual and must be repressed for the sake of the individual. However, this cannot be farther from Freud's most fundamental move of positing the theory of the drive, *triebe*, against theories of instinct: the rigid differentiation between a mental apparatus regulated by certain principles on the one hand, and instinct penetrating into the apparatus from the outside on the other, cannot be maintained in Freud's schema.

Instincts after Freud are no longer defined in terms of their origin and organic function, but in terms of the *real* determining forces which give life its determining direction and principles. Thus, 'instincts' are shaped by life and shape it in turn. Moreover, they have other aims than the furthering of life. The animal man becomes human only through the fundamental transformation of his nature that is not already given in the first place: 'the individual perishes from his internal conflicts while the species perishes in its struggle with the external world to which it is no longer adapted'.¹³⁸ The struggle for satisfaction or for happiness as Freud depicts it in *Civilisation and Its Discontents* is a struggle with death: it is only the death story (the individual learning to die in their own way, from inside) that will illuminate the life story: 'the moment one inquires about the sense or value of life, one [becomes] sick, since objectively neither of them has any existence'.[139]

Civilisation and Its Discontents was written toward the end of Freud's life, and it carries within it a structural theory of the mind. In it we see staged the grand duel between culture and the drives: the repression of aggression and sexuality as the main function and impetus of civilisation, and the death drive as a destructive factor that is channelled into the construction of civilised society yet threatens its dissolution at all times. There is a disquiet in culture, a malaise, an element of discomfort that seems to be fundamental to being-in-culture.[140] Dolar's reframing of the debate on *Civilisation and Its Discontents* is crucial here: the problem cannot be stated in the terms of culture versus nature, or culture versus drives; it cannot be reduced to the simple opposition between reality principle and death principle. The problem lies, rather, in the production of a surplus element that is a springboard for a repetition compulsion:

> Drives are endowed with a vector which compels them to return to the same place, the place of the crime, that is, the place of satisfaction, a satisfaction beyond use and need, and this is what epitomises the object of the drive. There is a blind automatism built into the drive which entails repetition, insists as repetition, the repetition of what procures pleasure – and ultimately, enigmatically, also the repetition of something which is beyond the pleasure principle.[141]

The discontent in civilisation can perhaps be redefined as the repetition compulsion that emerges in all six traits of culture: 1) the mastery of nature through prothesis and technology is a source of discontent, wherein knowledge becomes acephalic and heeds an automatism that serves no other purpose but itself; 2) the validation of the beautiful as the validation of an 'objectal excess' that has no utility; 3) the importance of cleanliness, which harbours a repetition compulsion insofar as the renunciation of bodily enjoyment (in filth and excreta) only leads to a surplus enjoyment; 4) the trait of order, which is also linked to compulsion beyond utility; 5) the valuation of spirituality as a process of sublimation, in which one satisfaction replaces another only to show that the drive from the beginning accepts stand-ins, deflections, partial objects and is in fact dependent on substitutions; and 6) law or justice. The sixth trait of culture – law/justice – is of particular relevance for this discussion of Brown's reading of Freud. This final attribute of culture relies on relinquishing individual satisfaction for the horde or community: there can be no freedom in society, and the primal father is the only image of a free individual.

The cultural bind, or the bind of the drives, is this constant duel between satisfaction and renunciation, satisfaction and repression: in the failure to attain its object, the drive keeps going, there is 'something that drives the drive and which is its true object. This surplus is what sustains cultural and social coexistence as well as marks it with an impossibility'.[142] Reading Freud's account of nature and culture as dualistic is in fact a misreading that overlooks the precise link that is posited between sexuality and drives. Freud's analysis of sexuality in the *Three Essays* provides the key to understanding the drive not as a substance but as that which is defined by the impossibility of substantialisation:

> It is not a substance that one would have to delimit and localise, say by positing sexuality as the firm determining force, a substratum that lies under all seemingly higher endeavours, a universal answer – it consists precisely in the very impossibility of such a delimitation or localization, it is a universal question rather than an answer.[143]

Freud's account of culture and the drives is not an engagement with two separate or independent entities: nature is a substratum on which the culture works, there are no opposed totalities we can call nature and culture; rather, the drive in Freud's account is what de-totalises both; it is the point of their impossible overlap, which simultaneously generates them as points of indifference. Brown's insistence that culture is an *a priori* that must be acknowledged not as a choice but as a historical condition, which the individual cannot and does not necessarily wish to escape, merely replaces one *a priori* (liberal individualism) with another. Brown regards Freud's view of groups – as formations premised on narcissistic love and ideal-ego introjections – as liberal because he pathologises 'group enthrallment as a regression from rationality, science and impulse control'.[144] This reading renders Freud's analysis of the function of repression normative; it makes it seem as though Freud is suggesting that repression is necessary for individual formation and threatened by group formations because they represent a 'de-repressed human condition'.[145] It is as though in Brown's reading, Freud requires love to be domesticated and privatised in order for the public liberal sphere to be possible. Freud then appears to be advocating the sacrifice of 'inherent individual freedom on the altar of love that which dominates it'.[146]

Brown's aim then is to defend group belonging, and *organicist* group belonging in particular, against Freud's 'western-centric' account that – on her reading – promotes the social contract as a mature and civilised social bond against groups ruled by a 'slavish devotion' to a leader. In other words, she reads Freud's analysis as a defence of deliberative rationality against unrepressed instincts.

Brown circumvents any engagement with the problem of the drive as it emerges in Freud's metapsychology and instead holds fast to the dualistic reading of Freud: nature versus culture, primitive versus individual, civilised versus uncivilised. This leads Brown to reject Freud's analysis of narcissist love or ideational projection in group formation because it is premised on the positing of group love, identification with a group through a leader, *against* the individual ego-ideal. Freud's analysis of love is premised on thinking of group enthrallment as opposed to rationality, as a regression from it. Her reproach to Freud is as follows:

> We do not actually love each other but are bound together through identification that is experienced as love, even as it is a way of living our love for the unattainable object. With regard to the second, for Freud, being in love inherently entails a certain regression, a withdrawal from the world and a loss of boundaries – a state of abandon as well as slavishness. Moreover, being in love entails a loss of the individual ego-ideal and of the conscience and inhibition it sustains.[147]

Brown claims that Freud understands group formation as being premised on the idealisation of that which is external to the group, the leader. The love of the leader is fundamentally a narcissistic form of love, an ideal-ego projected onto an object:

> Originally driven by eros, the (sexless) love for the leader or ideal develops into an ardent idealization of the loved object, starting as a gratification of the ego's own narcissism and ending with the idealised object taking the place of the ego-ideal itself and consuming the ego.[148]

Consequently, Brown argues that Freud understands love as a loss of 'individual' boundaries, a slavishness, and devotion to the group. According to her, Freud's theory of love pathologises group formations and serves individualistic liberal ideology. She claims that Freud's definition of organicist societies is liberal because it suggests that love ties must be contained in the private and domestic domain in order for society to complete its civilising mission:

> If love civilised is love domesticated, then ardent attachments of any sort – to a God, a belief system, a people, or a culture – must remain private and depoliticised if they are not to endanger civilisation and the autonomous individual who signifies a civilised state. Culture is thus dangerous if it is public rather than private, a formulation that is significant in distinguishing liberal from nonliberal states, and even more so, 'free' societies from 'fundamentalist' ones.[149]

This reading, however, misses the essential claim that psychoanalysis posits with regard to the nature of love as an external mark of the origin of subjectivity. Freud's analysis of love in *Group Psychology and the Analysis of the Ego* (1921) is an analysis of the introjection of an object into the subject in the process of identification. The introjection of an external element is not simply an assimilation or a replacement of one thing by an other – in Brown's reading a substitution of an ego-ideal for the 'liberal' ego – it is a space that generates a difference between an ego and an ego-ideal: the ego is nothing but this difference.[150] The key point to retain from Freud's analysis is that the constitution of the subject is premised on this junction of a contingent exteriority (cultural symbolic forms) with an intimate kernel. Furthermore, this introjection of an external object is always a forced one, whether in liberal or organicist societies; it is a 'forced choice' imposed by symbolic identification. The symbolic function leaves the subject without a choice; it is a choice between a void and a loss: the subject is forced to take up its position in the symbolic but at the cost of losing *not its freedom*, which is not a substantive capacity in the psychoanalytic framework, but any kind of substantial interiority or autonomy. Love is the particular instance where this melodrama plays out: it is a contingency that turns into a necessity, *tyche* transforms into *automaton*:

> The moment of subjectivation is precisely that moment of suspension of subjectivity to the Other (Fate, Providence, Eternal plan, Destiny, or whatever one might call it), manifesting itself as the pure contingency of the Real. Indeed, that strange force of love reputedly rules out any other considerations; it does not permit deliberation, the balance of gains and losses, of the pondering of the advantages of a certain choice-it just demands unconditional surrender to the Other.[151]

This fated encounter cannot be subverted and is pivotal for the very practice of psychoanalysis, where transference-love is engineered in the analytic session only for it to be traversed by the patient culminating with the end of analysis. Psychoanalysis in a sense rehearses, reproduces and isolates the very pathological state that underlines symbolic identification *tout court*. In the situation of transference love, the analyst occupies the position of the Other for the subject. But this Other has no call, no desire to which the subject must respond (unlike the ideological call of love of nation, family, religion, etc.). And it is only then that the subject recognises that the Other is a function that is always-already present for him/her. This process, which is the most fundamental contribution of psychoanalysis, reveals to the subject that they are always-already occupying a lack in the Other, that they are always-already responding to a lack in the symbolic and imaginary orders. In this sense, there is no pre-constituted liberal individual ego that loses part of itself in group identification: the loss itself is generated by the forced choice that the subject undergoes in occupying a place in the symbolic. Freud's insight was precisely that there is no ontological substantial ego prior to group identification; that in fact any identification is underlined by the disavowal of a negativity or lack in the symbolic. This disavowal is what generates a return of the image of an ego from an elsewhere. The ego is an inert alienating function, always-already an Other that resides in the subject's own house.

Thus, Brown's reading, in which she accuses Freud of harbouring a negative view of organicist societies, misses the entire point of Freud's account of the ego as an imaginary function. There is no escape from a slavish devotion to an Other, whether in liberal or so-called non-liberal societies; the same drama plays out in different fantasy formations.[152] Brown makes it seem as though Freud would maintain that there is a possibility of negating repression altogether, which constitutes an order of 'rational deliberation', whereas Freud precisely insisted that the function of repression persists even when the process itself is revealed to the subject. Repression isn't simply a function of a reality principle against a pleasure principle: there is a persistence of unconscious mechanisms that resists analysis. The importance of psychoanalysis lies in revealing that there are fantasy structures or libidinal investments already at work in any social order: the principle of individual autonomy is precisely one of the strongest ideological fantasies in modernity. Consequently, Brown's assertion that Freud maintains the 'conceit about autonomy in liberal orders', which states that the subject somehow precedes or 'is prior to culture and free to choose culture',[153] is a false one.

Ultimately, Brown targets what she describes as Freud's progressive-anthropological historicist narrative, which she reads as perceiving group dynamics and organicist orders as regressions of individuation. She reads both *Civilisation and Its Discontents* and *Totem and Taboo* as works in which Freud promotes an image of civilisation that relies on a distinction between nature and culture, a distinction between a natural state of 'sexual rivalry and primary aggression' on one hand, and sublimation and civilisation on the other. According to Brown, Freud reproduces a narrative of the primitive as 'a lone savage and submissive tribal follower'.[154] Furthermore, she argues that he normatively aligns 'maturity, individuation, conscience, repression, and civilisation' as opposed to 'childishness, primitivism, unchecked impulse, instinct, and barbarism'.[155] And it is this opposition that feeds into the liberal ideology of tolerance.

The problem with 'Freud's liberalism' in Brown's account can be reduced to two main points: it presupposes what she calls an 'ontological *a priori* individual' as the subject of politics; and, most importantly, it denies the right of organicist communities to exist in the contemporary civilised world. According to Brown, Freud's concern, 'in addition to ratifying the basic architecture of the psyche he spent years theorizing, is to affirm the individual as a primordial unit of analysis and action and thereby to pathologise the group as a dangerous condition of de-individuation and psychological regression'.[156] As we have seen, however, Freud's account of the ego as the illusion that emerges from the distance between the ego and ego-ideal, as a place of pure difference, is in no way compatible with an *a priori* understanding of the individual. Furthermore, according to Brown's reading, the progress of civilisation hinges on repression, and repression is defined as the individual repression of *instinct* for the purpose of group integration: 'for Freud there is only ever the individual, that is, the individual is both the ontological *a priori* and the *telos* of civilisation'.[157]

Brown's reading of Freud is perplexing on multiple levels. First, as is well known, in *Group Psychology and the Analysis of the Ego*, published less than twenty years before *Moses and Monotheism*, Freud is attempting to analyse the organicist vision of community promoted by Fascist ideology around him, together with the symbolic structures which it iterates. Was not the *Volksgemeinshaft* a libidinal fantasy of organic community, one that relied on a specific 'aestheticisation of politics' as Walter Benjamin described it?[158] Second, in a somewhat predictable Foucauldian fashion, Brown's whole approach elides the fundamental concept of psychoanalysis: the unconscious as a topology that disturbs the *Innewelt* and *Ummwelt*, the inner and outer domains. The unconscious is neither nature nor culture in Freud's view but can only be understood through a theory of *triebe*, or the drives – wrongly translated as 'instinct' by Brown. The unconscious functions through this mechanism of repression. And repression is not simply a form of self-deception or bad faith. It is a mindless state of mindedness that is non-teleological and that cannot be captured by our normal understanding of what is meaningful and purposeful mental activity, but rather through the compulsion to repeat or the return of the repressed. Unconscious mental activity – symptomatic agency – is at its core organised around *signifiers* rather than full-fledged meanings, beliefs, purposes, or propositional attitudes.

It is surely not coincidental that the great shift in critical theory, the rise of poststructuralism in the 1970s, is concomitant with the new self-transformation of liberalism – neoliberalism itself – and it is a shift that insists on dismissing the category of the unconscious. Foucault of course stands out as one of the most influential twentieth-century thinkers attuned to the new forms of neoliberal power actively promoting freedom against a previous regime of discipline and punishment perceived as repressive. As we know, Foucault, whose epistemology Brown is informed by, focused on discourses, bodies and pleasures. He argued for the insubstantiality of the subject in its nominal interiority and ultimately promoted a hyper-pessimistic activism of 'resistance' to power. Meanwhile Lacan, his direct contemporary, returned to Freud and Marx and conceived the task of psychoanalysis to be fundamentally political: the relation between social institutions and the unconscious informs a political topology that requires a psychoanalytic act, a *scilicet,* to incite a new form of knowledge; one that inverts the relationship between truth and knowledge and frees the former from the mechanisms of *jouissance* that dictate relations of exploitation in society.

After May 1968, while Foucault turned to ancient Greece, Lacan turned to Marx and Freud again to analyse the regimes of enjoyment, *jouissance*, that structure the capitalist social-bond. Lacan formed his concept of surplus-enjoyment on the basis of Marx's concept of surplus-value and Freud's concepts of lust, pleasure, *mehrwork* and that which is 'beyond the pleasure principle'. For psychoanalysis, then, the concept of *jouissance* is not simply about individual solipsistic enjoyment, a result of the attrition and breakdown of social bonds, of community, and so forth; rather it is precisely the site of an engagement with an Other, with the social link, etc.[159] Freud had already introduced this fundamental psychoanalytic insight: the dialectics of repression that govern enjoyment are always-already social.

The Freudian discovery of the unconscious is irreducible to a *Weltanschauung*, which Brown accuses it of being. A worldview, as Freud himself put it, is an intellectual construction that gives a unified solution to all problems of our existence on the basis of an overriding hypothesis, a construction that therefore leaves no questions open and gives everything that we are interested in its particular place.[160]

A *Weltanschauung* is seen by Freud as an *ideal desire* for humankind: by believing in it, one can feel secure in life, know what to strive for, and how to bear one's emotions and interests appropriately. This is to say, a *weltanschauung* is that which provides the subject with a homeostatic ideological fiction: the *homo legalis* (the subject of rights), the *homo economicus* (the subject of political economy), the *citoyen* (the citizen). For Freud, a unifying worldview stands in relation to a specific unconscious desire. The reality of desire manifests itself in the construction of a worldview; a worldview's *dispositif* (its mechanism and knowledge structure) is the fulfilment of this desire. This mechanism of the worldview is a continuation of the early analysis of dreams as symbolic formations (closest to neurotic symptoms, defined as any behavioural or psychosomatic symptoms that result from the return of the repressed) produced to satisfy an unconscious tendency or a wish-fulfilment. The mechanism of wish fulfilment works through distortion and censorship. In the dream-work there is a latent content, a warning, an intention, a preparation; but the manifest content of the dream, its form, its dream-work, is not simply an intention but an intention that is translated through an archaic mode of thought by the help of an unconscious wish. Analogous to dream formations, *Weltanschauungen* or worldviews as wish-fulfilments are not simply a psychological formation internal to the subject but a border between the subjective and social reality: i.e. there is no reality without a phantasmatic support; every worldview has a 'wish-fulfilment' or a specific structure of desire that sustains it. Every *weltanschauung* harbours an unconscious.

In this sense, psychoanalysis is incapable of being a *Weltanschauung*: 'it doesn't have an all-encompassing perspective, it is incomplete, and makes no claims to forming a unity or a system'.[161] In contradistinction to the religious worldview that claims to appease human desire, to soothe and satisfy it, psychoanalysis aims not at liberating desires but at exposing the complicity between certain desires and their interpretation: i.e. the aim of psychoanalysis is not to provide a satisfaction of desires but to uncover the mechanisms, the fantasy, that articulate unconscious desire in a specific *dispositif* or dictum of satisfaction. Psychoanalysis, then, through its method of analysis directs the subject to the problematic kernel of the unconscious mode of production that presents itself in the symptom. The form of interpretation of the world is possible only by subverting the praxis of interpretation already there, already at work; i.e., there is an intertwining of worldview mechanisms and unconscious mechanisms of satisfaction.[162]

The work of interpretation or analysis is summed up in the famous Freudian *Wo es war sol lich warden* (where the id [it] was the ego [i] shall be): where there is an unconscious regime of production, or *jouissance*, there the place of the subject should be revealed, a place where subjectification can take place. In other words, the subject is not a master of their own house. It is in the dream that you are at home, in slips of the tongue, in symptoms, in the sense of the unfamiliar or the uncanny.

Psychoanalysis in this sense cannot offer an interpretation of reality by giving it more meaning; it cannot normalise existing conditions; instead, it creates the conditions through which a transformative act can occur and thereby a transformation of the overall mechanism underlying the unconscious mode of production at work.[163] The reason why psychoanalysis cannot totalise reality or provide a *Weltanschauung* is its specific subject matter, the unconscious: this is a theoretical construct with material effects, a somewhat 'immaterial materiality'. And unlike the objects of the natural sciences, whose positive ontological characteristics are specified by laws enabling prediction, the limits of psychoanalysis follow from the status of its object, for the unconscious is neither a positive entity nor an ontological substance: it depends entirely on contingent and unpredictable traumatic events.

Brown's assertion that Freud assumes an ontologically *a priori* individual is in this sense unfounded. The unconscious mechanisms that govern the social order are not conceived as a struggle between an individual and a collective. Freud argues in *Group Psychology* that because the defining principle of psychoanalysis had always been the division between individual and group, which falls *within* the individual subject, then it was the group itself that was the proper site of psychoanalytic interpretation. For Freud, then, the subject is a joint entity – both psychic and social at once – and the principle of individuation is a collective reality present in the individual subject.

Lacan gave this reality the name *jouissance*. *Jouissance* has a collective nature: it does not belong to an individual as his/her exclusive right but rather to the group itself. In fact, the question of the Other (the stranger, the other culture, and so forth) in psychoanalysis can only be broached when we recognise that the Other is not without an unconscious, that the other is already a stranger in their own house, so to speak. This is far from the liberal discourse of tolerance, for it exposes an internal kernel of alterity, of otherness, that is universal in nature and against the recognition of which all kinds of fantasies are propped up, including the discourse of tolerance.

Moses and Monotheism is a direct commentary on group dynamics. Jewishness for Freud is characterised by a certain neurotic obsessive-compulsiveness. A surplus element characterises Jewish life as a particular interpretation of excitations and pressures caused by a determinate lack, by a missing element, a fundamental desire. In *Moses and Monotheism*, Freud defined Judaism as a specific phantasmatic reaction to the pressure of the super-ego. And what is a super-ego? It is the psychic agency that polices one's identity, one's place within the third-personal, part–whole relations that make up the cultural systems we inhabit. Super-ego discourse is ultimately about law and the subject's always 'exciting' inscription in law. The guilt incurred through the murder of Moses, 'which metaphorically repeats the murder of the primal father that first released humankind from life in the horde and inaugurated the rule of reciprocity, was what ultimately guaranteed the survival of the Jews as a people and tradition'.[164] This is Freud's precise point: the paternal law, or the name-of-the-father, supports the social bond through some form of murderous betrayal. There is an element of transgression and culpability that sustains the law and nowhere does Freud posit this observation as a normative assertion; rather, it is always-already the very condition of normativity. For Freud, the symbolic order is not animated when we publicly affirm a conception of the 'good', but when we are plagued and haunted by transgressions, transmitted in myth, culture, ritual, etc. This is why Freud seeks to analyse the phantasmatic structure that underlies symbolic orders, groups, religions and culture.

The fundamental target of Brown's critique in *Subjects of Tolerance* is to expose that culture-less liberalism is in fact a culture of exclusion that propagates itself through the logic of tolerance (we are tolerant while they are not). Because of the separation of culture from politics, which is a result of liberalism's own disavowal of its own culturalism, according to Brown, liberalism 're-depoliticises what erupts into the political as a cultural, religious, or ethnic claim'. Thus, the ideology of tolerance on this account is at the core of liberalism's 'universalist self-representation'. For Brown, then, it appears that the critique of liberalism must go through the path of re-culturalising politics in the face of the 'cultureless culture of liberalism', or to affirm the 'right' of culture to politics. Brown's critique of Western secular liberalism is legitimate and important, for it points to the manner in which the secular state constructs any politics that does not accede to the separation of public and private spheres as a religious or cultural Other, which has no claim on questions of political freedom. However, Brown's conscription of psychoanalysis into liberal discourse detracts from the potency of her critique of liberalism and does nothing to enhance it. Brown defines the civilisational discourse of Western liberalism as a colonial imperialist imperative that obfuscates attention to the process of global capitalism. Capitalism, however, cannot be assumed as an *a priori* social condition that is merely gestured towards. A critique of the liberal discourse on religion, for example, requires a concrete analysis of how capitalist real abstraction underlies claims to religiosity in the modern era and most importantly requires an analysis of the religious nature of the liberal secular state itself.[165]

Brown's critique of the discourse of tolerance does not move in that direction, for it only defends the claim for a more self-conscious liberalism that does not disavow its own culturalist bias – defined by Brown as the 'conceit of individual autonomy' – one that can accept that there exists a 'set of beliefs and practices [that] attach to values other than autonomy, for example to formulations of plurality, difference, or cultural preservation that do not devolve around individual liberty'.[166] In a sense, Brown is confronting liberalism with its own repressed element that is disavowed only to return from without. She presents liberalism with its own symptom in the hope that liberal secularism will recognise its secular prejudices. The aim of deconstructing the binary between 'moral autonomy and organicism, secularism and fundamentalism'[167] is to reinvent a new liberalism that is 'more restrained in its imperial and colonial impulses' and 'more capable of multicultural justice to which it aspires'.[168]

Brown thereby seeks to deconstruct the so-called separation of culture from politics in order to re-culturalise politics and simultaneously politicise culture in an era in which all we have is a 'culturalisation of politics'. Is not the 'global consciousness'[169] of neoliberalism premised on generating conflict from cultural difference, one that understands modernity as being essentially Western and hence adopts the Western bourgeois ideal? Culture – in this analysis – emerges as a concept which has no outside, fashioned along the lines of Foucault's notion of power; and politics is simply to be conceived as an internal loop of culture, just as Foucault's self-care is nothing but an internal loop of power back on itself.[170]

Is it not enough to deconstruct the liberal prejudice against the cultural Other? The deconstruction of a fantasy does not lead to its dissolution, but aids in fortifying it, buttressing its resistance to transformation. Furthermore, this critique of liberalism doesn't take into account the fundamental liberal assumption: individualism is premised on the notion of self-possession; the individual is an *a priori* for liberalism insofar as individuals are understood as proprietors of their own capacities (labour, freedom, and so forth). The liberal social contract is premised on the 'equal' exchange between proprietors and the aim of political society is simply to protect property and maintain an orderly relation of exchange. In this sense, the political state is meant to protect the *a priori* relations of exchange, which are in turn based on a notion of self-possession and personhood that is religious and abstract. The legal person, as we know from the Hobbesian formulation, is modelled along the incarnation of God in Christ: the person is an outward disguise, a mask; it is a prosthetic device, an outward appearance of a great multitude of men. And it is this legal person who comes to be defined as a proprietor of an abstract quality called labour-power. The person/individual is a real abstraction that dominates social life under relations of capitalist exchange: the political state is a means to safeguard this alienated form (the legal person) of the subject; it becomes the incarnation of the alienation of humankind.

Rather than dismiss the ego as liberal ideology in modernity, we ought to consider it as a symptom of the shortcomings of the name-of-the-father, of guarantees to symbolic authority. Fariyaq is Shidyaq's escape – *far* in Arabic literally means a fugitive, a runaway – and that escape is constituted through a pure *jouissance* of language. Fariyaq shows us that the ego is constituted by language and thereby only founded in a dimension of delusions and *paraplexis*. Shidyaq stages through Fariyaq's egoic-narcissism a new language; he attempts to create a new reader as an act of rebellion against accepted social norms and meanings. The madness of Shidyaq's writing stages a linguistic autarchy that betrays an ability to communicate intersubjectively, on a social level.[171]

Bustani's ideal-ego, Robinson Crusoe, is also a prosthetic device, a means to bypass the crisis of the symbolic in a post-war Beirut society. Crusoe's 'true story of civilisation' is paired with an obsessive-compulsive work on language, dictionary- and encyclopaedia-making, with the aim of purifying Arabic from its (allegedly) stagnant elements. Bustani poses a Hegelian questioning of habit as he attempts to synthesise an encyclopaedia encompassing all knowledge. Shidyaq, on the other hand, writes in response to Bustani's patriotism with anarchic egoism: of which *watan* (nation) does Bustani speak? Belonging cannot be defined in terms of blood and land: so, who provides the guarantee of belonging?[172]

2

~~Why is There Lalangue Rather than Nothing?~~
Love of *Lugha* and *Lalangue*

> Beings of language aren't organized beings, but there is no doubt that they are beings, that they stamp their form upon man ... it nevertheless remains true that they don't have any substantial existence in themselves.
>
> – Lacan, *The Psychoses* (177)

> Hysteria is a question centred around the signifier that remains enigmatic as to its meaning.
>
> – Lacan, *The Psychoses* (190)

Language perceived as a mirror, in which an image of likeness is constructed, is nothing but the language of the social contract: a tool for communication to be possible and justified by a legitimate authority. This 'image' of language is one that is constructed by grammar specifically. It is grammar that constructs a unity of totality. And in grammar language is seized in a glance, all at once, as an imaginary totality. The question of mastery in language – its correctness and incorrectness – lies at the heart of grammar. As such, it is also a substitute question for the legitimation of the sovereign and the social contract.

Arabic grammar in particular has been concerned throughout its history with the problem of presumed 'corruptions' in or of the language: Arabic is eternal, like the soul, and it is to be guarded against error. In fact, it is the very fear of error, of corruption, of 'low' language (*ammiya*) that renders the first treatise of Arabic grammar possible.[1] It is always the fear of the neophytes (the new Muslims, conquered people, and so forth) that renders the codification of correct linguistic norms necessary. The fierce debates between Arabic grammarians and logicians – exemplified in the famous medieval contestation between As-Sirafi and Abu Bishr Matta ibn Yunis – concerning the category of meaning shows how heavily guarded was the Arabic grammarian tradition against philosophy, against a 'foreign logos': while As-Sirafi considered meaning a 'semantic aspect of a phonetic expression', Yunis claimed meanings referred to 'logical operators of the mind'.[2] Despite the consensus reached by the introduction of logic into Arabic linguistics, grammar largely remained Arabo-Islamic without foreign influence.

The beauty of Arabic grammar, conceived as an eternal synchronic, lies in its untarnished state, a pure language that does not submit to diachronicity, that seems to have subverted the historical break between grammar and linguistics inaugurated by the scientific revolution. The discipline of linguistics, and in particular the structural linguistic turn of the twentieth century, moves away from the philological model of comparative grammar and shares the anti-Aristotelian assumptions of the Galilean mathematisation of nature.[3] What modern linguistics shares with scientific discourse is that both come up against a real that is not representable, yet they insist on its formalisation. The real of science is formalised by mathematical logic, while the real of language (the agrammatical limit to the grammatical) is the 'impossible to be said', which forces itself upon speakers of a language and linguists alike.

Linguist Anne Banfield's formulation here is succinct and crucial: 'The real is the state of affairs that can be imagined as other than it is because there is no reason why it is the way it is. But it is not other than it is. In this sense, it is impossible for it to be otherwise and continue to be itself'.[4] This impossible-to-be-said is also the forbidden-to-be-said: not everything can be said *and* there is a prohibition against saying everything; however, this prohibition (like the incest taboo) does not cease to write itself. The speaking subject is reminded constantly of their exile from language (and the sexual relationship). And the linguist who studies language deliberately ignores homophonies and parapraxis because they resist formalisation. Yet this disregard is the precondition for the scientificity of linguistics.

Consequently, the grammarian's passion for language is driven by a desire for its treasures; it is a desire for an *agalma,* for from the beginning the grammarian knows that they shall never conquer the object of their passion. Like the miser and hoarder driven by the desire for accumulating wealth, the grammarian's drive for enrichment can only be satisfied if the 'wealth' of language is removed from social circulation; ossified in lexicons, textbooks and dictionaries; and reserved as a fetishised object of enjoyment, of *jouissance*.[5] But what is the *agalma* of language? Is the *agalma* the trigger of the love relation, of the self-same relation sought out between two speaking subjects, who repeatedly fail to be joined together? Furthermore, what would the *agalma* be when the language itself, *fusha* Arabic, is not really a spoken language at all?

Lugha in its etymology carries the meaning of *laghuw*: incoherent speech, babble and error.[6] In Bustani's nineteenth-century Arabic dictionary, it also has the meaning of annulment, erasure and deletion. To be in a state of *laghuw* is 'to drink endlessly without being able to quench thirst'.[7] In other words, *lugha* oscillates between pleasure and beyond pleasure, an identifiable object of desire that it constantly addresses and makes present through speech. This would mean that *lalangue* would represent an adequate translation of *lugha* – not language as a medium for communication, but the language of the unconscious, in which there is no simple transformation of words into images (or signifier into signified).

Lalangue in its psychoanalytic understanding is speech that penetrates and flows uncontrollably through its speaker. It is speech as a parasite, which imposes itself and divides the speaking subject. The constant equivocation, through homophony, within the word itself in Shidyaq's texts, and the way in which he strips the signifier of its identification-producing effects, can be seen as aiming to dam up of the flow of *lalangue* on one hand, and on the other to unsettle meaning as the space within which the subject exists. 'Like snow falls during the night in order to whiten the surface of the world, my letters fall upon the paper in order to blacken it',[8] writes Shidyaq. He warns the reader of the useful uselessness of his writing, for its solitary pursuit is based on the opposition of the letter to signification.

I will show in the following chapters that the insistence of *lalangue* is evident in Shidyaq's fiction novel *al-Saq 'ala al Saq*, where equivocation, puns and an endless babble of the tongue repeat in one *Maqama* after the other.[9] *Al-Saq* is a difficult book to enjoy reading, for it only speaks of the *jouissance* of the writer himself, an enjoyment that emerges from the constantly failed pursuit to master language: 'as I tried to conquer her, she conquered me'.[10] *Lalangue*, or *lugha,* is then one of the limits of language, and the seduction of Arabic is greater with the continuous failures of its pursuers. When a subject believes in meaning and pursues it, he seeks further a mimetic identification with language – only to find that he is in fact always-already exiled from language.

Linguisteriks

Ahmad Faris al-*Shidyaq* can be considered the modern Sheikh of Arabic par excellence, the foremost linguist of his age; and his writing, in its distinct fixation on equivocation, reveals the true passions of linguistics, the love of language, which at first sight conceals itself in the distinction between *langue* and *parole*. The linguistic model or approach to language primarily assumes that equivocation is a function that can be explained by the rules of stratification in a language (in every language), which renders an abstract concept of Language conceivable as the object of linguistics. Equivocation is thus understood as a result of a schism within the field of language: between *langue* and *parole* (the syntagmatic and paradigmatic) and between the different strata of a language (sound and sense, writing and word). Ultimately, from the perspective of linguistics, equivocation is dissolved within the idea of language as a self-identical and invariable formal determination. As such, equivocation makes way for what is univocal under the guise of language understood as a relational system of differences and the problem of equivocation is resolved through stratification within an object identified as language: 'in order for language to be constructed it suffices for these elements outside the orbit of the ordinary to be relegated into the farthest limit by an adequate naming'.[11] This conception of language always assumes isotopy and a univocity by which language is seen as One, as identical to itself. This is why language in the linguistic account is a unity that underlies all multiple languages, 'a language, as the possible object of a proposition which can be universally validated ... claims to be always distinguishable from what is not a language, always distinguishable from another language'.[12]

Shidyaq expresses this perception in his arguments for the modernisation of Arabic through the proper identification of its linguistic strata which would not only render translation possible but also the formation of new words and concepts. The rules of derivation in Arabic are universal to any language and similar to that of Greek and Latin in this view.[13] Shidyaq's observations on *naht* and derivation rely on identifying systematically and categorically the linguistic strata of Arabic and on re-organising the dictionary in a manner that removes obscurity – which results from incorrect rules of derivation – and allows for Arabic to become a 'scientific language' adequate for the modern world.

The linguistic and grammarian move is premised on procuring as much stratification as possible – phonemes, words, phrases, sentences. However, it cannot do away with the resistance of equivocation, or the 'real of the equivocal'.[14] This is evident in Shidyaq's lengthy critiques of Arabic lexicography in *al-Jasus 'ala al-qamus* and various other essays.[15] His literary and non-linguistic texts, however, reveal that there is another component to his passion for Arabic that requires analysis: that which is in language and yet persists in equivocation. Despite the fact that his texts precede the Freudian and psychoanalytic account of language, we can discern in the lapses, the absences in his writing, an unstated question for which he offers an answer.

To articulate the meaning of the symptomatic reading – a reading of what is present in the text but not directly visible – the intervention of psychoanalysis becomes necessary. Lacan's corrective to structural linguistics, to both *langue* and *langage*, is fundamental for understanding the function of equivocation in Shidyaq's language. So is Charles Sanders Pierce's theoretical apparatus, which redefines the study of logic as semiotics and teaches that every process of signification involves a triadic relation between the signifier (or sign), signified (or object) and an interpretant (or subject) – who is the most complex link in the chain of signification.[16] Pierce's semiotic account set the grounds for structural linguistics in the twentieth century, for Ferdinand de Saussure, Émile Benveniste and Claude Lévi-Strauss.[17] The main claim of the semiotic approach is that signification cannot be divorced from the subject who utilises it and is in turn defined by it: signification is fundamentally concerned with symbolic structures, and discourse is nothing but the logic which structures the social link. The semiotic and structuralist accounts are fundamental for Lacan's formulation of his theory of the subject.

Lacan provided a correction to structural linguistics through the isolation of the signifier from the sign and his introduction of the category of the subject of the unconscious. Lacan in his theory of language posits the signifier as matter transcending itself into language, as a contingent element without which language would be unthinkable. He thereby rejects both conventionalism and neuro-linguistics that understand language as an organ of communication.[18]

The subject (which is not the ego here but the subject of the unconscious) is a missing link in the chain of signification. As Lacan famously put it, 'a signifier represents the subject for another signifier'. Signification in this sense is understood as a process that the Real forces upon us: the Real is that which insists on forcing its way to recognition as something *other* than the ego's creation. Although the semiotic schema largely influences psychoanalysis, a point of difference is important to point out. For Peirce, signification is an infinite process, an endless series of representations that are largely conscious.[19] By shifting the subject from being a transcendental producer of signifiers to being determined by them, Pierce, Saussure and later on Frege offered an important groundwork for the Lacanian elaboration of the unconscious as that which is 'structured like language':

> The unconscious, in being 'structured *like* a [Lacan's emphasis] language [langage]', that is to say *la langue* which it inhabits, is subject to the ambiguity which distinguishes each language [*langue*]. One language [*langue*] among others is nothing more than the sum of the ambiguities which have been allowed to persist there by its history.[20]

Lacan's understanding of signification is primarily concerned with signification as an unconscious mechanism or mode of interpretation that is already ongoing but of which the subject is unaware. It is important to insist here that Lacan's subject of the unconscious is distinct from the conscious subject of semiotics. I borrow here Lorenzo Chiesa's precise formulation: 'The subject of the unconscious is, for Lacan, both the unconscious subject, a psychic agency that is opposed to the agency of consciousness (or, better, self-consciousness) and the subject of the unconscious, the subject subjected to the unconscious'.[21] The unconscious tangibly manifests itself in consciousness, what Freud had detected in slips of tongue, *aphanisis*, dreams and other symptomatic manifestations. And the symptom is precisely that which escapes the meaningful processes of symbolic as well as imaginary structures and signals the formations of the unconscious. The discourse of psychoanalysis has since its inception investigated the rift between consciousness and intentionality. Before the category of the unconscious, it was assumed somewhat that the subject would 'consciously say what they want to say'.[22] Building on the linguistic separation between the subject of enunciation and the subject of the statement (or between and language and speech, *langue* and *parole*), psychoanalysis proceeds from acknowledging that the I who speaks is not equivalent to the grammatical subject of language. There is a fundamental disjuncture in the subject, which is split between the I as ego of imaginary identification and the subject of the unconscious.

The linguistic separation between *langue* and *parole* renders the study of grammar possible, however, the language that psychoanalysis proposes to listen to, the language of the unconscious, is that element in speech which is not simply identical to *langue*, language. The language of the unconscious is a formal attribute of language, which reveals that language can only be understood as substance if we accede that language is not identical to itself.[23] Lacan follows Freud closely by stating that the subject as such is uncertain because he is divided by the effects of language. Through the effects of speech, the subject always realises himself more in the Other, but he is already pursuing there more than half of himself. He will simply find his desire ever more divided, pulverised, in the circumscribable metonymy of speech. The effects of language are always mixed with the fact, which is the basis of the analytic experience, that the subject is a subject only from being subjected to the field of the Other, the subject proceeding from their synchronic subjection in the field of the Other.[24]

This account of language as a divisive force implies that there is something that demands to be realised in speech, which appears as intentional, of course, but has a strange temporality and does not have the form of propositional statements. Lacan's subject of language, the I that speaks, is the ego – the ideal image – and everyday language is 'empty speech' in comparison to the 'full speech' of the psychoanalytic encounter. The subject of enunciation is split by speech and in speech: because of speech the subject is never fully present to himself.[25]

What occurs, what is produced, in this gap in language, is the unconscious. The unconscious presents itself *as* discord. It was in this way that Freud first encountered what occurs in the unconscious (through condensation and displacement or metaphor and metonymy): the unconscious is this discontinuity in which something (desire) presents itself as a vacillation. Speech, or communicative language, always assumes a relationship between a subject and Other (from small to big Other) but this relationship is not simply one that communicates meaning, meaning for Lacan is 'like the imaginary, always in the end evanescent' for it is tightly bound to that in which the subject is 'ensnared'.[26] For Lacan then, the meaning of meaning is that it does not mean anything: meaning is that gap which lies between culture and nature.

The subject is always subjected to a language that is already there and alienated by it because he can never fully articulate in this language his true desire, which nevertheless presents itself constantly in the subject's speech: the subject always says more than they intend to say.[27] This split of the subject does not mean that the unconscious is equivalent to a repressed entity, an alternative ego; but it implies that in any act of speech there is a double address: that which is said, and that which is not said. The unconscious addresses an Other with the truth of their desire, which cannot present itself except negatively.[28]

This does not imply that the unconscious expresses itself in discourse. Rather, psychoanalysis maintains that all unconscious phenomenon have a linguistic mode: 'every analytic phenomenon . . . is structured like a language'.[29] This means that all unconscious phenomena reveal that there is an autonomy to the logic of the signifier which separates it from the domain of the sign. The signifier does not refer to any one object but 'insofar as it forms a part of a language, the signifier is a sign which refers to another sign'.[30] This opposition of signifiers – day and night, man and woman – read through the logic of the autonomy of the signifier (signifier is a sign which refers to another sign) defines language as a chain of differences that are non-relational: signification is premised on a distortion of referentiality and constituted by a constant displacement.[31]

The signifier is therefore different from another signifier and indifferent to itself: signification is a system of pure difference. Lacan's *objet a*, the object-cause of desire, is the placeholder for this pure difference. As such, the unconscious is governed by the law of the signifier, by linguistic rules, and is therefore not a simply a psychological irrational force; rather, it is governed by its own logic and grammar: 'The unconscious is neither the primordial nor the instinctual, and what it knows of the elemental is no more than the elements of the signifier'.[32] In other words, and to be concise, Lacan's statement that the 'unconscious is structured like language' implies that language is irreducible to the domain of intersubjective communication or meaning-making, which is in itself nothing but an imaginary identification or fantasy: 'the signifier doesn't just provide an envelope, a receptacle for meaning. It polarizes it, structures it, and brings it into existence'.[33]

Lacan introduced *lalangue* as the register in every language that is the site of equivocation. *Lalangue* disrupts the comparative model of languages: languages are not to be compared to one another; the site of comparison can only be in relation to that which *cannot* be said, a site of negativity that is disavowed by the linguistic understanding of Language as an organ of communication. Language, understood by linguistics as a tool or organ, is only an imaginary account of that which cannot be communicated: a negative thrust that is only discerned in the lapses, slips of tongue and *aphanisis* of the speaking subject. The speaking subject, or the subject who is said to have linguistic competence, is always-already a split subject in the psychoanalytic account. It is a subject divided between the statement of enunciation and what is enunciated: speech is constituted by signifiers that are irreducible to the phonemic sounds articulated but which are constituted by a desire that only expresses itself negatively, as a missing element that is deprived of symbolic support (articulated by language).

We can discern this disavowed element of *lalangue* in Shidyaq's linguistic approach, it is a linguistics afflicted with a passion of language that bears witness to the modern question of the subject as the subject of the Other: i.e. there is an unconscious desire implicated in this passion for language. The I that speaks is the ego, but the ego is not the subject. The ego is an ideal imaginary image and its everyday speech is 'empty speech'. The subject of enunciation is split by speech, in speech and because of speech the subject is never fully present to himself. I is an ego and the ego an other. The ego emerges as one of the core philosophical and political questions of modernity. It is a symptom of a pre-Cartesian universe: it is a symptom of modernity, persisting as an inert specular image that haunts the split subject of modernity.

Shidyaq's writing is egoistic and modernist only if we understand modernism as the current of the return of the repressed in modernity, the return of pre-modern ghosts and apparitions, which are essentially linguistic and give rise to endless repetitions and speak of the unspeakable.[34] Shidyaq presents his writing as a posthumous tribunal of his life and the whole century. Although penned in the mid-nineteenth century, the style is descriptive, and shares the modern 'mythical method':[35] there is a listing of the world of things (including human organs) and a writer who stands in the middle as a public figure with a mock-epic tone, intent on recuperating some past values while only imagining a modernity to come, whose heirs would be the selected ideal readers he seeks as his audience.

Shidyaq is particularly modern in so far as we understand:

> modernity as never being contemporaneous with itself, since it constantly projects, anticipates, and returns to mythical origins, but that also teaches us more about the 'present' which it historicises . . . Such a modernity resists any attempts to supersede it and any effort to declare it obsolete, even if this effort comes from a so-called post-modernism.[36]

In this sense Shidyaq's writing, as we will see, proves the precedence of the postmodern in modernity rather than its coming afterward. In fact, the four books of *al-Saq* are presented as the result of a futile pursuit of an absolute Book. This One and absolute book of language, not only sustains

Shidyaq's fantasies but is also itself a systematically futile attempt to reach for the absolute.

Medusa: The Image of Umma

Shidyaq's writing exaggerates the modern Arabic slogan '*lugha* is the mirror of the *umma*'.[37] If language is a *Gestalt*, an ideal image captured at a glance or an imaginary identification, is it then *lalangue* that is the image in the mirror? Without which there would be no possibility for the *umma*, the mother tongue, to reflect on itself? Reflection as a mode of thinking is best defined by its inability to meet any demands for unity. The image and its reflection can never offer anything other than a metaphysics of reflection. However, the dialectic of identification that emerges from mirroring, from mimetic doubling, always implies a third: reflection ought to reflect upon itself and the mirror's mirroring be included in mirroring itself. The reflection of self and image in mirror is faced with a non-mimetic kernel, a Real of enjoyment that cannot be reduced in an epistemic fashion to a condition of knowledge. Between the object and its reflection, there is an uncanny element that presents itself despite representation.

The Greek myth of Medusa's gaze offers a key to the problem of the metaphysics of reflection. The mirror of language at once solidifies the looking subject and shatters it into fragments. We know well that the sight of Medusa's head stiffens its spectator with terror, at once turning them into stone and making them experience the horror of castration. Freud and Sandor Ferenczi both devoted separate discussions to the symbolism of the myth of Medusa.[38] In both of their accounts, the symbolism of Medusa is linked to castration. Castration is a form of lack that is decisive for subject–object relationship: it is a lack that affects both feminine and masculine positions, and it involves the subject identifying with a symbolic lack of an imaginary object, an imaginary phallus.[39] The child (here both male and female/the subject) loves the mother and seeks to identify itself with the desires of the mother (other); however, the subject believes that the mother does not lack anything, that she is a desiring being just like the subject. But this is where the role of the father comes in: the mother, in fact, desires something (the father's phallus) that the child does not have; as a result, the child attempts to identify with this lack. The function of the name-of-the-father, the law, is to prohibit this imaginary incestuous identification and to institute the symbolic law (the real object of mother's desire is a forbidden phallus). However, the law is not something that comes from the real father[40] but it is already there, constituting the symbolic order and limiting the mother's desire. The subject's struggle with imaginary identifications, with *Gestalten* or *imagos* that represent him/her for an Other, makes way for a symbolic imposition that renders the process of sexual identification and differentiation possible. Castration is thus a normative phase[41] of the assumption of the subject's sex; however, it is a matter that the subject always seeks to repress, and at the site of this repression anxiety is substituted:

To decapitate = to castrate. The terror of Medusa is, thus, a terror of castration that is linked to the sight of something. Numerous analyses have made us familiar with the occasion for this. It occurs when a boy, who has hitherto been unwilling to believe the threat of castration, catches sight of the female genitals, probably those of an adult, surrounded by hair, and essentially those of his mother. The hair upon Medusa's head is frequently represented in works of art in the form of snakes, and these once again are derived from the castration complex. It is a remarkable fact that, however frightening they may be in themselves, they nevertheless serve actually as a mitigation of the horror, for they replace the penis, the absence of which is the cause of the horror. This is a confirmation of the technical rule according to which a multiplication of penis symbols signifies castration. The sight of Medusa's head makes the spectator stiff with terror, turns him to stone – if Medusa's head takes the place of a representation of the female genitals, or rather if it isolates their horrifying effects from the pleasure-giving ones, it may be recalled that displaying the genitals is familiar in other connections as an *apotropaic* act. What arouses horror in oneself will produce the same effect upon the enemy against whom one is seeking to defend oneself. We read in Rabelais of how the Devil took to flight when the woman showed him her vulva. The erect male organ also has an *apotropaic* effect, but thanks to another mechanism. To display the penis (or any of its surrogates) is to say: 'I am not afraid of you. I defy you. I have a penis'. Here, then, is another way of intimidating the Evil Spirit'.[42]

An encounter with Medusa, in the Greek myth, serves an *apotropaic* function: it is a symbolisation that works not only to ward off a threat (of castration) but more importantly – and as Lacan points out – to induce an affect of anxiety. Medusa's face of frozen angst mirrors the subject's own: the abyssal gaze in her eyes is the source of fear incurred in the onlooker. It is as though the subject just encountered his or her own eyes detached, coming at them through the gaze of an Other. Medusa is an impossible sight that threatens the subject: one's own eyes looking at oneself from an elsewhere. The real of Medusa's head, this primitive object that appears as a vanishing point in the ego's imaginary hall of mirrors, induces a sense of vertigo: it is a sign of an excess feeling that comes with loss. Loss, as we know from Lacan's seminar on anxiety, is an imaginary experience of the Real, which corresponds to a lack as a symbolic recuperation of that loss.[43] Medusa's head – like Oedipus's castration – is frightening because the subject and object (the subject and their image) are not dialectically differentiated; they are frozen in a false synthesis that threatens with petrification.

Medusa's head is a horror to witness because it faces the subject with the truth of their castration, a truth that the subject has had repress, but one that only comes back as something from without, an intrusion from the Real. There is a very important distinction to be made here, one in which we can distinguish Lacan's move beyond Freud: the fear of castration is not simply a fear of femininity (the fear of being in the passive position against which Freud reinforced the traditional figure of the father i.e. patriarchy); rather, it is a fear of being faced with the Real (the Real of the drive and not the Real of the desire of the Other). Medusa's head is horrific and terrorising because it displaces the real being of the subject, by which the subject can no longer be in the position of an answer to the Other (choice of sexual identification) but an answer to the Real.[44]

This truth that the subject cannot face is that castration creates the lack on which desire is instituted and that desire is the Other's desire. It is the desire to be subjected to the law.[45] Furthermore, the subject's assumption of their sex (their identification in relation to the phallus as signifier) is always premised on a deviation, an impasse that is constitutive of sexuality – woman loses what she does not have while man gains what he does not want – this impasse is premised on sexuality emerging from the very *aphanisis* of the subject and the emergence of the signifier.[46]

Castration anxiety, or anxiety *tout court*, materialises from the sexual impasse at the core of formation of subjectivity. It is an affect that emerges from the subject's desire *to never lose their lack*. Given that anxiety concerns the category of the subject, anxiety is then fundamentally a political problem.[47] The anxiety about assuming symbolic identification, which we can discern in the fear of encountering Medusa's gaze – or as I am suggesting the image of the *umma* in the mirror – is not an anxiety of separation but one that emerges from being *too close* to the demanding Other. Lacan's observation of Freud's analysis of the *fort da game* is crucial here:

> What provokes anxiety? It is not, contrary to what is said, either the rhythm or the alternation of the presence–absence of the mother. And what proves it, is that the infant *takes pleasure* in repeating this game of presence and absence: this possibility of absence is what gives presence its unity. What is most anxiety-provoking for the child, is that precisely this relation of lack on which he establishes himself, which makes him desire, this relation is all the more disturbed when there is no possibility of lack, when the mother is always on his back, and especially by wiping his bottom, the model of the demand, of the demand which cannot fail.[48]

Anxiety, then, does not emerge from the threat of absence of symbolic authority of power, but from its over-proximity, from experiencing it at the core of one's being.[49]

Modern linguists of Arabic, like Shidyaq and Bustani, express these anxieties of over-proximity. Shidyaq depicts them as physical afflictions, ailments in his bowls: he has epistemological anxieties, sexual anxieties and anxieties about the originality of his language and ideas. Bustani's ruminations and obsessions with the origins of language, culture and society betray a similar anxiety, which he can only resolve by beseeching Robinson Crusoe as a true story against the evil ways of the devil that corrupt civilisation.[50]

Encyclopaedic *Prolepsis* and the Anxiety of Knowledge

In the Arabic-speaking world during the nineteenth century there occurred a distinctly modern encyclopaedic endeavour to reduce language to grammar – which is to say, language transformed into a medium for communication, in which words and meanings have to correspond to clear images.[51] The alphabetical ordering of words in both the encyclopaedia and the dictionary presumes that language is a set of signs that combine together in larger units; each word is a combination of both form and meaning. This idea (which is arguably Saussurean) presupposes that nothing outside a language predetermines the connection between form and meaning, and it falls short of accounting for how the supposed structural interdependence of the system of a language came about. Bustani's shorthand answer to the source of interdependence is that the language, being Semitic in origin, was 'miraculously preserved by God' and that the language carries the pre-established meanings of its speakers. By engaging in lexicographic and taxonomic activity (encyclopaedic work largely defined), in fixing meanings for words for the coming future, Bustani creates a discourse that presents language as neutral in itself, a mere communal instrument.

Bustani's approach uses a synchronic understanding of language: it freezes a historically evolving system at an arbitrarily chosen point, to reveal an ahistorical *etat de langue*.[52] Bustani has to suppress history (by reducing it to big chunks of times of decline and progress), suppress diachrony and emphasise synchrony. This is for the purpose of instituting proper conditions for subjective reform, enhancing the use-value of individuals, through pedagogies of education and teaching that are based on lexicographic and neological reform. Language with Bustani becomes a *sign* of civilisation and a means for the preservation of the self (a conception that is close to say Spinoza's proposition of self-preservation as virtue). Arabic needs to be cleansed from un-clarified concepts and useless terms: terms that are useless for self-preservation. Bustani, for instance, argues for removing the endless synonyms for one meaning in Arabic – 'the hundreds of names for camels and their attributes', as well as the 'inappropriate European words' (*al kalimat al ajnabiya*)[53] – because the functional meanings for utterances becomes a fixation on self-preservation: communal self-preservation in our case.

The purification of language is simultaneously a purification of the present from the burdens of the past that institutes an understanding of language as a 'means for civilisation'⁵⁴ and a 'tool for scientific knowledge'.⁵⁵ This conception of language as a medium comes hand in hand with the perception of history as a *telos* of progress. History is guided by a final cause but one that is always delayed; almost like Kant's ideal of progress as a purposeless purposiveness, the *telos* is an end of a construction that is only carried through the work of perfecting or completing itself.

Bustani chose Ibn Athir from the 'books of the Arabs' to push forth the idea of History (as a universal category) as a mirror of progress throughout Time. Bustani quoted Ibn Athir: '[H]istory mirrors the achievements of people of time past and their industriousness and pursuit of knowledge are etched in its mirrored reflection'.⁵⁶ For Bustani, History is made singular: it is what remains eternal as a final cause while human civilisations age and pass away. History, like language, is a mirror of God: it is a mirror of the dynamism and a *telos* of a pure actuality; it retroactively restitutes a predetermined end. This is why in Bustani's logic there is a debt and guilt at the core of the historical process (a concept I discuss thoroughly in Chapter 3). History figures in Bustani's liberal nationalism as political-theological account of a restitution of debt towards God's mercy: it is the place of reckoning with a symbolic debt.

This brings us back to the game of mirrors. History is a mirror on which the image of guilt is frozen. And it carries the *true* image of a people, as does their language. However, there is a curious dissociation between an image and the mirror. In a sense, the image that is in the mirror exists *in* something else. As such, whilst history projects a unifying image of a fragmented subject, the encyclopaedic account of knowledge carries out a similar function. Encyclopaedic writing attempts the prefiguring of language as language that is yet to come, a complete language. In other words, the alphabetical ordering of words and their meanings is meant to act as an overarching taxonomy and systematic description of 'all the inquiries and knowledge that exists in the world'.⁵⁷ Bustani accompanied most words in the dictionary with their English and French counterparts in order to 'tie the sciences of the Arabic language with those of European languages'.⁵⁸ The transliterations and translations with which the *Da'ira* is abundant signify that Arabic will be kept at bay by other languages: these will act as its regulators because knowledge is one. In other words, Arabic as a language is bound to translation in its exposition of knowledge. The entries in the encyclopaedia that are not accompanied by a translation but by a transliteration – such as proper names, linguistic categories (like *tafrigh, tadmin*), names of things Bustani defines as no longer in use (*tiyn*) – are words that, Busatani predicts, will no longer be used in the centuries to come.

Seeing language as a 'mirror of the *umma*' ultimately transforms language into the medium of progress. It is the tain of the mirror, however, that makes any reflection possible. The alphabetical ordering of knowledge in the encyclopaedia, I argue, constitutes this tain. The alphabet is itself yet another image of language: it organises an 'arbitrary' allocation of signs to signifieds. In other words, the reader of the *Da'ira* does not presume in his mind that *Tiba'a* (printing),[59] is preceded by *Tabataba* (name of a Zaydi dynasty) and *Tabashir* (chalk) and succeeded by *Tibaq* (a kind of *Badi'*) when the use of a word and its antonym occurs at once. Rather, the encyclopaedia is meant to organise knowledge by replacing original works such that the reader is no longer required to see things in the world: books have now replaced things, and knowledge is solely a process of predication. The *Da'irat* is in this sense similar to other enlightenment encyclopaedias, such as Diderot's and Alembert's *Encylcopedie*. Bustani himself stated that the *Da'irat* 'replaces hundreds of books'.

Encyclopaedias are abstractions of original books that they aggregate into one mass of knowledge: they are the fantasy of taming knowledge into its instrumental ends. Modern scientific knowledge, however, is acephalic: it is headless, has no aim but itself. Bustani's determination to overcome anxiety induced by the modern abstraction of knowledge expressed itself in an obsessive pursuit of taxonomy, a neurosis of accumulation and hoarding use-values. The *Da'irat* therefore manages knowledge, while knowledge 'manages the organisation of society' (*rakn li-intidham ahwal al-hay'a al-ijtima'iya*).[60] Knowledge then has both 'moral' and 'material' worth for every *umma*. And every category within the encyclopaedia, every entry or definition, is one part that mirrors the totality and unity of all of knowledge – a knowledge "whose paths the Arabs have previously found very hard to traverse'.[61]

This ordering was meant to offer a navigational technology to the readers allowing them to observe knowledge as though it were 'something to be contained, surveyed, and thereby made manageable'.⁶² It has been suggested elsewhere in scholarship that the Enlightenment encyclopaedia 'collapsed knowledge into information'.⁶³ Indeed, *prolepsis* characterises the modern encyclopaedia in the sense that although the very existence of an encyclopaedia acknowledges the futility of completing a collection of knowledge; all encyclopaedic texts continue to aim at 'the encyclopaedic unity of all of knowledge as a deferred ideal'.⁶⁴

Foucault has argued that, for Diderot and the *philosophes* in Europe, the encyclopaedia was supposed to confidently represent the world of existence. Foucault contended that:

> the continuum of representation and being [is] an ontology defined negatively as an absence of nothingness (absence *deneant*) a general representability of being, and being manifested by the presence of representation-all this is a part of the overall configuration of the classical episteme.⁶⁵

However, once we take the element of *prolepsis* that is inherent in the encyclopaedia, as well as the meta-narrative embedded in any encyclopaedia to justify it as a system of representation (e.g. Bustani's own entry for *encyclopaedia* in the *Da'ira*), what do we make out of the need to represent the representation itself?

James Creech argued in his rereading of Foucault's epistemological configuration that the modern encyclopaedia is defined by its lacking of a definite epistemological measure, that it is always tethered to the failure of offering a measure: a stable epistemological measure remains a 'desideratum and a projection'.⁶⁶ In this sense, the logic of the encyclopaedia is one of a *revoke* that is sustained by language as a prosthetic device: 'Prosthesis is thus an integral part of what is being represented as an encyclopaedia. Recognizing a lack and preferring a supplement is therefore, literally, a part of the Encyclopaedia's definition of itself. That is what the Encyclopaedia "is"'.⁶⁷ There is an element of anticipation of the object, which is knowledge, in the epistemological model of the encyclopaedia. Creech compares Diderot's encyclopaedic organisation of knowledge to Lacan's analysis of the mirror stage as formative of the ego as an imaginary alienating function. The encyclopaedic mirror does not reflect an image of nature, as some philosophers like Rorty would maintain, but offers an imaginary identification, an *imago,* of knowledge as a pursuit of interminable failure. There is in the Enlightenment encyclopaedic project, which I have argued Bustani's *Da'ira* belongs to, a particularly modern form of desire for knowledge: 'the object of its lesson is less about the content of its articles, than its desire'.[68]

The encyclopaedia is a project that presumes total representability, including both represented and representation in it; but it functions as a system of knowledge through a blind spot: the *prolepsis* of a system of all of knowledge generates an anticipation, a kind of *jouissance* perhaps? 'The *Da'ira* is meant to replace hundreds of books' because it 'presents the reader with all the important knowledge in the world'.[69] By claiming that the encyclopaedia replaces hundreds of books for its readers and that the 'human being is an abnegation of forgetting (*al-insam mahal al-nisyan*)',[70] Bustani gives the encyclopaedia the role of recuperating knowledge – not simply through reminiscence, but as a system in which 'we' (the readers) desire knowledge in the present *and* desire that knowledge already in the future. The arbitrary nature of the alphabetical ordering of words in the *Da'ira* is meant to relieve the reader's memory and sharpen his reason through a system of *renvoi*: of referencing that severs man from the world, 'like blindness, both makes possible and requires figurative, orthopaedic representation in the mirror'.[71] In the encyclopaedia, 'memory is oriented not to a past that it simply stores but to a future that it produces'.[72]

Bustani's encyclopaedic work is characterised by a 'proleptic ideality',[73] in which the Ego gleans the surface of the mirror of representation. As he tells us in the Preface to the work, it was a long arduous path of work that required complete self-renunciation and dedication. Encyclopaedic work is the reformer's and the idealist's path of altruism: its fruits can only be reaped in the future. In the article in the encyclopaedia on the *Da'ira* itself, Bustani is compared in his efforts to the work of an entire State:[74] can this not be analysed as a pedagogical altruism that sublimates an aggressivity towards the Porte, the Ottoman imperial rule?

The encyclopaedia in this sense therefore carries both a political and ontological significance. It carries a faith in representation, in knowledge as a system of representation, and it challenges the political system of representation. The *prolepsis* that is inherent in the genre of representation, the encyclopaedia itself, reflects the *prolepsis* in the *telos* of progress. It ultimately places the encyclopaedist in front of a demanding if not impossible task: the Herculean task of representing knowledge as a unified whole in language.

Bustani's argument in defence of the need for an encyclopaedia is as follows: the desire for knowledge is ever-increasing; this necessitates a unification of all knowledge into one system of representation in order to secure it against the travesties of memory, because 'the human is prone to forgetting' (*al insan mahal al nisyan*).[75] However, since the encyclopaedia 'is a book for all religions, sects, and groups',[76] must knowledge therefore be apolitical? Or is politics only possible once the encyclopaedia is complete? The encyclopaedia hoards knowledge for a future that only promises to be more unfamiliar; it harbours the anxiety of events that may not fall under the valence of the system of predicative knowledge. While Bustani still mentioned the legacy of Arab encyclopaedists like al Dumayri, Ibn Khalliqan and others, the *Da'ira* in its ontological makeup as a modern encyclopaedia comes to replace all these books and claims that it does so because of their original absence: there is a disorder in knowledge that modernity has finally come to restitute, but knowledge cannot safeguard society from the imperatives of modernity, its infinite *telos*. The *prolepsis* that characterises the modern drive for knowledge – knowledge for knowledge's sake – has no measure; its only quality lies in the *jouissance* attained from the enjoyment of the ideal of knowledge.

Metathesis and *Parapraxis*: From Phoneme to Signifier

Shidyaq's mode of writing is contemporaneous to Bustani's but struggles with the game of mirrors from a different perspective. He does not dwell on the directly present image of words but on the unthought in the process of reflection. His literary works and anti-dictionary lexicons – *The Spy on the Dictionary* (1882) and *The Secrets of the Night in Metathesis and Substitution* (1867) – bear witness to an obsession with what underlies the process of signification itself. In Shidyaq's writings, we do not find a resolute subject whose words reflect them, a 'Master' whose language knows no impossible. Rather, language as a mirror refuses to recede into the background, creating an overflow of words, an excessive surplus whose only function appears to be *jouissance*. Shidyaq's distinct voice exposes the underlying process of reflection, as when a mirror mirrors itself: the grounds of certainty can be established neither by the onlooker nor within the act of reflection. Words cannot be reconciled to determinate objects in the world: the I does not only think, but is spoken-through by language.

In nineteenth-century sources, the word *umma* stands at a distance from the modern *watan* (nation). However, both carry the meaning of a path of predestination, an infinite task of travelling forward, as it were, toward an origin. The *umma*, in its profane and non-Islamic usage, was to be affirmed by harnessing self-reflexive thought. It is not surprising, though it is uncanny, that the word *umma* shares a root as well with *umm* (mother). *Umma* in Lacanian terms would be called the desire of the mother: we find warnings of a loss of, or in, language coupled with fear of a loss of an *umma*, which does not really exist beyond this relation of desire. The mother in turn desires language, as psychoanalysis tells us, and the law is desired for the purpose of taming her sons. In other words, addressing the *umma* poses the question: what do you want of me? It is a question that is fundamentally about the anxiety of procreation, of the paternal function as posed from the position of the feminine, of a crisis in symbolic identification.

Shidyaq's response to the question was to literally make himself into a book by inventing a split-fictional character: the 'Fariyaq' and 'Fariyaqa', through which he attempted to make a name for himself or make his proper name common again. In other words, Fariyaq/Fariyaqa allows Shidyaq to relocate himself in the meaning that he symbolically lacked. Shidyaq's split double is the answer to the parasitic nature of words, for language is a verbal parasite, a kind of parasitical cancer from which there is no escape.[77] The symptomatic repetition of phonemically similar words in *al-Saq* is interrupted by abrupt sounds like 'shh!shh!' 'tiff!tiff!' 'azwa!azwa!', which speaks of attempts to silence the speech in Shidyaq's head. Shidyaq's emptying out of words in the middle of dark nights, his 'darkening of the sheets of paper in the darkest of nights', are an attempt at a liquefaction of language, at resisting the seductions of *lalangue*.

In Shidyaq's writing, we see language taking on a life of its own, wearing infinite layers of clothing that could be peeled off one after another. Unveiling language's secrets, a task to which he committed his life's work, rarely if ever resulted in reducing the subject of enunciation to the enunciated, the signifier to the signified. In other words, as Shidyaq produced written texts, he found himself not to be speaking on behalf of language but was constantly exceeded by language itself. Language in his works does not appear as a code, but as a constant slippage of signifiers.

In 1855, Shidyaq depicted grammar and the grammarian's craft as a site of excessive libidinal enjoyment. In the introduction to *Sir al-layali fi al-qalb w al-ibdal* (*Secrets of Night in Metathesis and Substitution*), he writes,

> Although the predecessors have worked on this noble language, I for one have loved it passionately and un-dividedly (*ashiqtuha 'ishqan*), and have been occupied with it endlessly until I have become her slave, for her my withering away has been a blossoming (*azharat laha dthibali*). I have spent nights on end probing her mysteries and secrets. I have dedicated to her my undivided attention and no other need has diverted me from her. She has been my solace in solitude, the source of my consolation in sadness, and has brought happiness to my state of misery.[78]

The goal of the *Secrets of the Night,* or the explicit aim of its passion for language, was to locate the sources of equivocation. The stated aim of pursuing equivocation is to remove confusion from the vocables of the language, the source of equivocation being *metathesis* in language, or the transposition of sounds and syllables in a word. The problem of *metathesis* for Shidyaq, when undetected in the dictionary, is that it allows for the eternalisation of speech errors.[79] *Metathesis*, according to him, originates from *onomatopoeia*, the sounds of nature.[80] However, it is striking, he says, that *metathesis* occurs precisely when there is a cut with nature: 'one of the strangest attributes of this language is that most cases of *metathesis* occur with words that carry the meaning of a cut, a scission, a break, a gap, a rupture, and a separation'.[81] Shidyaq proclaims that this discovery of his – the realisation that the origin of equivocation in language lies in scores of undocumented speech errors which are all linked through a cut with nature – was revealed to him by 'divine inspiration in the darkest and loneliest of nights'.[82]

Metathesis and substitution, or *parapraxis*, carry the concealed secrets of language, they are a seduction that cannot be resisted, that overtakes

Shidyaq and speaks on his behalf, *parapraxis* are paraphrases of the same *unstated* meaning: i.e. there is a display of the extraordinary fecundity of language, its mode of regenerating itself. The proliferation and prolixity of the signifier renders Shidyaq's language a series of paraphrases with no recourse to any metalanguage. He shows us that there is no way to speak about language in language itself, despite writing being the very struggle to do so. The language of which Shidyaq speaks, is not a mother-tongue as such, it is not a spoken language in any sense, but an excess that he seeks to write, it is language as a lucubration of knowledge, written in the darkest of nights, in solitude and with the desire to be language's sole legislator, its master and sheikh *al-lugha*.

Shidyaq delves into *lalangue*, into the bottomless, erratic nature of language, and of Arabic in particular – the object of his love and torment, also described as bodily torment. This outburst of *lalangue* coinciding with a standardisation of language, and this love–torment relationship, is ambivalent. While Shidyaq strives for master signifiers, he also sees that they do not work anymore; he looks for phallic meaning but finds that meaning vacillates. This ambivalent relationship is inflected by Shidyaq's preoccupations with sexual difference. He invents his own feminine double, and stumbles onto the sexual non-relation, which he tries to subdue but cannot quite do so. The questioning of identity and meaning of language, the questioning of sexual (non-)relation, is inscribed within the transitional shift of modernity, and ultimately constitutes it.

In tandem to the Protestant missionary's theologically based philological attempts at tracing Arabic to the Adamic languages of paradise,[83] Arabic intellectuals became preoccupied with reducing language to grammar: the grammatisation of language was fundamental for instituting a national pedagogy, which was one of the main preoccupations of the modern Arabic intellectual movement. Intellectuals of the nineteenth century expressed an urgency to standardise language, cleanse it of incorrect syntax and turn into a 'language of science' (*lughat 'ilm*). Some even maintained that the reasons for Arabic 'scientific regression' (*ta'akhur 'ilmiy*) could be found in the terrible state of 'Arabic letters'.

Shidyaq, in contrast, maintained that the 'Arabs can only derive Civilisation from their language while the Europeans derive their language from Civilisation'.[84] During the frenzy to collect and order the language and set down its grammatical rules, Shidyaq penned hundreds of pages of *anti*-dictionary essays and critiques, in which language emerged not as a concept of study – determined by the modality why is there language rather than nothing? – but by the modality of existence: why is language like it is and not otherwise? Although Shidyaq framed the linguist's task as a seeking of mastery over language, the problem that he set out to answer, contra the philologists of his time, is not the question of existence/inexistence of language (its origin). His questions were these: why is it that all cannot be said? How is it that words fail, that they repeat in order to fail? What does this failure support? What does it sustain?

The master of language or the 'inventor of the magnificent science of grammar',[85] Shidyaq tells us, is not like a sovereign sultan but comparable to a despondent lover: 'a poor man who fell in love with the subject'.[86] Falling in love with language fundamentally means that the grammarian questions the nature of reference in language:

> If, for example, he saw the sun rising, he would say, 'How are we to understand the "rising" of the sun here? Is it "literal" or "metaphorical," and would the metaphor here be "conventional" or "linguistic"?'[87]

In other words, the question is, what causes the sun to rise? The revolution of the earth around the sun, but perhaps also God as the cause of revolution would need to be considered. That is, there are strata of metaphor that need to be considered: 'There are also three- or four-step metaphors and some with more steps than the stairway of a minaret. Some of these stairs are smooth, others spiral, some winding, and others something else'.[88]

The epistemology of 'multiple steps of metaphor' that drives the lover's quest for sense in language is only secured by the immortality of the soul. The grammarian tells Fariyaq his pupil that 'when I found that grammar has an "inchoative" but no "terminative", I drew an analogy between that and the soul and I ceased to be confused'.[89] The rhetorical sciences, sciences of figurative usages, also have a similar structure of inchoation: the study of language – which owes itself to 'the existence of women' – is a search for an absolute beginning: where to begin? How to think the moment of origin as an absolute beginning? With every grammarian, with every rhetorician, there is a falling in love again, a repetition compulsion that characterises the love of language: 'the originator of this science went on thinking about these rhetorical figures until he came to the end of his life . . .. After him, another, similarly enamoured, arose and fleshed out many areas left by his predecessor'.[90] And so on. This repetition compulsion is the source of all rhetorical sciences, the point of origin of every love affair with language.

It is a form of love that binds the grammarian to language. Complementary to the sultan or prince who rules by the power of the sword, the grammarian, or the 'inventor of rhetorical figures',[91] commands a love for the language. But it is a love that torments and affects the body at the most curious of locations: not only the oral and anal aural (the throat and ear, loci of the voice and listening) but also the anal orifices.[92] These locations or orifices in the body are particularly interesting insofar as they lie between the inside and the outside of the body.

Language in Shidyaq's account does not satisfy a need for meaning, it does not simply serve as a function of consensus and ideal communicative speech à la Habermas. Rather, the language of which Shidyaq speaks is an affliction that strikes at the most *extimate* of locations. It appears that the aim of human speech cannot be reduced to the task of understanding – a task to which grammarians dedicate their lives. The effect of illocutionary speech is not simply about reaching a rationally motivated consensus. Rather, language brings forth a specific form of negation into the world; as a symbolic function, it shores up an unsymbolisable real that is experienced as a source of pressure, a demand that afflicts the speaking subject at its most extimate locations. It is this unsymbolisable element that affects the body, a 'too-muchness'[93] that is felt as an excitation, a pressure experienced at an extimate location, which is neither inside nor outside the body but a topological space – a point of transition that intensifies the body and its sensations.[94] The experience of the letter is literal: its touch is felt at the sites of the anal and oral drives.[95]

Shidyaq recounts the progression of grammar in terms of an incessant stratification and subdivision of categories that strike at the orifices and at the loci where sound generates. It is as though the orifices resonate, reverberate and echo at every strata of language. At every instance of grammatical subdivision, there is an excess sound that cannot be delimited within the organs of the body. In other words, metaphors are symptoms of the existence of a complex system of signifiers that are displaced along the signifying chain, from the 'tongue-smacking' to 'the anal-resonatory':[96]

> Certain scholars said that metaphors may be divided into the literal and the analogical, the literal into the categorical and the presumptive, and the categorical firstly into the make-believe and the factual, secondly into the primary and the subordinate, and thirdly into the abstracted and presumed, with some claiming that this must be sub-divided into the Aeolian, the ornitho-sibilant, the feebly chirping, the tongue smacking, the faintly tinkling, the bone-snapping, the emptily-thunderous, and the phasmic while the Aeolian itself may be subdivided into the stridulaceous, the crepitaceous, and the oropharyngael, the crepitaceous into the absquiliferous, the vulgaritissmous, the laipecous, the crepitaceous into the panthero-dyspneaceous, the skrowlaceous, and the oropharyngeal into the enteric, the dipteric, the vermiculo-epigastric, the intestinal, the audio-zygo-amatory, the anal-resonatory, the oro-phleboevacuative, the capro-audio-lactative, the ovo-(or assino-) audio-lactative, and other may-be-sub-divideds.[97]

The problem of metaphor is thus none other than equivocation. But it is an equivocation that directly inflicts the body, defines its extimate location and enframes them. Despite the grammarian stratification of levels equivocation is set loose as that which resists all subdivisons and persists within them. The different types of metaphor listed even share a similar phonemic sound in Arabic, a distinct vocal sound, the movement from stratification [a movement from up to down] is supplemented by a movement from down up. By way of giving an example of the importance of using all these metaphorical tropes for one to prove their mastery of Arabic, Shidyaq claims that ingesting the rules of grammar can only lead to vomiting and voiding. Equivocation forces itself out of the body, while grammar afflicts the body with mortality.

The student of grammar is told by his teacher about the deaths of different grammarians from bodily afflictions: al-Farra', Sibawyhi, al-kisa'i, al-Yazidi, al-Zamakhshari, al-Asmaʿi all perished from unresolved problems in grammar that affected their bodies. For example, al-Asmaʿi died 'from goiter on his neck from worrying about the gluttoral stop'.[98] After hearing this, Fariyaq is distraught and wonders,

> did all the grammarians too die before completing the rules for that science? And does the fact that I've studied it at your hands relieve me of the need to go over it all again with someone else here? And is the student obliged to learn grammar as it is understood by the people of every country he travels to, or is it a science that has to be learned only once?'[99]

The grammarian confirms that the science of grammar will be correct once Fariyaq understands the rules of the book – the only book, the unnamed book. Learning the grammar of other languages will never relieve the subject from the agrammatical of language. What 'book' is it then that the grammarian refers to? It is surely not a lexicon that safeguards language from error, for error is what occurs in speech and cannot be prevented. Can it be that the errors of speech, which generate from the prohibitions against just saying anything, is coincidental with the fact that not everything can be said?

The puns of one language may not correspond to the puns of another; however, the pun is always founded on the existence of the signifier. The pun acts as a swivel for a symptom:

> A swivel which supports a symptom, a pun which doesn't exist in a neighbouring language. This is not to say that the symptom is always founded on a pun, but it *is* always founded on the existence of the signifier as such, on a complex relation of totality to totality or, more exactly, of whole system to whole system, of universe of the signifier to universe of the signifier.[100]

This means that the puns in one language correspond to the logic of the signifier, to the Real and not to puns in other languages. In other words, the 'universes' of the signifier are an indefinite division that cannot be added up or made whole.

The artifice of grammar, given its failure to deal with the problem of equivocation, is to establish the correctness and incorrectness of language, which satisfies nothing but the vanity of rulers. However, the study of grammar exposes a realm of that which is impossible *not* to say:

> The brilliant pupil continued to read grammar with the his *shaykh* until he got to the chapter on the 'doer' and the 'done' [the subject and object of verb] when he objected to the fact that the doer was 'raised' while the done was 'laid', claiming that the terminology was corrupt, for if the doer was raised then someone else must have raised him, whereas in fact it was the doer who did the work, the evidence being that we may observe a man working on a building raising a stone or the like on his shoulder, in which case the stone is the thing raised and the doer is the raiser, likewise the doer of the . . . is the one who raises the leg. At this point the tutor told him, 'Steady on! Steady on! You're being foul-mouthed. In the scholarly gathering – which is quite different from the princely – you're supposed to demonstrate good manners'.[101]

The grammatical question, which is about the specific delimitation of the 'doer' and 'done' of the verb, reveals that the doer of the deed and the done conceals an impossible that cannot be said: of fucking and being fucked in this case, or of the sexual (non-)relation. In fact, the very title of the book, *Leg Over Leg*, seems to originate from the impossibility of defining the sexual relation in grammatical terms (the doer and done). It is from the impasses of the sexual relation that a forceful explosion of speech, which cannot be contained, occurs: an unconscious voice that always disrupts and plays the role of a disturbance. Shidyaq begins from the purist preoccupation with grammar – the *do*'s and *don't*'s of language – only to come to the field of speech, which ceaselessly comes up against *lalangue*.

The 'incorrect' in any language is this impossible limit that only reveals itself as what cannot be said: a *lalangue* where desire flashes and the sexual non-relation is exposed.[102] This takes us back to Shidyaq's declaration at the beginning of the book that pleasure or enjoyment, *al-surrur*, is not to be derived from the sexual relation but from the burning fire of speech. The *jouissance* of which Shidyaq speaks is none other than the *separation* between body and language. Language, after all, is not only about making sense; 'but on the way to making sense, it always produces more than the sense catered for, its sounds exceed its sense'.[103]

3

Piercing the Bull's Eye: The Sexual (Non-)Relation

Shidyaq wrote in an era when capitalism had already made its way into the Ottoman Empire. Scribal work was already an inheritance to be refused, the discourse of the master was in recession and the crumbling symbolic order presented itself at every corner: in the home, where cultural practices of generosity impoverished his family; and most importantly in the traditional schools (*kuttab*), where learning grammar was harder than 'scratching your own balls'.[1] Rejecting the impotent work of scribes and grammarians, Shidyaq invoked metaphors of ejaculation to describe his version of *linguisteriks*. The writing of his pen is described as a 'cut' (*shiq al-qalam*): an incision into the symbolic sphere, from which a sense of pleasure is derived,[2] yet one that does not satisfy. Instead of the rampant *seraglio*, the paradise of pure enjoyment, the liberalising sphere of empire is experienced as a zone of impotence, a place in which pleasure can no longer be derived from coitus, if it ever has been. Pleasure cannot be derived from the sweet taste of sin even; rather, paradise itself, the promised paradise of satisfaction, is like the 'fruit of the *zaqqum* tree', a tree that grows in hell whose fruits taste bitter and 'its nectar like pus'.[3] The foul taste of a world in which masters can no longer be identified is experienced at once as a penetrating force and an excessive pressure. Shiyaq wrote, 'I once thought the world is like the vulva for both are stuffing in shape, I say it's more like the anus in its circularity'.[4] He compares the release experienced through the written word to a precipitation from the bottom up, a painful emptying out that through the 'narrow slit' of the pen.

Writing is a literal emptying out of the nozzle of the pen. It is a result of offering oneself to the desire of an Other who is perceived as a seductress the pursuit of whom is the pursuit of divine providence itself: 'my books had taken against me as a wife does her husband and I have decided to have nothing more to do with them'. He continues ' my intention in writing this book has been to approach closer to them and use it to appease, not anger, them'.[5] The book is thus dedicated to God himself via women, for 'one cannot behold the whiff of woman without glory of the creator'.[6]

Scribal work, Shidyaq's traditional training, is enslaved to the arbitrary rule of the law; it requires a reproduction of 'signs' and 'not good language'.[7] Lamenting his inability to be a clever fellow and simply accept his craft, Shidyaq makes the claim that ignorance lies in *savoir-faire*, in scribal work that relies on the writing of signs; while true pleasure in language lies in opposition to the knowledge found in *savoir-faire*, for there is 'no abjection worse than servitude'.[8] There seems to be a distinction, then, that is posited between ignorance in knowledge, ignorance in *savoir-faire* and a truth to be found elsewhere, in his burning speech. Shidyaq finds that the theft of knowledge, which the scribe suffers at the hands of the Emirs and notables, is debasing, in place of which he prefers the debasement of the love of language:

> Love is an abasement that makes bodies grow thin.
> No one would choose it.
> Did he not suffer from it.
> My Lord, O lord!
> O object of my desire!
> Take unto you none but me.
> And don't forget me for another.[9]

Writing, then, is a cut introduced into the symbolic order, a blackening of paper, a material 'precipitation' of the signifier – like how snow falls and 'brightens the weather', the 'descent' of Shidyaq's words brightens his thoughts; and this precipitation 'falls out of the [writer's] head into the reader's head'.[10] This direct emptying out of words, their ejaculation, is meant to inseminate the reader, and procreate a new symbolic – one that is posited against the Emirs, Metropolitans and monks, and other guardians of society. Shidyaq's egoism strikes at all the guarantees of custom and tradition and of sovereignty in society. The retreat from scribal work and the refusal to be 'tethered to the robes of an Emir' led Fariyaq to travel (to Alexandria, Malta, Tunis and finally England) from one official appointment to another: he was appointed, first, as a Dream Interpreter in the Oneiromancer's Chambers; then, as a physician who would clean out foul breath (generated from the presence of Metropolitans and foul-mouthed grammarians); and, finally, appointed as a companion to a Bag-man (wandering salesmen), a merchant, who would eventually go insane.[11]

Fariyaqa, his companion, is portrayed as an average woman from Damascus who had known no other company than her servants and who, through her travels with Fariyaq, comes to gain a knowledge that serves to destabilise the symbolic function of the marital couple. She is a woman who cannot be satisfied. Fariyaqa is almost sterile, like language, and she renders Fariyaq impotent and instigates in him fantasies of sodomy. Her 'backside' was all Fariyaq had for company in the evenings; and contrary to common opinion, 'there is nothing in the backside to indicate anger . . . The backside is one of those things that people have gone to great lengths to exalt, magnify, and aggrandise both materially and immaterially'.[12] The fetishism of the backside, for which Shidyaq provides many examples and more than a few poetry verses, can even be 'applied to all parts of the body'.[13] He proceeds to describe the particular Arab obsession with conquering the backside, 'this lofty structure'. A golden-gilded toilet adorned with flowers and silk brocade does not attract an Arab as a much as a great 'quantity of flesh and fat' on a woman's behind does: 'for a man's eye, despite its small size, is never satisfied, even when filled with something a thousand times larger and broader than itself'.[14] Shidyaq continues,

> Should he hear a peep from that place, he'd think the sultan must have sent him an orchestra to congratulate him on such a terrific triumph and comprehensive conquest and imagine that the lute would never have acquired the most plangent sound of all instruments had it not been fashioned in the

likeness of a half of that place, and that it had it been formed from both halves together it would be hard to speak Arabic complete with grammatical endings; likewise the dome takes its shape from it and from it ambergris derives its smell, that the Arabs were so enamoured of it that they added the letters of its name [anus] to six-letter verbs, which indicate a request for an action or that a thing is considered to possess a certain quality, that all the breadth of a man's chest and all the width of his back are worth nothing compared to the breadth of that thing, that when the big-buttocked women press eminent princes with their requests, the princes are brought low.[15]

The power of the posterior sack is an enigma. The pleasures gained from kissing it are many: 'in common parlance people have given it the names of kings and sultan, men of power and immanence, and leading imams, and for some (forgive me lord!) the Most Beauteous Names are as nothing before it, albeit their daily magnificat is to chant, "O Lord Glorious be thy Name!"'[16]

The praise of the buttocks, which is found to be comparable in name and form to an angelic form, brings princes to their knees. Shidyaq proceeds to borrow a description of the buttocks as *al-sawma'atan* – a monk's cell, a sanctuary – and to argue that the letters that make up the word *dubr* (which is the opposite of *qubl*) 'have their own meanings, and no matter how you switch them around, they'll give you a new meaning each time'. Employing numerology, Shidyaq argues that the 'numerical values' of the letters always add up to even numbers and that the entry for buttocks in Fairuzabadi's *Qamus* is 'the richest in that work'. This leads him to claim, 'the abstract and figurative always derive from the concrete'. The Arabs have compiled around 90 terms for backside, while the sun and moon don't have as many names; even the Emir does not enjoy this many 'names and sobriquets':[17] why is it, then, that the buttocks become a signifier of such importance for Shidyaq?

We cannot ignore that the buttocks become central after conversations with his wife, Fariyaqa, and in the discussions around her anthropological observations of strangers and foreign peoples and lands. The buttocks present us with the problem of hospitality. From the moment Fariyaq and Fariyaqa board the 'fire-ship', the obsession with the buttocks is enflamed.

It is indeed in their travels that Fariyaq's anxiety about remaining 'faithful' to Fariyaqa, the Levantine wife and to Mount Lebanon's culture of hospitality, emerges. Fariyaqa comes to embody at once 'the ignorant woman' and the spirit of a new age; she is confined to the customs of traditional society but expresses a sharp, if brittle, intellectuality. It is as though Fariyaq wishes to both exclude her and make of her an example of the rash new modern spirit which he condemns: after all, what woman turns her backside to her husband when he fails to answer her questions? Fariyaqa's questions and her histrionic praise for traditions, her incessant questions about soft-skinned men, flirtatious women and hundreds of other 'foreign' habits, become the site upon which Eastern hospitality itself fissures and breaks apart.[18] The false universality of hospitality (which Fariyaq complains about with regards to his mother and father as well) is revealed in the anxieties of Fariyaqa. How much can she cope with? How militant can her hospitality be without sliding into a *hostis* (hostility)? What is then the line between hostility and hospitality? Can the buttocks be the site of intersection of these two halves, 'the bull's eye' to be pierced by the 'animal that has been endowed with the power of speech'?[19]

The problem of sodomy arises as a point of intersection: there is an anxiety over tradition; there is anxiety over the impotency of emirs and princes, who simply cannot fuck the buttocks away; and there is an anxiety over paternity and procreation, which expresses itself in this depiction of the buttocks as an angelic form with which copulation is a formative fantasy for the Arabs. This fantasy cannot be interpreted simply as resulting from Shidyaq's repressed homosexuality: indeed, Shidyaq is ambiguous about the question of homoeroticism throughout *al-Saq* and there is not much to be gained from making this claim. Freud had already argued that the problem of sodomy and even homoeroticism itself as a phenomenon arises from the subject's inscription in a triangular desire that results from the familial complex. Desire *tout court* for Freud is fundamentally concerned with the problems of symbolic investiture, maternity and paternity, procreation and legitimacy. Am I the legitimate child? What do you want of me? These are questions addressed to an Other.

It is important to note here that this does not in any way anchor desire in the 'natural' function of reproduction; rather, it is to say that desire emerges in the interstices of symbolic identification.[20] The Old Testament tale of Sodom and Gomorrah tells the tale of a city of constant transgression, of incest and sexual cannibalism that threatens the dissipation of civilisation. God's angels are not spared from the hostile hospitality of Sodom's people. Lot and his daughters, after being exiled from their destroyed city, engage in incestuous transgression, drunk and unconscious. The story opens up the question of hospitality, of its necessity and impossibility, as do Shidyaq's fantasies, which offer a variation on the problem of hospitality.

Fariyaq in his exile refuses his hosts who even permit him flirtations with their daughters and wives and condone his desiring of backsides (instead of the reproductive sexual activity stipulated for the marital couple). His refusal is a demand for a more radical exile than the one he is already in. It is only in his writing, in the urge to create a name anew for himself, that symbolic paternity can be reconfigured. There are no surrogate fathers to be found in his hosts, only crazed, lustful and hypocritical figures. There is no 'real' paternal role Fariyaq can take on with the Fariyaqa who does not cease to tell him that he is not a real man and that he could never understand woman:

'I shall travel, leaving behind no man shall I miss'.
'Am I', I asked, 'one of the unmissed?'
'You're not a man', she said.[21]

Fariyaqa continues: 'The way you poets drool over poetry deceived us into thinking you were both sayers and doers, but it turns out the only thing you do well is describe'. He responds, asking, 'And who are the good doers?' She replies, 'Those who are no good at description'. Fariyaq presses her further: 'So where does literature have its say?' Her final response: 'In scholars' sitting rooms, not women's dressing rooms'.[22]

It is Fariyaq's literature, then, that blocks him from satisfying the symbolic role of husband and father. In literature Shidyaq measures a distance between the real and symbolic: there is a lack of a relation, which pushes him to a love of language as a love that resists corruption, a saintly kind of love. This love of language is the source of pleasure and pain, however. The impossibility of fusion, of the two becoming one, of sexual pleasure, is resolved in language: language itself becomes a means of pleasure, or to be more precise, sexual pleasure is only possible through language.[23] In the modern *episteme*, there is a fusion between the sexual and pleasurable; this is in contrast to the ancient and pre-modern *episteme*, in which pleasure was perceived according to the material qualities offered by things to bodies: i.e. pleasure functioned during these earlier epochs according to the principle of incorporation.

Jean-Claude Milner, following Foucault closely yet challenging him fundamentally, argues, 'in the ancient doctrine, pleasure has as its fundamental paradigm the starving man who eats, the parched man who drinks. Against this standard every pleasure is measured and legitimated'.[24] Pleasure under this paradigm was measured by the criteria of incorporation: the fulfilment of the five senses, the passage from the exterior to the interior. Until Plato introduced the 'Idea' of the Good, pleasure was largely conceived as determined by a principle of devoration: of incorporating into the body the material quality of a thing. The law of hospitality, of welcoming a stranger into one's home space, also functioned according to the same principle of incorporation: the stranger is treated as a guest but remains a stranger; guests do not have to renounce their nature as strangers; like the ancient model of eating and drinking, the ingested substance remains essentially distinct.[25] The trouble with pleasure is the fundamental occupation for Shidyaq: pleasure (*al-sirr w al surrur*) cannot be found in coitus; it cannot be found in marriage nor in foodstuff; neither in relations of hospitality in the social 'body'; nor can it be found in the affirmation of social belonging, place of birth, sex, or productive labour.

Voiding Verbiage: On Pleasure and Pain

Chapter 13 of every one of the four books of *Leg Over Leg* has a specifically allotted place by Shidyaq. The number 13 in numerology, as we know, is a destructive number: destructive insofar as it is meant to signify the establishment of new order.[26] Shidyaq gives a special place to the number 13 and resorts to numerology often to argue for the importance of certain words.

The thirteenth *maqama* of book one of *al-Saq* is a polemic against a fictive Islamic scholar and his views on pleasure and pain, the name of whom refers to at least two figures from the Islamic tradition, Ibn Rushd and Ibn Hazm: Abu Rushd 'Brains' Ibn Hazm. It is during a sleepless night that an insomniac Shidyaq comes to consider the matters of the human condition, the problems of stimulation and excitation, of pleasure and pain and their beyond. These chapters (the thirteenth chapter of every book) are always penned during sleepless nights and narrated by a Faid-Hawif ibn Hifam, a name created by Shidyaq through letter substitution and that rhymes with al-Harith ibn Hisham who is a narrator in al-Hamadthani's *maqamat* series. The stories are narrative fictions written as short episodes and have a realist descriptive tone, they are usually parodic, ironic and comical. In Shidyaq's variations on the *maqama*, we can note that the character of the Fariyaq is introduced to resolve the moral and philosophical predicament with a poetic verse that remains open to interpretation. The thirteenth *maqamas* are titled as interruptions that are meant to shake the reader and disrupt them: 'a *maqama* to make you sit',[27] 'a *maqama* to make you walk'.[28] The rhymed prose of these fragments addresses two sets of 'muddled matters':[29] pleasure and pain, marriage and desire.

Shidyaq entitles Ibn Hazm's book *Kitab Muwazanat al-halatayn wa-murazant al-alatayn* (The Book of Balancing the Two States and Comparing the Two Straits). This is of particular interest because it is concerned with comparing 'man's two states of wretchedness and *leisure*, of joy and care, of gain and loss, of sorrow and *pleasure*, from childhood until he arrives at *maturity*, then desiccated *senility*, all set out in facing tables using a columnar system that comparison enables'.[30] Shidyaq's contestation with the Honoured Sheikh – 'God sanctify his soul and elevate his rank and worth to the highest point above the earth'[31] – proceeds as follows:

> He gave undue weight to pleasure and failed to treat life's evils in equal measure. He even asserts that pleasure is to be had from both deed and thought – unlike pain, in which thinking is of no import – claiming that were he to picture himself cavorting with a ripe young wrench, and she with him, he'd be so shaken by ecstasy he'd be entirely carried away, chest and flank, bed and bench. However I doubted his words upon this point, thinking to myself, 'Glory be! Every writer, however great, must on occasion be out of joint', in my case, when I pictured the drunkard, the drowser, and the

yawner, as I lay there trying to sleep, all that picturing didn't compensate for the actual thing by even a jot, and I found no pleasure in it, either a little or a lot. I tend to the belief of a certain madman that the pleasure of sleep is not felt by the sleeper, either while, after, or before it prevails – a knot those who hold to the humoral theory remain incapable of untying by talking or thinking, or even with their teeth and nails.[32]

Ibn Hazm's mistake, according to the insomniac Shidyaq, lies in the assumption that pleasure can be gained in thought as much as in deed, that imagining a pleasurable act releases unnecessary excitation and restores a more homeostatic state in which sleep can be restored. In the particular example of imagining an act of coitus, Shidyaq finds it hard to conceive of pleasure resulting from such a fantasy, for there is something that seems to exceed both pleasure and pain in the function of fantasy. The reduction of the human condition to two binary columns, which the pre-modern theory of the humours proposes, fails at explaining the persistence of compulsions and anxieties, the persistence of excess elements beyond homeostasis:

> the people of the earth, without exception were fast asleep, while I alone among them all no repose could reap, that all my neighbours were at rest, while I am alone distressed . . . In a desperate agony of thought, cares thronging me from side to side, my worries ranging far and wide. All things possible and impossible to my mind occurred, every situation over which I'd ever worried (if only once and many years before) recurred.[33]

In order to pursue further this problematic of satisfaction through thinking and its relation to pleasure and pain, Shidyaq questions his 'neighbours' for an answer – a metropolitan and member of the clergy, a village school teacher, a jurist, a poet and the scribe of an emir – only to resort in the end to Fariyaq, who solves this mystery with a verse of poetry. The metropolitan 'whose adornments, worth, and culture were lauded and cheered at a length equal to his beard'[34] when faced with the two columns (of pleasures and pains) did not 'catch the implication or grasp their signification'. The school teacher suggests to place the columns on two scales in order to compare the weight of the arguments, this empiricist naivety leaves Shidyaq seething with anger at 'men of perspication', who were indeed 'the most feeble in mind among God's creation'.³⁵ The jurist, whose task ought to have been to reveal the rational 'distinctions among things that might otherwise be the same' and who by 'seeking guidance from one of the schools [of jurisprudence], which, by insisting on the impossible and making from the non-existent something necessarily existent' demanded that Shidyaq calculated the number of letters in each column. The weightier they would be, the jurist argued, then the better composed in essence, i.e. the measure of pain and pleasure is a measure of them as qualities. The jurist refers to Aristotelian logic, in which 'it is inconceivable to posit the impossible', only to propose a ludicrous numerological calculus of the weight of words corresponding to qualities of pleasure and pain. Now, the poet – 'the great flatterer, a mouth-twisting faux-Arabic patterer' – pontificates that 'the good things of this world may be the fewer', as he had written more panegyric poems than sonnets. The scribe tells Shidyaq that happiness and unhappiness lie in the emir's contentment and resentment; it would require a ledger of the emir's states over a period of time to provide an answer for the human condition.

With this final response, Shidyaq is infuriated. None of those of high rank and office, none of those in positions of mastery, can provide an answer. He then beseechs the young but poor Fariyaq, who scrambles his answer on a scrap of paper, 'which he pulled from his tattered coat and on it wrote without a qualm' that good compared to evil is a drop in an ocean.³⁶ Fariyaq states that man from his first sprouting of his hair and nails can find no pleasure and no joy,³⁷ and that 'pleasure cannot come from thinking, nor from recollection; that's naught but an illusion, when you think upon it well, one that may occur to the dimwit or victim of delusion . . . this world of ours, to those who know, is naught but loss and tribulation that we must endure. Man's born enslaved, not free and so he dies, of that you may be sure'.³⁸

With this response, Shidyaq is finally satisfied and to Fariyaq exclaims, 'Shame upon the people of this earth, should they fail to recognize your worth!'³⁹ Fariyaq's wisdom, then, lies in the claim that pleasure cannot be derived from imagination, from maturation, nor from procreation. Pleasure does not come into *being* through imagining or perceiving that which is pleasurable: pleasure is not found in thought. Rather, it is only to be found in the speech of the speaking being or beings that are qualified as speaking animals; it is only found in language – *if* we understand language as the very split between *parole* and *langue*, in 'verbal voiding', as Shidyaq deemed it. Man is destined to conditions of unfreedom because even when pleasure is attainable, it does not fulfil; rather, it splits the subject into two: there is something in the subject that enjoys regardless of whether they know it or not. This enjoying thing can be discerned when language proves to be excessive, providing an excess to sense-making, for 'its sounds exceed its sense'.[40] It is no coincidence that Fariyaq constantly provides the answers that Shidyaq seeks only in poetic form, through the alliterations of sounds: the poetic form provides an excess of sound over sense-making.

On one level, the poetic form paves the way for the onset of phonology, on the level of meaning (reduction of sounds to differential entities); 'but on the other hand, on the level of phonic substance, sounds are not to be reduced but to be maintained, elaborated; their music can be heard . . . they can be the material of an art of sounds apart from their sense making-properties'.[41] There is a parasitical nature to sounds: they are like 'the parasites of the phonemes'; the sonority of sound is parasitical on the 'fleshless, boneless, and bloodless'[42] phonemes.

As Shidyaq looks for sense, from the legislators of the symbolic (jurists, scribes, and so on), the guardians of language, he stumbles constantly on the erratic nature of *lalangue* (comparable to what occurs with linguists like Jakobson and Saussure in the twentieth century). The poetic effects, voiced by Fariyaq in one *Maqama* after the other, are the sources of repetition: they mark a discontinuity that serves an aesthetic effect that distinguishes a different function for language from communicative speech. Shidyaq *listens* to the voice of Fariyaq, the mythical creature that does not really exist as such, who is silent until asked to intervene. The answers that s/he provides are always transmitted as letters, scribbles on scraps of paper from the tattered pockets of his jacket; the answers are letters, signs from the Fariyaq who is 'subject supposed to know'.

The written word that Fariyaq provides is nothing but the flipside of Shidyaq's speech, always an indirect verification of Shidyaq's complaint: Fariyaq is an Other who always provides the answer sought, affirms

Shidyaq's fantasies, never providing an interpretation that would lead to a knowledge outside the bounds of what already is. Fariyaq is an avatar of Shidyaq's ego: s/he has a knowledge but knows that s/he knows. Fariyaq knows the extent of discordance that Shidyaq feels with his own existence, the sense of exclusion from his own experience. Fariyaq lives the particularities and contingencies of Shidyaq's existence; s/he lives in his place, acts as his narcissistic double. It is as though Fariyaq's function is to provide a direct link between the manifest content of Shidyaq's desires and wishes and their latent forms thereby leaving no space for desire to manifest itself as the distortion between the latent and manifest. However, there is something about Fariyaq, about his solitude, his inertness, and his unrelenting availability to synthesise all of Shidyaq's whims, which can only provoke laughter. There is something humorous in his choice of constant impoverishment. He is like Bartleby:

> to Fariyaq then I went, to find him o'er his copying bent, on his visage the first signs of transmogrification, eyes, as I beheld, deeply sunken, hands suffering from desiccation, cheekbones as though from the face's surface hewn, skin as tight as the shade of noon, so that I deplored his state and came close to staying silent for pity at his plight.[43]

Why is the 'subject supposed to know' comical? Is it because his knowledge is a burden he would rather not carry? Or is it because there is something that escapes it, a splinter of excess that doesn't make sense? Or is it because the 'subject supposed to know' is at a standstill, not open to the dialectics of self-consciousness? Is it because the 'subject supposed to know' is nothing but a mythical creature? Or is it because all he can offer is literally a letter (the written word) in response to Shidyaq's questions? Is it because Fariyaq is really impotent in the face of Shidyaq's *jouissance*, only present as a detour on Shidyaq's circuitous path back to the impasse of his own enjoyment?[44] Is it because the 'subject supposed to know' cannot be loved by Shidyaq, who appears to be fundamentally incapable of love? It is surely not insignificant that the moment Fariyaq provides an answer, Shidyaq literally experiences an explosion of speech: a *linguisteria* in which occurs a repetition of the free flow of language, slippages of the signifier. Neither Fariyaq, nor Fariyaqa, nor anyone else is able to hinder and suspend this process of infinite metonymy and repetition: it appears that Shidyaq is in a constant search of that which can interrupt the symbolic, halt the endless failed representations of the subject.

Right after his *thirteenth* chapter, 'The Obstruction and Levelling', Chapter 14 is entitled 'The Sacrament'. In it, Shidyaq returns to what he calls a necessary voiding of verbiage:

> Ahahahah! Ahahahah! Thank God! Thank God I'm done with the composition of that *maqamah*, and with its number too, for it was weighing on my mind. Now all that remains for me to do is to urge the reader to read it . . . now I have to squeeze my sconce to extract some more nice thoughts, figures, and choice words, at the same time avoiding chatter, a process that scholars refer to, I believe, as 'voiding verbiage'. But hang on a minute, and I'll ask them! What do you call words that are so bursting with meaning that they drench the reader, so that I can fetch them for you? If you don't tell me the name right away, don't blame me if I use their opposite. I exist, and it is my custom to look for what exists, not for what doesn't. Given that the term 'voiding verbiage' exists and its opposite doesn't, it is perfectly appropriate for me to turn to it in preference for some other term.[45]

He claims that the emptying out of words, their excrescence, is a process of naming: 'for when someone sedate bestows a name on something, it comes out as sedate as he is and cannot thereafter be converted into something different'. Shidyaq proposes that the process of naming is one of inheritance, of transmitting a symbolic identification, 'the words of kings are the kings of words. By the same token, poetry written by a woman is bewitching to the mind and teasing to the heart as a woman'.[46] The only exception to the law of the name, Shidyaq argues, 'is the donation of the child by the father, meaning the donation by the father of the material used to form the child'[47]: i.e. the semen. While the father cannot directly conceive his child, cannot literally be pregnant, neither he nor the mother can determine the name of the child: i.e. they cannot secure his symbolic function through paternal law alone. From this observation on naming, the narrative shifts suddenly to Fariyaq's own progeny, his writings, which are depicted as bastard children, born out of wedlock and for whom he must be expiated from sin. This necessitates a visit to none other than a priest who questions Fariyaq's poetic impulse for its corrupting element: the insistence on the articulation of desire. The priest says,

> I hear you're fond of poetry and tunes, which are among the worst causes of evil and passion. Has the Recoiler ever put it into your mind to court in verse a woman firm of breast, rosy of cheek, the *kolh* in her eyes so clear to see, her buttocks wobbling free, slender of waist.

A long, detailed description of a woman's body ensues, leaving nothing to be desired (from belly button to saliva). After the priest's description, Fariyaq is led to claim that they are after all 'fellows in craft'. However, the priest insists that the poems must be burned, the verses destroyed, for they 'incite heedless to err'. To this, Fariyaq replies,

> Does it make sense that all that effort of mine [poetic writing] should be thwarted for the sake of the heedless? Not to mention that I do not want them to read what I write anyway, because if they don't understand it, they'll ask the scholars, who will proceed to hold it up in scorn, accusing me of mistakes and shortcomings. They never see merit in the writings of the young and humble, and even if they do, my only reward will be, 'God shame him! God destroy him! May his mother be bereaved from him! May he have no mother and no father!'[48]

How did we arrive at this from voiding verbiage – which was incurred by Fariyaq's written letter in response to Shidyaq's laments? Fariyaq is in the position of 'subject supposed to know', as I am suggesting, as well as in the position of social impotence unable to inherit a symbolic function and only able to bequeath one in the emptying out of words: words that drench and burn, sting and puncture a hole in meanings already given. These words are his legitimate children that render him a bastard child. What sort of paternal authority then does the *Sheikh al-lugha* – as Shidyaq has been called – have? The test of lineage appears to be formative to Shidyaq's assumption of his role as a writer, voiced through his ego's double Fariyaq and challenged by Fariyaqa, as we will see shortly. The 'test of lineage is one of the ways that a culture frames or encodes' the question of social existence: how does an individual come to consider him/herself as legitimate?[49] How does one make a name for oneself? In the context of the 'decadence' of the nineteenth-century social order – or the crisis in symbolic investiture depicted by Shidyaq himself – within which Shidyaq lived and wrote, *Leg Over Leg* can be seen as the means through which he makes a name for himself. However, the name that he makes emerges as internally doubly split: we have Shidyaq, Fariyaq and Fariyaqa – a trinity that results from an internal doubling (Shidyaq and Fariyaq) and then a split into two (Fariyaq and Fariyaqa). The symptomatic eruption of verbiage is fashioned along the metaphor of voiding (what Lacan would call the anal object, one of the forms of *objet a*): it is a gift sent to the Other whose desire remains unknown to the subject. There is an *oblativity* at work in Shidyaq's seeking for an answer, through which he offers himself as a gift in order to qualm the panic of anxiety that haunts his entire *oeuvre*: what am I? Who am I? What do you want of me? The desire of the Other cannot be discerned and remains concealed from the subject; to the enigmatic desire of the Other, the subject offers his/her being as a sacrifice. This dialectic of desire, of subjectivity and otherness, is concluded with a manifestation of love. In this case, it is the love of language that emerges as the effort to arrest the signifier, respond to the mute desire of the Other:

> Love masks the external origins of subjectivity, concealing them not behind the illusion of an autonomous subject as a *causa sui*, but, quite the contrary, by offering one's being to the Other, offering one's own particularity in response to external contingency. The remainder of the Real beyond the signifier demands the offering of that remainder in the subject, the part of the 'individual' that could not be subjectified, the object within the subject. With that gesture, the remain der is dealt with and the Other is sustained. The opacity of the Other is made transparent by love, the lawless becomes the lawful.[50]

Indeed, the 'love of language' to which Fariyaq constantly clings is a *rejection* of tradition and pre-established customs, religion and cultural symbols: in his own words 'I am not a chain man'.[51] The only chain Fariyaq cannot but be ensnared in is the chain of signifiers. In his presence, priests, monks and notables alike confess their sins: priests with big noses desiring the wives of their hosts and priests whom Fariyaq aids in escaping monasteries described as wretched and unliveable. The Chapters of

Fariyaq's Quixotical episodes (beginning in Mount Lebanon and moving to Egypt, Malta, France and England) have titles that are 'to be deciphered as signs';[52] they are like 'smoke to fire', a sign representing something for another sign. The chapters are like dreams governed by the labour of condensation and displacement, metaphor and metonymy. The content of these chapters cannot be translated into the common language of intersubjective communication. There is no simple latent content to a symptom or a dream, no inner concealed meaning; the secret of the symptom lies in its form, in its formal nature and not in its content; it is ultimately a *signifier* through which an unconscious desire is expressed or articulated. Through the symptom, a lack is both affirmed and denied: there is a disavowal and an avowal at the core of the function of repression, and a gap between the pursuit of desire and the production of pleasure.

Undercapitalised Parasites and Antediluvian Capital

Nowhere outside languages could Fariyaq secure a direct connection to God. As a trader and a Bag-man, he was accused of heresy: the Gods of the market, it appears, were not his God. In the course of trying a career as a merchant, Fariyaq exchanged all his goods for new ones because 'all things new have an appeal'.[53] This, however, was conceived as a heresy by the bishop of the district, 'one of the big-time fast-talking market traders' who submitted him to a public hearing:

> God's horsemen against the infidel! They shall roast in Hell! How dare this accursed rascal, this raving *lunatic*, choose a path other than that laid down for him by his master's ecclesiastic, that followed by his very own patriarch? How dare he, in his impertinence, brazenness and infamy, have dealings with that miserable travelling peddler and barter away to him what has been passed down to him from his ancient ancestry? Bring him to us in disgrace! Flog him in the nude! Throw him in the fireplace! Feed him to the fishes! Make him eat ashes! Cut out his tongue! [54]

We cannot ignore that Fariyaq's plight may be a metaphor for Shidyaq's own brother, Asa'd al-Shidyaq, who, due to converting to Protestantism at the hands of the American Missionaries in Beirut, faced torture and imprisonment under the orders of the Maronite patriarchs and eventually died.[55]

It is more important to note that the metaphor Shidyaq uses for religious conversion is of trade and exchange of commodities: the exchange value of commodities shares a similar status to that of religious inheritance. To be more precise, the traditional barter system against which Fariyaq rebels is based on a model of God's propriety over all things, God-the-Father who is removed from the sphere of circulation. The conception of propriety that Fariyaq seems to argue for 'blasphemously' is that of private property, which works against the principle of paternal inheritance; it is a notion of ownership rooted in fraternal metaphors rather than paternal lineage or inheritance.[56] In the court hearing, the discussion goes as follows:

> The Trader: Woe unto you sucker! What made you barter away your goods?
> The Fariyaq: If they're my goods, as you have just submitted, what's to stop me?
> The Trader: Misguided Man! They're your goods in the sense that you inherited them from your forefathers, not in the sense that they're yours to do with as you please.
> The Fariyaq: This is against custom and truth, for a man may do whatever he likes with his inheritance.[57]

Fariyaq had exchanged old cloth for new dyes, old colours for the new, to which the Trader retorts: 'Blasphemer! He blinded you so you couldn't distinguish amongst the colours'.[58]

Fariyaq finds it hard to believe that his senses had deceived him and wonders why it is that the Trader is immune to this kind of deception:

> The Trader: May you perish! Though I was once a human being just like you, I am now an authorised agent of the Market Boss, who has let me in on the amazing powers that God had bestowed on him.

Fariyaq wonders about this 'Buff [Boss] of the Market *Difgwace* [Disgrace]': what if he is cursed by the *jinn* or falls sick or goes mad? 'How does he distinguish between good and bad products?'

> The Trader: May you perish! He is never afflicted by such attacks, he is the keeper of the mighty gate . . . has sole charge of this plot of land, for it was entrusted to him by its all mighty owner

Fariyaq: when was that?

The Trader: May you be crucified! About two thousand years ago.

The Fariyaq: you mean to tell me that the 'boss' has been around for two thousand years?

The Trader: Atheist! It came to him by inheritance.[59]

Fariyaq continues to probe the boss's inheritance and is told that it had been bequeathed him from a person who is not from his family, which strikes Fariyaq as odd: how could a person inherit anything from a stranger? For the money of a stranger without an heir ought to go to a public treasury. At this point, the Trader condemns him for questioning the 'sacrament' of inheritance, the original sin of accumulation. This cannot but remind us of the analogy that Marx had posited between original accumulation in capitalism and original sin in theology:

> This primitive accumulation plays in Political Economy about the same part as original sin in theology. Adam bit the apple, and thereupon sin fell on the human race. Its origin is supposed to be explained when it is told as an anecdote of the past. In times long gone by there were two sorts of people: one, the diligent, intelligent, and, above all, frugal elite; the other, lazy rascals, spending their substance, and more, in riotous living. The legend of theological original sin tells us certainly how man came to be condemned to eat his bread in the sweat of his brow; but the history of economic original sin reveals to us that there are people to whom this is by no means essential. Never mind! Thus it came to pass that the former sort accumulated wealth, and the latter sort had at last nothing to sell except their own skins. And from this original sin dates the poverty of the great majority that, despite all its labour, has up to now nothing to sell but itself, and the wealth of the few that increases constantly although they have long ceased to work.[60]

The blasphemy of which Fariyaq is accused pertains to his engagement with the circulation of commodities with the Bag-men (a mercantile bourgeoisie involved in global circuits of commodity circulation), and his selling of labour-power to a sphere of market exchange that 'has no boss'.[61] While the Market-men are 'the boss', they are commodity owners who are simultaneously owners of money eager to valorise the values they have acquired by buying the labour force of others. The sacrament of accumulation lies in protecting the position of the hoarder, of the collector of goods, who is simultaneously the keeper of tastes. The Market-men are outraged by Fariyaq's encouragement of new 'tastes' through his replacement of old colours with the new.

Fariyaq asks for proof of this sacrament, and the proof provided (from a book) by the trader offers a story of homoerotic origin. The sacrament is not the result of matrimony between man and woman, a 'normal' lineage of inheritance instilled through reproduction rather:

> The owner had once loved a man, so he'd given him a number of gifts, among which were a cup, a basin, a stick with a carving of two snakes on the end, a robe, a pair of shorts, a pair of sandals, and two keys. And he said to him, 'all these things I give to you. Use them and enjoy them'.[62]

The use-value of commodities however is not the source of their exchange value: i.e. inheritance cannot be the source of original accumulation; the hoarder (or Market-man) accumulates by stepping into the position of equivalence even at the expense of the object.

In the disagreement over the meaning of inheritance, the trader claims to be the 'warden of inheritance and its preserver'. He assumes the position of the guardian of the debt of inheritance, 'its trustee' and the 'sponsor' of all inheritors. Fariyaq is called a 'deviant' for daring to exchange his inheritance for other goods, to which he responds: 'exchanging one thing for another isn't evidence of error or deviance if the thing exchanged and the thing it is exchanged for are of the same kind'.[63] Fariyaq then defends the exchange relation in terms of its role in the fulfilment of a desire for the commodities, while what the Trade-men desires in contrast is money and exchange value itself.[64] This brings us back to Marx again, who called capitalists 'rational misers' in his analysis of commodity-based exchange relations:

> As the conscious representative of this movement, the possessor of money becomes a capitalist. His person, or rather his pocket, is the point from which the money starts and to which it returns. The expansion of value, which is the objective basis or main-spring of the circulation M-C-M, becomes his subjective aim, and it is only in so far as the appropriation of ever more and

more wealth in the abstract becomes the sole motive of his operations, that he functions as a capitalist, that is, as capital personified and endowed with consciousness and a will.[65]

The Trade-man in conversation with Fariyaq claims that he is after all the viceroy of an eternal will of God that had set down the rules of commerce. Marx's argument about the miser and exchange value is relevant here,

> Use-values must therefore never be looked upon as the real aim of the capitalist; neither must the profit on any single transaction. The restless neverending process of profit-making alone is what he aims at. This boundless greed after riches, this passionate chase after exchange-value, is common to the capitalist and the miser; but while the miser is merely a capitalist gone mad, the capitalist is a rational miser. The never-ending augmentation of exchange-value, which the miser strives after, by seeking to save his money from circulation, is attained by the more acute capitalist, by constantly throwing it afresh into circulation.[66]

Indeed, can we not see the Bag-men and The Trade-men expressing a necessary antinomy of capital: the desire for commodities on the one hand (C-M-C), and the drive for accumulation on the other (M-C-M'). According to Fariyaq, he could not understand his fault for he had only exchanged an old colour for a new one. And how can inheritance be safeguarded 'when both benefactor and beneficiary have died and the whole gift has been lost? How can just the keys be left, when the door is gone and they are useless without it?'[67] The Bag-men who Fariyaq had joined 'bank' on emotion and motion (*al-his w al-haraka*); they glamorise the ceaseless movement, the motion of objects of taste on the market;[68] the circulation of commodities requires that one's 'heart loves' that thing or 'feels drawn to it' or 'desires' it'.[69] Indeed, the Bag-man questions Fariyaq's allegiance to the see 'whether or not love for new goods beats strong within it'.[70] The Bag-man demands from Fariyaq that the price-list of commodities burns its letters through his heart:

> When you read the price list, do you feel that every single letter in it has been imprinted on it (meaning your heart), so that, even if it weren't there, those same letters could take its place? Does it sometimes ignite and burn,

and then at others go out, only to return more strongly, like the celebrated phoenix? Do you feel too that it's being prodded by a prodder, prickled by pricker, squeezed by a squeezer, constricted by a constrictor, ripped by a ripper, and pressed by a presser? . . . What is meant by 'burning' here and by 'prodding' and 'squeezing', is ardour, enthusiasm, and obsessive interest, and that imagining that what isn't there is present and that fantasy is real . . . because intense imagining and obsessive interest help a person put up with trials and tribulations.[71]

Fariyaq's labour as a Bag-man would then require that he accept that the figurative and the real, the tangible and intangible, become interchangeable if not indistinguishable: social relations premised on commodity exchange allow for one to 'reckon hunger as a dining table, the bier a throne, the impaling stake or cross a pulpit'.[72] The Bag-man declares in misery that their fate is 'trudging high and low over the earth, offering to make any mortal who crosses his path his partner and co-financer. He goes on his way, until his time is up, and nothing pleases him than to die thus engaged. The Bag! The bag! No other trade or labour have we than it'.[73]

Fariyaq's departure from his native land of Mount Lebanon, away from the misers of the Church, the Metropolitans and Market-men, and his acceptance of the cause of the Bag-men, and their dedication to creating new desires for goods, is caused by this confrontation between the religious creed of the 'Market-men' or 'undercapitalised parasites', as he calls them, and the changes brought about by the 'Bag-men'. In this narrative, we can note a shift from a local economy of mercantile capital, of hoarders and misers, to a more global one characterised by constant motion and movement and circulation. Fariyaq escapes the monopoly of Market-men over social life, their attitude towards hoarding in particular and their claims over exchange-value, only to be fated to join the league of the other idol worshipers. Both the Market-men and Bag-men, share in their trade imagination (or fantasy) and division, *al-mukhayila w al-qasm*.[74] Their capital[75] is only gained through warfare, depicted by Shidyaq as a feud and combat over grammatical categorisations structured along these lines:

> It is likely that the thing to which you refer falls under the rubric either of the trope attributive or the trope lexical, or the trope tropical or the expression

periphrastic, or it may belong to the category of referring like to like, or opposite to opposite, or under that of 'expressing the intrinsic while intending the extrinsic'... or it is to be approached via the door of irony, or the aperture of allusion, or the peephole of person-switching, or the rent of redundancy, or the casement of carefully crafted composition, or the inlet of implication, or the tear in 'tight weaving', or the spiracle of the quasi-paradoxical simile... or the knot-hole of the substitution of what is known for what is not.[76]

The grammatical dispute is, after all, a dispute over the exchange value of language, and bloodshed ensues from these idolaters, these protectors of idols (Shidyaq lists different kinds of protectors of idols for three pages on end). Shidyaq wishes to 'roll a boulder' against the Market-men who stand in for the exchange-value of commodities and against the Bag-men who create new fantasies of use-value for novel commodities. Neither of these trades, according to Shidyaq, require knowledge of quantification: 'neither measuring or counting – unlike that of the practitioners of the natural sciences, engineers and mathematicians'.[77] Theirs is a pseudo-science, which is not inherited or transmitted, but simply a set of practices that anyone can partake in. The claims to social status, to inheritance and lineage, are pure ideology, because 'anyone who wishes to wear an outer garment or robe, with drawers underneath or with wrestler's breeches, can make them himself with any colour he pleases and of any shape he likes'.[78]

The question of taste is fundamentally related to the goodness or badness of a commodity. And the pure quantities that are represented by the senses are qualified in particular commodities, and these in turn become the vehicles of imagination. The hell of exchange relations, of the exchange of commodities, is a hell on earth, while the accumulation of value is an affair of heaven. Shidyaq's response to this hell was to state that God couldn't have wanted it this way: the value lies in a common humanity, in those that work 'in anticipation of only heavenly reward. All people are God's children, and the person God loves the best is he who is of greatest benefit to his children'.[79] The problem of inheritance is translated once into the terms of an economy of exchange, and back again into the anxiety over procreation: who shall inherit the earth but the sinners who live in it? The boss of the Market-man exclaims,

So long as the market is well and its boss is safe and sound, the rest of the world is too. Business is going well, and the market's up and *running*, bellies are full, mouths are *munching*, stomachs are *digesting*, molars are *crunching*, hands are *snatching*, joys are *everlasting*, fortunes are *accumulating*, bosses are *prohibiting*. Providence is *protecting*, women bearing ex-votos in droves are arriving, pious bequests are all-*encompassing*, the mouths of the Fates are smiling, and all's well that ends well. To market! To Market! There's the box of delights, there the trove of truths! Into the chest! Morning and evening the chest is best![80]

The boss of the Market-men, read here as the stand in for the capitalist drive, has only to devote himself 'to the taking of opium', for he does not sleep: he is an insomniac who also had 'stuffed his ears with pages from the market ledgers so that he wouldn't hear the scream of those who called on him for help'.[81] The boss of the market cannot hear, does not listen, is silent, mute and knows only one thing: for the market to work, new desires must be created; the market doesn't work the other way around (i.e. through people's desires); the commodity has to be sold in advance. And it is not simply the synthesis of use-value and exchange-value; rather, what is at stake in the synthesis is inevitably 'faith':[82] an 'as if'[83] situation, which assumes that commodities are incorruptible in any exchange, existing as values beyond the use-value of their physical properties. There is a peculiar religious nature to this world of exchange, which will be approached again in Chapter 4.

Feminisation Fantasies: Am I a Man or a Woman?

Shidyaq presents his life through the voice of a masculine Fariyaq – a mythical creature that may not even have existed to begin with – and his doublet or feminine pseudonym, Fariyaqa. Fariyaq and Fariyaqa are both missing halves (of a creature that autocopulates, a hermaphrodite) of something that was not whole: a mythical creature haunted by the impossibility of the sexual relation between man and woman and by their radical difference, which is in turn constitutive of both.[84] The book, which is relentless in its shocking libertine depictions of sexual fantasies, is addressed to young women as a source of learning about habits, morality and the dictums of sociality. Through Fariyaq's licentious fantasies, the reader is exposed to the irrationality of the moral law of mutual respect in society, to the compact between law and desire in liberal modernity:

> I swear this book contains nothing reprehensible, unless you find the Fariyaq's sometimes pushing his way through a troupe of *ghaniyas* or forcing himself upon them as they rest safe in their bridal pavilions or in a garden or in the corner of a house or on their beds to be so. This was, however, something I was unable to avoid, for the book has been compiled as an account of his doings and to provide knowledge of the circumstances that influenced him, it having come to my attention that many people have denied that the above named even exists and claimed that he belongs to the same category as the ghoul and the phoenix, while others asserted that he appeared but once throughout the *age* and thereafter vanished from the *stage*, and more than one held that he was transmogrified a few days after his birth and that it is not known what shape he adopted or into what form he mutated. Another party has claimed that he joined the race of the monopods and another that of the monopodettes. Still others have said that he joined the *jinn*. Some have insisted that he transformed into a woman, for when he saw that the female enjoys a happier state in the world – this 'women's world', as it's known – he let not a night go by without praying to his Lord to turn him into a female and God accepted his prayer (and He is capable of all things).[85]

Acknowledging that the book itself may indeed be 'inappropriate to women',[86] Shidyaq argues that two things had pushed him to this end: to 'show off the beauties of our noble language' – which is always experienced by him as a demand from an Other under which as a linguist he is doomed to suffer – and to 'awaken the desire' in those indolent readers to *listen* to this language. 'Dear *reader*, then, and dear *listener*, dear shame-faced *abstainer* and dear *blind-eye turner*, tell the trouble maker among you, "To the bitter, nothing is sweet"'.[87] Shidyaq then wishes to vex his reader, by the ailment of which he suffers, the *jouissance* he experiences from the 'tyranny of the pen'.[88] The written text is meant to finally satiate 'that sexually voracious mistress of mine, that beetle-bodied mistress of mine, that flat-breasted, small-buttocked mistress of mine, and that soot-bedaubed mistress of mine'.[89] This insatiable woman is one in the presence of whom Fariyaq is rendered impotent and one who renders a king or emir impotent, handing in both his 'sceptre and *baton*'[90] and only able to recite to her poetry. In her presence, a *vizier* 'would toss her his ring in submission',[91] a judge would 'bestow on her . . . all his possessions'.[92] And if she were to visit a physician who happens to be 'treating a man of impotence, he'd prescribe him a rub with the cartilage of her nose-end'[93]; an astrologer would 'throw in his astrolabe in surprise and stupefaction'[94]; a philosopher would find 'he'd no good sense left to stop him feeling *fraught*'[95]; an architect's shapes would be muddled and 'his mind befuddled'; a logician would be led to 'violate analogy, flail in ambiguity'; a grammarian would 'lose all sense of active and passive, decide that knowledge of such things was simply *invasive*'; a prosodist would 'find himself replete' and recite 'I want to do you, I want to do you, I want to do you!'[96]; a poet would 'hang out his tongue and drool with delight'.[97]

It is evident here that Woman is not fashioned along the image of an eternal feminine that draws all (scientists, philosophers, grammarians, linguists and poets) toward her in an act of elevation, as the Romantics would have it; rather, the feminine here is depicted more as a 'femme fatale', as a threatening and repulsive force and an erotic attraction, a spell under which all will fall. Shidyaq continues, addressing the reader in first person, that if indeed this woman would touch either him or his reader, she would 'strike them from all growths, lumps, perturbances, and swellings'.[98] Here he lists eighty different words, synonyms and homophones for skin protrusions and abnormal growths that Woman can cause, after which Fariyaq descends into a diatribe against this castrating Woman who is 'man-mannered',[99] and who not only levels all protrusions but also impedes any growth, even further castrates Man. The feminine Other as such is experienced as a paternal function, a manly intrusion, a penetration that renders Shidyaq himself in the position of the impossible woman: an almost saintly woman who conceives *Leg Over Leg* in an act of immaculate conception.[100]

It is this particular 'true' feminisation of Fariyaq that renders it a 'duty' to relay his story to young girls in particular. The young and earnest reader whom he calls forth is also feminine, a reader who has to be conceived in a manner similar to his book. Shidyaq's 'difficult circumstance' in accommodating to social relations, his 'hardships of travel and consorting with foreigners and learning their languages, especially the graying of his hair and his passage from the youth to the age of maturity',[101] and his feminisation – these are proposed as stories of instruction for a family of readers that he constructs. But what is Shidyaq's writing instructing its reader about? What kind of reader is Shidyaq calling for in his text?

Shidyaq often slates the inept reader who cannot interpret his words asking them to put down the book. The book is only meant for the earnest, insomniac, knowledge-hungry and in particular those who can identify with the sense of exile and homelessness that Fariyaq and Fariyaqa experience everywhere. Rabaté's concept of a 'genetic-generic reader' – versus a semiotic account of an ideal reader – is helpful here. The 'genreader' is meant to partake in the burial of old-sense that Shidyaq undertakes, his revolt against tradition, and his insistence on making a name for himself beyond familial inheritance. Shidyaq seeks the name-of-the-father, a paternal metaphor, the injunction that names him as a son. But the more he seeks a male figure of authority (grammarians like Sibwayhi, priests of Mount Lebanon, noblemen and emirs, scholars of Oxford and Cambridge), the more it becomes evident that they are impotent: a master's force and power are always accompanied by a comical impotence that Fariyaq/a reveals. It is, then, the injunction of the Name-of-the-Father that motivates the writing of Shidyaq (and not simply his intentionality as an author): an injunction that is experienced as uncanny, for the bare truth of power lies in its particular impotence. Shidyaq's sardonic obsession with titles, lineages, and names (the legitimacy transmitted by the Name-of-the-Father) expresses the pressure exerted by the symbolic functions on the subject, there is no lack of titles around Shidyaq, but an immense pressure that generates from their over-proximity. This can be discerned in the bad luck (*al-nahs*)[102] or the jinx that Fariyaq suffers from. This ill fate is cosmic: 'how ill-omened was the star under which he had been born and how much bad luck his pen had brought him'.[103] God who is usually at a removed distance from humankind, can enter into contact with Fariyaq, in his dreams, in his private contemplations, but most importantly in grammar and rhetorical sciences, which owe their existence to God. And the pursuit of them is none other than the affirmation for the love of God: the pen is his curse and cure, the source of his *jouissance* and suffering.

Leg Over Leg: The End of Procreation

Shidyaq's passion for Arabic – 'the means to all the sciences [*al-ʿulum*] of this world and the hereafter'[104] – signifies a particularly modern turn of Arabic from a language of elsewhere, of an imagined past, to a language of the self and to a 'language like no other'.[105] Shidyaq describes his relationship to Arabic with the *jouissance* of a lover's submission to his object of desire: 'as I tried to conquer it, it conquered me'. The very elements of praise in Arabic, its concealed secrets – its eloquence and articulation, its *fasaha* and *balagha*, and its reason and wisdom – are those same aspects of language that constantly 'defeat' its speaker. But what is this language that cannot but be experienced as a conquering of its speaker by an Other? It is a terrain that cannot be conquered and is both internal and external to the speaking subject who can only experience its presence negatively, as a defeat experienced with euphoric pleasure. *Lugha* is an object of desire that cannot be conquered and towards which the subject yearns with an enjoyment in its delayed attainment.

In Shidyaq's writings, *lugha* is depicted as an unattainable object of desire, a 'fathomless sea' of concealed treasures, an untameable woman, and an object of love. The love of language that torments Shidyaq's movement reveals the plight of the modern subject, who in the wake of the dismantlement of the ancient regime seeks a master signifier to make them whole again. It is in this pursuit that Shidyaq stumbles upon the problem of subjective enunciation: the I is not whole but both whole and nothing at the same time, a 'non-totalizable source of negativity introduced into the world'.[106] The very act of writing is perceived by him as a 'cut' in the symbolic order introduced by the 'nib' of his pen, *shiq al-qalam*.[107] Having been trained in traditional scribal work – the copying of books – Shidyaq's four volumes of *Leg Over Leg* are introduced as acts of disruption: Raising of a Storm,[108] Rolling of a Boulder,[109] Lighting of a Furnace,[110] and Unleashing of a Sea.[111] In these works we see the function of writing as a disruption in the symbolic order and a symptom of a surplus to imaginary identification.

Leg Over Leg begins with the 'raising of a storm' against an age in which true masters are no longer to be found – men are no longer men, and women no longer women – in a way that reveals that neither of these categories was stable to begin with. It is an autobiography relayed in the third person, the double that Shidyaq creates for himself and whose life is narrated in the four volumes is named Fariyaq, a conjunction from *Far*is and Shid*yaq*. The Fariyaq we are told is neither man nor woman; he is a traditionally trained scribe from the feudal Lebanese mountains who inherits the craft from his father, who was a participant in a failed rebellion against taxation policies of the provincial prince, and who suffers the fate of death leaving Fariyaq with a devastated mother. Fariyaq is a character ridden by knowing too much about the waning symbolic order of feudalism and the tragic fate of liberal individualism in, respectively, the Lebanese mountains and European society. He is one who does not accept that the function of writing is solely limited to the *savoir-faire* of scribal writing.[112] Scribal work no longer could offer a viable source of income in a shifting economy of printing presses at the time. As a scribe, Shidyaq finds himself all the time an estranged guest, a stranger, constantly moving between different hosts (Bag-men, merchants, clergymen) only to mock their ways, to laugh at them and criticise ruthlessly. By refusing to accept the symbolic function of the host (in Malta, Cairo, Tunis, England) as surrogate father, a substitute figure for the law of the father, Fariyaq refuses to conform to the social order of modernity. This refusal to conform can be read as a modernism against modernity, defined by 'typographical reproduction and authorial certainty'; however, with Shidyaq, what we witness is a return to a form of pre-modern instability, a destruction of the old sense, an insistence on a real revolutionising of the old world.[113]

The spectres of modernity, its ghosts and apparitions, conceal a disavowed element already at work in modern society. Whether it is the thrust of emancipation as Marx and Engels declared in their *Communist Manifesto*, or the undercurrent of egoism as detected by Freud (in which the I as soon as it is enunciated as an ego disappears in the very act of that enunciation), the ghosts of modernity, its phantasmagoria, reveal its split nature and the conjunction of two subterranean trends. Jean Michel Rabaté argues that egoism is a direct 'outcome and main symptom of early modernism'.[114] The dissolution of a unified social psyche, which is the watershed of modernity globally 'is defined by the conjunction of two movements: individual scepticism in the realm of society and culture, and in epistemology, a split between subject and object, mind and matter'.[115] Shidyaq's paradoxes, his witty inversions of common-sensical beliefs still held by previous doxa, are based on a gap: a lull introduced between 'the world of empirical object and the mind, free to reconstruct a world out of nothing'.[116] Shidyaq's internal split between Fariyaq and Fariyaqa introduces a double split: a rift that questions the division between the *Umwelt* and *Innenwelt* and relays the plight of the modern subject, of the I as an internal other.

If we accept that modernism, even before postmodernism, is a movement that was defined by experimental writing that rejected parochialism and undertook the 'revolution of the word' but was characterised by a polyglottic prose and hard-to-decipher allusions, then we can place Shidyaq within this movement – expanding its limits beyond early twentieth-century figures like Joyce and Conrad. If the European modernist movement was defined by World War I, then the social conditions surrounding Shidyaq – a liberalising Ottoman empire, the impact of which was a sectarian civil war in Mount Lebanon and the wretched conditions of the working class in London and Paris that he witnessed – have had a similar influence on his work. Literature, after all, exhibits the trials of self-consciousness at a historical moment and 'fictional texts can, in their own way, not only convey but produce forms of speculation which are directly expressive of a determinate historical reality. They allow us both to understand it and to imagine it'.[117] Pierre Macherey maintains that since the 1800s, literary philosophy has employed a 'digestive fantasy' to define a whole range of that century's poetics: 'the author swallows everything, digests the whole of reality, and everything that occurs or does not occur in it, in order to bring it up in a completely dematerialised form after an almost alchemical operation'.[118] The metaphor of digestion is befitting for Shidyaq's metaphoric tropes and literary devices.[119] However, the result of the digestion process and indeed Shidyaq's many indigestions is not just the literary text as a product that offers itself as an object of study; it is also a process of literary production that has a fecundity to it which is inexhaustible, and the object of which is the generation of a form of knowledge that is not a rediscovery of what is already there but a construction of a new discourse: it is a knowledge that carries within itself the conditions of its own objectivity.

Shidyaq's literary *oeuvre* does not simply translate into his psychobiography (in a crude psychologism) or his direct social and historical *habitus* (à la Bourdieu); rather, the particular object of his literary production appears to be an element that cannot be interpolated in the symbolic register, but which presents itself as a negation of the symbolic, bores a hole in the established culture, takes away from its received knowledge. Carrying out this invasive function against culture, the written work, or literature, can be understood as a testimony of an obsessional subject on the structures that determine him or her, a standpoint of a subject failing to be interpolated by ideology.[120] We see in Shidyaq's text a refusal to serve any master or cause. However, it is a refusal that is experienced as an excessive libidinal pressure; it is as though the moral pressure to abstain from pleasure excites and is transmuted into a moral duty to enjoy: Fariyaq's 'gossip needs fresh butts to feed its endless discourse'.[121] Shidyaq oscillates between fantasies of feminisation, of being protruded and probed, and of sodomising others. His fantasies of sodomising the wives of his hosts and copulating with the women of the villages in which he resides are intertwined with constant slander in which the very act of writing is experienced as an ejaculation:

> The Fariyaq, however, was not elated at having to practice this craft, believing that any earnings that might reach him through a slit as narrow as that in the nib of a pen must themselves be straightened (Alack! Alack!). True, many a person has obtained a living expansive and *agreeable,* as well as good fortune unabated and *reliable*, from a wellspring that, though broad by comparison with the pen's nib, when measured against their greed and extravagance, was narrow (What a pity!). However, the Fariyaq was then a greenhorn, with neither practice nor experience, given to judging what is distant by what is close – and nothing is closer to the eye of the scribe than the nib of his pen and the paper before him, or closer to his heart than the words he is writing. A clever fellow is he who accepts the craft that he practices, to whom the shame of hard work is no burden, and who does not crane his neck to look out for things at which he does not excel (No the flesh! No to the flesh!)[122]

It is with irony, of course, that Shidyaq expresses his lack of cleverness, for it is precisely the problems of the flesh that irk his literary *oeuvre*: the sexual relation proves to be his utmost concern, for Woman – like language –

can never be satisfied, rendering him impotent and unable to terminate his acts. The book itself is dedicated to Woman and God, while Fariyaq is himself: neither man nor woman, but a eunuch and hermaphrodite at once, an un-manned man, a manly woman, a female saint, and a creature ridden with fantasies of sprouting horns.[123] Fariyaq is an Oneiromancer who interprets women's dreams, a master of Arabic who believes that 'learning grammar is easier than scratching your own balls',[124] and an impotent husband who cannot satisfy his wife's desire and fantasises of a surrogate husband to carry out the deed.[125] Fariyaq's love–hate relationship to woman as well as Arabic is ridden with sexual fantasies of sodomy, defecation, nightmares of horned monsters, and a pervasive sense of sorrow. In a lament against his women Fariyaq says:

> Honesty's a rarer thing in women then in the *male*, for men are always preoccupied, their situation *frail*. They're distracted from pleasure, for work and toil they *must*, and good sense and brains turn them from *lust*. Women have no worries but how to excite longing and stir dissension among *men*, with no regard for where or *when*. You'd reply, 'Not so. In fact women are more respectable and *modest*, less greedy and *dishonest*, more given by nature to *chastity,* further by inborn temper from *hypocrisy*'. If then, fate should ever reunite us and we talk at large of *loyalty*, of affection and *sincerity*, I'll give you arguments against which you cannot *prevail* and demonstrate how far superior is a man to any who wear the *veil* – those treacherous *treasonists,* those fibbing *fabulists*.[126]

Fariyaq proceeds to threaten Fariyaqa, his wife:

> And if you hold fast to denial and disdain, the cudgel will be there to make sure you're *whomped,* as will the hand, to slaps and punches ever *prompt*, and if you grab my forelock or the front of my *gown*, and broadcast my shame all over *town*, I'll hang you like a crucifix from a *nail*, or throttle you till you *wail*.[127]

This fantasy of submitting Woman to punishment, making her feel the burdens of the moral order, is directed against Woman as a figure who demands more than he can ever give: as though submitting woman to pain is the only way to yield their pleasure or *jouissance*. It is remarkable that Shidyaq's fantasies increase exponentially on the day (or night of his marriage); he claims that surely the aim of marriage, about which the 'Almighty Creator said: Multiply and fill the earth', can be nothing but suffering, 'for if the earth were to fill with people it would necessarily be ruined, not made prosperous'.[128] The symbolic functions of marriage, of being a good husband, a loving father, a notable scribe and a good citizen, are experienced by Fariyaq as persecuting forces: I don't love him/her, I hate him/her because s/he persecutes me. Delusions of persecution as we know from Freud are always experienced through a process of projective identification: internal perceptions are disavowed only to appear as threats from the outside.[129]

The impossible Woman, the object of hate that persecutes and whose desires cannot be met, generates in Fariyaq a prevalent sense of sorrow, or a depression:

> Sorrow is, in principle, beneficial. It prevents random and seductive hopes and desires from driving out insight and good sense. This calms the mind and prevents it from mooning about at the water holes of the *inconceivable*, and things settle down to a point at which the soul can wean itself from the *unachievable*.[130]

What is unachievable is the sexual rapport between Man and Woman. Sorrow is an emotional state that arises from the impotency Fariyaq experiences in relation to the feminine other – the symbolic sphere of marriage, family and language. Sorrow is his sole refuge and is experienced as an internal decomposition of organs:

> The clearest and most creative of thoughts are those that occur during one of three states: the first is the onset of sorrow, the second in bed just before falling asleep, and the third in the latrine. The last involves the breakdown of concentrated matters exhaled by the bowels and the intestines, and the breakdown and exhalation taking place in the lower part has the effect of breaking down, at the same time and place, whatever may have coagulated in the higher folds of the brain. Some of this matter then departs in a downward direction while some of the images formed by the brain rise, like steam rising from the earth to thicken a raincloud.[131]

The anger, sorrow and anxiety generated by the demands of the symbolic order (Fariyaq as husband, as scribe and Sheikh of Arabic, as an esteemed man of letters) are not clearly distinguished from moral states (devotion and valour). It is as though the confusion of mental states and moral virtues, when properly described in the world, allow Shidyaq to designate his true faith: psychic life can lead naturally into ethical life, but one that is only experienced as suffering.[132] The clear degraded state of *bourgeois* morality that afflicts Fariyaq can only be countered by retrieving some individualist ideal that is best experienced in the mechanics of bowel movement, a movement of decomposition, of voiding and verbiage and most importantly as a feminisation of himself. There is an internal decomposition that Fariyaq experiences: a decomposition of the *bourgeoisie* that is repressed for the maintaining of social conformity but returns incessantly in his writing – a return of the repressed.[133]

Fariyaq (and Fariyaqa) stand at the cusp of a great misfortune: the demise of an old social order, evidence of which in the book abounds (corrupt clergymen, illicit sexual affairs, ignorant emirs and corrupt nobility, greedy merchants, women with horns, men with horned turbans, desirous peasants and lustful monks); and the crisis of liberalism in the periphery of empire (how to locate the self in the entanglements of community, how to define formal concepts while preserving moral value). Shidyaq alludes to divine signs to justify his fated tribulation:

> I declare: The Fariyaq was born with the misfortune of having misfortune in the ascendant everywhere, the Scorpion raising its tale to strike at the Kid, or Billy Goat, and the Crab set on a collision course with the horn of the Ox. His parents were people of notability, nobility, and righteousness (Bravo!Bravo!) but while their prospects for the world to come were *expansive*, their prospects in the world in which they lived were not with these co-extensive, and their reputations were, of their *purse*, the *inverse* (Boo!Boo!).[134]

He proceeds to recount how his parents' generosity and commitment to village customs had rendered them so destitute that they could no longer send the Fariyaq to Kufa or Basra, the renowned contending schools of Arabic grammar. He thus had to attend a local *kuttab* in the village with a teacher who had read nothing but the psalms, a poorly-translated book into Arabic that 'consists of no more than word puzzles and riddles (Have at it! Have at it!)',[135] despite which children are taught to read it without understanding; in fact, they are 'forbidden to understand the meanings of the letters, s-t-u-p-i-d'[136] and 'it seems our masters, lords of the next world as of this, do not want their wretched subjects either to understand or open their eyes but instead try as hard as they can to leave them wandering in the labyrinths of ignorance and stupidity (Barf! Barf!)'.[137]

These masters then wilfully keep their subject ignorant, and also reduce language to scribal copying, conceived by Shidyaq as a means for instantiating the arbitrary rule of the letter. Scribal work has no regard for the author and works towards the legitimising of a nobility 'barely able to sign their noble name. (Aiee! Aiee!)'.[138] Shidyaq's refusal to limit his writing to the traditional scribal mode was precisely because he recognised the original impotence of the masters for whom the scribe works:

> The country's ruler employed scribes but only those whose writing was ugly to the eye and whose words were disgusting to good taste (Oy! Oy!), this being a kind of public declaration that good fortune is not dependent on good handwriting, that to administer the *law* does not call for language without *flaw* (abtholutely not!).[139]

The arbitrary rule of law in the Ottoman lands is one that drives Shidyaq's fictional *oeuvre*. Alain Grosrichard captures this relationship between law and literature in his reading of Montesquieu's *Persian Letters* and is relevant here in assessing Shidyaq's writing: 'Fiction has the last word: it is fiction which can spill out over the present historical conjuncture, which at this point is nothing more than the corruption of monarchical morals and the vacancy of power'.[140] *Leg Over Leg* abounds with tales of corrupt merchants, emirs and governors, and monks. 'There is no abjection worse than servitude',[141] Shidyaq declares, especially when masters wilfully wish for ignorant servants and spend their time outside of social intercourse with their subjects: 'The poor man's brain is not so much narrower or smaller than that of the emir that it cannot hold cogent opinions that may be lacking from that of the other, even if the latter's turban be larger and thicker'.[142]

Thick-turbaned Masters and Horned Women

The problem with masters, as conveyed in *Leg Over Leg*, is that they are domestic despots at odds with a society of free men. However, Fariyaq himself counts as one of these free men in so far as he speaks of the *discomforts* of a society of freedom. It is these very 'discomforts' that the domestic despots disavow and Fariyaq exhibits, for he occupies at once the position of a bastard child (seeking the maternal and paternal metaphors) and the virtuous saintly woman who immaculately conceives. In Book One of *Leg Over Leg*, Shidyaq compares himself as a writer to a pregnant woman impregnated by the 'fathomless sea' of Arabic, as a Saint would be impregnated by a divine force:

> Unlike a woman, my head was pregnant with it
>   For a year, and the whole year was a season of storms.
> But it took only three months to be born
>   And quickly it learned to crawl and grew into a delightful youth.[143]

Not only was the book conceived in this manner, a seed implanted by the infinite power of Language (or God), it is also a prodigal son that blossomed quickly into youth and skipped its childhood. However, the delivery of the child did not happen through the usual route; it is experienced rather as a defecation. Shidyaq often describes fantasies of Woman having a vagina with a straight link to the rectum, and who can thus defecate while enjoying anal intercourse.[144] Fantasies of women who are not wholly Woman, either missing a feminine attribute or having an excess of it, correspond to Fariyaq's claim: 'I used to wish God had created me a woman, or turned me into a woman'.[145] Shidyaq's fantasy of feminisation evident in the unmanning of Fariyaq, of him wanting to be a woman and being coupled with a feminine Fariyaqa who carries the same name, is also experienced in terms of voices and languages entering his body. The literary text he writes is inflicted by a delusion of grandeur: it is the result of a direct insemination by God composed in a 'night as dark as pitch, which is why it emerged so filled with animus and darkling allusion'.[146] The book itself, Shidyaq continues, incites its reader and nourishes them; it is like an eternal garden of paradise in which fruits are abundant (to feed one's children) and women of all shapes and sizes (described metaphorically as vaginas in particular) are ready for 'cunsummation'.¹⁴⁷ The ideal reader that Shidyaq calls forth is a new reader, one that cannot be limited to the nationalist and patriotic but one that releases Fariyaq's refusal to serve any master or any cause beyond owning a new language that can welcome all others. In comparing his book to others and in specific lexical or grammarian texts consumed by 'categorisations', Shidyaq claims that his book has:

> done the opposite: We save the inquirer the task of delimiting and defining. We have no blemishes you will find. Any like us in our art nor any co-worker. For this art is an orphan to find whose brother is impossible, and it is unique so be well-disposed toward it.¹⁴⁸

The book, then, is an orphan, a bastard child, a singular product with no clear paternal and maternal lineage, a stranger whose acceptance (by the reading world) relies on a certain sense of hospitality or reciprocal sociability that begins from avowing alterity and being open to the logic of the signifier which has precipitated into words. This reader, like Shidyaq himself, must be an insomniac, seeking self-mastery and egoism as a sense of own-ness and *not* egotistical self-interest.¹⁴⁹ It must be a reader who is open to receiving the logic of the signifier that structures the social link. In a chapter entitled 'Snow', Shidyaq compares his words to the falling of snow that 'gives birth to a clearing and brightening of the weather'.¹⁵⁰ Shidyaq proposes that the reader of his words 'if he finds himself getting chilly' must eat more of the snow to put 'his brain through warm up exercises',¹⁵¹ for Shidyaq only tells the 'truth'.¹⁵² The truth of what, however? Is it the truth that is on the side of the subject who speaks or on the side of the structure of signification by which he is determined? Perhaps it is the truth that lies in the gap that Shidyaq exposes between the statement of enunciation and the subject of enunciation.

Words precipitate onto the pages of books, but unlike snow that 'falls on what is black and makes it white... my words fall on paper and make it black'.¹⁵³ However, despite the difference in colour, in both cases the effect is ephemeral: 'the sun rises over the snow, it melts, and the same is true of my words, for almost nothing will remain of them in the reader's head after the passing of moonlight or the rising over him of one

Shining Orb'.[154] It is as though his words are experienced as a natural force; however, it is the logic of the signifier that afflicts the text. He claims that the titles of the book's chapters 'unambiguously' signify the content of each chapter 'as smoke does to fire'.[155] Not only are the chapter titles semiotic signs of what lies within them, but also language itself is experienced as an invasion into Shidyaq's own body, an impregnation inflicted by the signifier in a solitary and dark night. Shidyaq employs a 'semiotic' analogy only to move directly beyond it. Language for him acts like a toxin that inflicts him regardless of the concern for meaning. Shidyaq again brings to mind Schreber's *Memoirs* that speak of the 'crisis of symbolic power', and its transfer as 'experienced as sexuality, as the very matter of sexuality'.[156] This crisis of the symbolic is a crisis in the 'production of credible symbolic identities',[157] and the failure of repression for which Shidyaq's writing becomes a symptom.

The letter itself penetrates his body and the book is a result of imagining himself a woman undergoing copulation, the pain of labour, only to emerge with a testimony of the *jouissance* inflicted on her by the desire of the Other. The book is a progeny of Shidyaq's direct insemination by God. His offering himself to the desire of an Other had allowed for the written text to pass through him, like a message from God:

> I could not tell if my head gave birth to its feet first or blew it out of its
>   nose or
> Spat it out or dumped it in the latrine.
> I suffered over it in groans may the Lord protect
>   You, suffering such as cannot be measured haphazardly
> And cut its umbilical cord to suit only the people of discernment
>   To whose name alone it is dedicated
> It had no wet nurse other than
>   My thoughts, and even so I thought it too well suckled.[158]

The problem with the domestic despot, we know since Aristotle,[159] is that he exercises power as a form of paternal authority and rids himself of all involvement in the work of the slaves (his wife and children included). Despotic power is at odds with political power because the despot removes himself from the social sphere and releases himself only to a life of pure pleasure and enjoyment. Moreover, the problem with the domestic despot is that they disavow a certain childhood within, one that is perceived as endearingly unique – by Shidyaq – through the singular Arabic nouns (*qaqaq* which he employs formed from the conjunction of two consonants) that designate a child's excreta or waste. The social construction of paternity and of family is inhospitable to the infantile origin of society, one that is peculiar in its waste, the trash of sociality at its origin:

> Know, God set you to rights, that greater pleasure is to be found in your carrying your child on your back and wrapping his sweet legs around your neck than in increasing the length of your gown, widening your sleeves, and winding your turban or than having your servants standing by with their hands on their hearts. Know, God increase your understanding, that the reason Arabs gave names to the actions of small children was that they wanted you to notice those children and pay attention to them – to the degree that they coined for their excrement two strange words that have no like terms of structure in the entire language, namely *sasas* and *qaqaq*. Know, God grant you success, that the *mister,* the *monsieur*, the *Herr,* and the *signor* enjoy greater peace of mind and better material conditions than you.[160]

The problems of the social construction of the family, of the law, which seem to occupy Shidyaq's text, can be discerned first in his attempt to make sense of the paternal and maternal relation between children and adults, and then in marriage itself, read as a 'decapitation' of men: 'Master and slave[161] alike are by their love, *prostrated,* rich man and vagabond, in their need for them, *conflated.* They cast men into perilous *places*, confused situations and *constricted* spaces'.[162] Love and marriage take up a significant portion of *Leg Over Leg*, as upon marrying Fariyaq realises that in matrimony love dare not speak its name but as that which speaks through him is only the impossibility of the sexual relation. The trauma of the wedding night, in which Fariyaq must consummate his marriage – and must show the 'bloody proof of virginity' to the sounds of a crowd outside his door – registers as a main episode in the unravelling of the problem of desire : 'Open the door bolt-holder! . . . Enter the dome, enterer! . . . Widen the wound, lancer! . . . Swizzle the swizzle stick in the kohl-pot, swizzler! . . . Dive into the deep sea diver!'[163] While marriage and the family centred around the couple are seen as driven towards the purpose of reproduction, Shidyaq exposes that there is a register of desire, which invokes a cultural domain (still anchored around the maternal and paternal) that is not anchored in the natural function of sexual propriety. The economy of desire presented in Shidyaq's writing shows that despite the fantasy of an absolute unrestrained liberation of 'natural' desire (pages on end describing different copulation postures, endless lists of different names for partial objects of desire, bodily organs, the anus, the vulva, the pudendum and so forth), there is no such thing as a raw, pure and natural desire; but always a mediated desire, one that is mediated by the symbolic Other of language and the law.

Leg Over Leg reveals the problem of the modern divided subject of desire – desire with a specific focus on the fantasy of sodomy:

> the backside is one of those things that people have gone to great lengths to exalt, magnify and aggrandize both materially and immaterially . . . How, one must ask, can one and the same thing be used as a means for contentment and ire at once? It is a blatant contradiction.[164]

While Shiyaq's fantasy projections expose the limits of the law, Bustani, as we will see in the coming chapter, formulates a complex psycho-theological framework that grounds the law in an eternal debt to a merciful God who watchfully reaps the sacrifices of labouring bodies.

4

A Liberal Psycho-theology

By the late nineteenth century, the Ottoman Empire had begun to sow the seeds of its *tanzimat* reforms that were largely liberal in nature and had transformative implications for property rights, legislation and governance, as well as taxation and military conscription. The peasant uprisings of Mount Lebanon (1820s, 1830s, 1841, 1845 and 1860) occurred in the context of drastic land reforms and the encroachment of private property and industrial capital on the premodern tax-farming system, as well the institutionalisation of waged labour. This was concomitant with the rise of the Maronite Church as a landowning power, and the demise of the traditional power of Druze and Christian feudal overlords in light of the influx of European mercantile and industrial capital, the establishment of wage labour through trade and the silk industry, reformed Ottoman property and tax laws, Ottoman–Egyptian commercial rivalry and the rapid urbanisation of Beirut and Damascus.[1] It is from within this historical context that the liberal nation form, or *watan*, surfaced in Bustani's writings as a regulative ideal for a society in crisis. The conversion of the political violence into the paradigm of 'civil war' within one nation rendered a natural history of the nation in a way that made it appear as history's point of departure rather than as the result of a historical process.

Commenting on the 1860 events, Bustani wrote a series of eleven nationalist pamphlets, entitled *Nafir Surriya* (The Clarion of Syria) and signed anonymously *muhib lil watan* ('loving patriot'),[2] and in that same year a translation of Defoe's *Robinson Crusoe*.[3] Throughout these pamphlets, and using Crusoe's story as an allegory for civil society in a post-war temporality, Bustani formulated a form of liberal nationalism in defence of the 'true religion' (*diyana haqiqiya*), Protestant in spirit and corresponding with a political economic logic that ties it to the history of capitalism.[4]

This wedding of religion and political economy is most strikingly evident in the way the concepts of guilt and debt were used to separate out a universalistic conception of religion from sectarian political identities, according to which Bustani's conception of nationality rendered the moral guilt accumulated in the wake of sectarian conflict into a quantifiable debt that underpins a project of national revival through cooperative labour. The political theology that underlies Bustani's liberal logic, and which will be the focus of the analysis throughout this chapter, raises the question of the nature of the rule of law in relation to violence; in other words, it exposes the fine line between law-making violence and law-preserving violence. Furthermore, Bustani's worldview provides us with an understanding of the kinds of symbolic investiture that iterate the performative nature of rites of initiation into community in *fin-de-siècle* Beirut, ones that restrict the potentialities of politics from within a 'psycho-theological' framework.[5] Psycho-theology, formulated as an analytic tool by Eric Santner, points to the 'theological excess' that underpins modern life, one which informs everyday subjectivity. Reversing the Freudian reading of religion as a psychological state imposed on the outside world, Santner suggests that the question of cultural difference, what makes an Other a stranger, is experienced theologically, as an interjection of an alterity into the self, and is a process that is entirely irrational and excessive, and has the structure of a fantasy.

Bustani has received much attention in the historiography of *nahda* since Albert Hourani's *Arabic Thought in the Liberal Age*, and it has been well-established in scholarship that Bustani represents a liberal and reformist strain of *nahda* thought. Historian Usama Makidisi has argued that Bustani represents a prescient discourse of 'ecumenical humanism' through his call for religious tolerance and coexistence during the outbreak of sectarian violence.⁶ He reads Bustani's discourse at the time as one that is recalcitrant to the adoption of 'Eurocentric understandings of modernity' by arguing for the maintenance of 'religious co-existence' in the face of the 1860 events.⁷ Makdisi writes, 'Presciently, Bustani asserted that the mixture of religion and politics would lead to an inflexible political system that could not adapt to new realities, anticipating almost word for word modern-day criticisms of the sectarian political system that dominates Lebanon'.⁸ Refuting modernisation theories' claims regarding the primordialness of sectarianism, and presenting Bustani's liberalism as a visionary solution, Makdisi argues that sectarianism is indeed modern and can only be overcome by the proper separation of religion from politics, one that Bustani 'presciently' adopted early on.⁹ This reading remains to be merely descriptive; it prescribes his logic rather than analyses it, for it accepts the liberal antinomy of religion and politics as it is laid out in Bustani's writings and does not analyse it. I argue, however, that Bustani's 'secular' stance is based on a politico-theological worldview that in turn is premised on an idea of universal religion: it is a form of liberal nationalism that binds political economy with religion while propounding the separation of religion from politics.

Makdisi shows how Bustani formulated quandaries regarding memory-work precisely because he deemed the 1860 events a civil war within the boundaries of one nation.¹⁰ But what Makdisi misses is the problematic logic of 'civil war' – one that Bustani propounds – as a category of analysis itself, and of the return to 'national co-existence' and the rule of law as the solutions for violence. Makdisi represents sectarianism as an unfamiliar interruption of existing social relations, one born out of foreign European interferences and from within Ottoman liberal reforms (also read as external interferences in Mount Lebanon), both premised on an orientalist perception of Mount Lebanon as pre-modern. However, this does not explain the impulse to abstraction that characterises liberal 'anti-sectarianism' as exhibited in Bustani's writings – an impulse that cannot be analysed without attention to political economy, largely defined as the symbolic system of relations of exchange and production in society. Why sectarianism emerges hand in hand with a liberal universal conception of religion, and how they both become constitutive of the social bond itself within a national sphere, go unaddressed in existing scholarship.

Jeffrey Sacks, in a more recent reading of this work, recognises a relation between religion and the body politic; however, it is one that is premised on a structure of loss and mourning: 'the text [*Nafir*] remarks its relation to loss – it repeats the losses, by telling us that it has lost the capacity to represent them'.[11] Sacks offers a parallel reading to Makdisi, for he analyses Bustani's demand for the separation of religion and politics as one that 'enacts and obscures the linguistic, epistemic violence' of modernity.[12] While Makdisi praises Bustani's liberal humanism, Sacks suggests that his humanism was always-already an interrupted project that points to the impossibilities inherent in representation or in 'the finite event language is'.[13] Neither of these readings takes account of the ideological element implicit in Bustani's liberal secularism. Furthermore, a close reading of his works shows that the representation of loss incurred by civil war did indeed occur, but through a logic that converted the material losses into moral gains, one that placed the citizens of the nation in a position of eternal indebtedness to both the 'civilised world' (*al-'alam al-mutamaddin*),[14] and God.

Postlapsarian Nationality

In 1860 Bustani proclaimed the political violence, a 'black mark on the nation's history',[15] as a testament to sectarianism and 'partial interests'.[16] He called for a universal religious sentiment, a 'true religion',[17] to cure the ailment of partisan interests; however, the ailment and the cure in this case prove to be identical. True nationalism, like true religion, was essentially a guiltful relation: Bustani posited the idea of a perpetually-indebted national subject as the only penance for the 'barbaric' and 'uncivilised' political violence.[18] As such, his demand was for equality across religious groups – but not within them, in contrast to the peasant's demands in 1860 – under the claim of safeguarding public interest (*al-huqquq al-'umumiya*).[19] This demand for coexistence and national reconciliation accepts the logic of sectarian division as long as it is a relation between social groups *within* one nation. Consequently 'civil war' (*harb ahliya*)[20] was characterised as a natural catastrophe, an aberration to the normal order, and as a direct result of God's punishment:

> *Ya abna' al-wat an*, the vilest of all things in this world, is war, and the evilest and foulest of all wars is a civil war between citizens of one nation. This type of war usually results because of petty causes and lowly desires. Not only does it oppose the principle of justice and impose on the rights of the guardians of society, it also counters and refutes all the good, honest, and dignified rights and sensitivities of humankind, such as the rights of neighbourliness and national fraternity; and gratitude, familiarity, and unity that are directed to the neighbour, brothers in the nation, and anyone who deserves the rights of man and the rights of humanity.[21]

In the same manner by which a father strikes his son with one hand and embraces him with another to dispel vengeance and promote love, so has God almighty done to the nation.[22]

Entitling the eleven *Nafir Suurriya* pamphlets as *wataniyat* – nationalist pamphlets written in response to the unprecedented 'civil war' – Bustani addressed the citizens of the nation (*abna' al-wat an*), whom he depicted in the image of Cain, 'the murderer of his own brother, wandering and lost with no one in his pursuit'.[23] Presenting the 'civil war' as an act of fratricide, Bustani drew out a covenant of blood as the basis for the *watan* (nation) to come after sacrificial violence, for the war had rendered everyone to a state of homelessness, seeking God's kindness and mercy (*al-lutf w al-rahma*).[24] Unrequitable mercy was God's alone, and all other acts of charity were to be considered requitable debt, 'to be paid back from the account of the nation' (*min kis al-watan*).[25] Bustani warned his readers to beware of perceiving their post-war state as a repetition of the experience of the Israelites in Exodus: 'the blinded heart of the Israelites in Exodus is not an example to be followed but a lesson from which you must learn'.[26] In the pamphlets, he drew out a scene of conversion, from hatred (of each other) to love (of the nation and God) and from fratricide to sociality. These same *Nafir* pamphlets were reprinted in 1990 after the end of the Lebanese Civil War by another 'anonymous patriot' (*muhib lil watan*), who argued in the preface that Bustani's proposed diagnosis of society's ailments and its cure still holds true for post-1990 Lebanon.[27]

The anonymity of the signature, both of the author and of the editor of the reprints, attests to the recognition that the sole author for the discourse of nationalism is the abstract figure of the citizen who shares equal rights and duties with others. The anonymous signature of the text functions here as a 'performative utterance',[28] as a 'speech act', as J. L. Austin defined it; it is performative precisely because its meaning is not garnered from the author's intentionality but because it is posed as a constative utterance: the anonymous patriot calls forth at the beginning of every pamphlet the presence of a 'we', a body of citizens (*ya abna' al-watan*). But who is this we that is hailed forth? The foundational nature of the *Nafir* asserts a 'we' through a calling forth of a civil society forged in the name of the people. It beseeches in the anonymous signature the laws of nature (the need for self-preservation, the division of labour) and the name of God.[29] Civil society in its liberal rendering has to be normatively declared against society: 'it is a society against society, that is an association of dissociated and continuously dissociating egoisms, that is thus a paradoxical union of desocialization held together through competing property and profit interests'.[30] It is thus not surprising that citizens are depicted in these pamphlets as independent animals that require a division of labour for sustenance:

> *Ya abna' al-watan*, sons of the nation, the bountiful season of summer has now passed, and the little needs that you had during it shall now increase. You can no longer suffice by sleeping in the wilderness and using trees as your cover and bright stars as your guards ... the frugal season of winter is here, and it will present you with endless needs to survive its cold, snow, and blizzard.[31]

> *Ya abna' al-watan*, the ants have gathered harvests for the winter and built tight fortresses for protection from its dangers. The bees have as well done the same and prepared intricate dwellings abundant with nourishment ... while our fellow humans, the sons of Adam, can barely gather what is required for the fulfilment of their daily needs. They are homeless with no abodes to dwell in, and no garments to protect them from the harshness of cold weather ... A consideration of their future state is crucial as well as distressing![32]

Nationality in this specific sociohistorical context is depicted as a form of artifice that in a postlapsarian age requires religion, labour, industriousness and exchange to survive as a social contract. 'Civil war' exemplified a return to a state of nature that had to be amended by a return to the laws of nature and seeking refuge under the name of one God. The social contract, articulated in these Hobbesian terms, could only be sealed through the recognition of natural laws as the foundation provided by God as father. In other words, in the moment of founding the social contract, of calling forth the *abna' al-watan*, God is beseeched as the last instance: the creator of nature, and the external guardian of the act of foundation that the *Nafir* declares. Derrida's analysis of the function of God as a signifier in declarative acts that found institutions is important for understanding Bustani's formulation, for 'God comes, in effect, to guarantee the rectitude of popular intentions, the unity and goodness of the people. He founds natural law and thus the whole game which tends to present performative utterances as constative utterances'.[33]

In the *Nafir* pamphlets, God is invoked at every juncture as the events are folded into a praise of his abundant mercy and grace: the violence must breed forgiveness and compassion, and, most importantly, the violence binds its survivors into an eternal symbolic debt to God. In turn, the violence is given a mythical diagnosis: it is *al-gharad al-aʿmma* (the blind drive),[34] *al-marad al-khabith* (the malignant disease)[35] and *wisawas alqaah al-shay.tan* (a satanic haunting, an evil apparition).[36] Sectarianism, the assumed cause of the violence, is portrayed as a spectral apparition, and Satan's evil is presented as a necessary supplement to God's good.

Through the identification of sectarianism as the specific form of transgression of the laws of community, the nation emerges in Bustani's writings as a religious community of faith from within which those with partisan interests ought to be forever banned.[37] In other words, the incitement to transgression (sectarianism) is circumscribed in the very logic of the law (nation as a religious community of faith); it is constitutive of the function of sovereignty, not an exception to it; there is an element of excitation to the function of the law of community, not only repression. Moreover, the socio-symbolic order of community is directly constituted by 'the psychic agency that sustains our attachment to the norms of a community', that 'functions not so much as the level of belief as in the form of a pressure or urgency that can, in turn, incite transgression of and, thus, apparent distance to, those very norms'.[38] The pamphlets iterate the urgency of love for the nation lest violence erupts in its ebbing:

> We have frequently mentioned the nation in our pamphlets because it is the most resonant of words to the ear of a loving patriot, and one of the most beautiful *muwalada* words in Arabic. Surriya, otherwise known as *barr al-sham*, and Arabistan, is our nation, its expanse being its valleys, fields, coasts and mountains. The people of Surriya from different faiths, kinds, races, and divergences are the people of our nation. The nation is like a great chain connected by its many links: its beginning is our home or place of birth and whomever it includes; its end is our country with all those in it. Its centre of gravity is our heart and the centre of our heart's gravity is it.[39]

Drawing out the socio-symbolic community of this nation, Bustani described its force of traction, 'it reaches out and grasps and encircles its sons with great force and gravitational pull, forcing them towards it when they are estranged from it'.[40] The symbolic order of the nation – posited contra sectarianism – both binds the subject into solidarity with the family/community/institution in a direct covenant with God, and opens the real possibility for his or her own transgression of these bonds. 'We call for living watchful religions . . . that lovingly and considerately perceive of sects as members of one family, their father the nation, mother the land, and sole creator God'.[41] This form of religious faith in the nation posits sectarianism as a transgression through its very prohibition. In other words, the nation is understood not only in terms of territorial sovereignty but also in terms of a forging of a social contract, a body politic, that must relinquish its right to kill for self-preservation to the law.

Comparing the war-ridden society with the Israelites in exile, Bustani warned the citizens of the nation of the threats lying in wait.[42] Yet the only revelation to come out of this Exodus was the acceptance of guilt as the sole horizon for the citizen subject. It is only God with whom the citizen, represented by the figure of Cain, can have an immediate relationship, yet not even God can offer atonement for the guilt, for he can only predestine it. Atonement is only to be garnered in the daily pursuit of bread and from the expenditure of flesh and bone: Bustani repeated again and again, 'you must only accept to live from your own toil and sweat'[43], 'unemployment and indolence are the worst of vices'.[44]

While urging his fellow citizens to return to labour in the aftermath of war, Bustani contended that the urgency of production did not simply come about from the 'measure of time in terms of gold',[45] or wealth, but from the measure of life itself in terms of time: 'Life is worth time itself'.[46] Bustani's writings draw out a post-war temporality in which the weight of flesh and bone becomes the subject of a political economy that is to be measured in abstract time. His call for 'love of the nation as an act of faith' urges citizens to act *as if* the nation already exists, *as if* the economy exists as a self-contained sphere, in order for society to progress in time. Every now moment in the temporality he drew out owes itself to another now, thus the now is constantly passing over into the past and every now is frozen in an act of reproduction of a schema of debt. This perception of the economy as an objective sphere of kin relations allows for the separation of the political from it, for politics appears as a corrupting force, an aberration to the natural equilibrium of liberal economy.

Moreover, the time that had been 'wasted' in 'civil war' was to be incurred as debt in the national ledger of gains and losses, *khasa'ir wa arbah al-watan*, which were calculated in the pamphlets under two headings: the 'moral losses of the nation' and the 'material losses of the nation'.[47] The losses were calculated in direct monetary costs and as moral losses (*khasa'ir maddiya w adabiya*). Despite all these losses, however, Bustani urged the nation to emerge from sacrifice for it had received a 'blow from the hand of God',[48] one that was comparable to a 'father striking his son'.[49] The lesson of the violence, or what Bustani deemed to be the gain from it, was a sacrifice made to God, one that has opened a path of linear sequential time along which the nation must progress following the call of a 'true religion'.

Bustani's political theology relegated political violence into the past and affirmed the historicity of both God and religion: 'It is not in our benefit to look back at the past, rather we must focus our attention and energies on the future for the purpose of alleviating the bad effects and unwanted results of the atrocities'.[50] This political theology reaffirmed an understanding of history as a plot or an unfolding narrative; in order to allow time to move on, citizens had to maintain a faith in a conception of community as that which comes after sacrificial violence.

Given that the citizens of the nation had been sacrificed through the political violence, they could now emerge as innocent victims who had been spared the wrath of God. The result of this survival can only be to profess love for the neighbour – 'be protective fortresses for each other rather than enemies'[51] – for God and the nation, and forever repress hate. In a true expression of the spirit of Protestant ethics,[52] Bustani urged his fellow citizens to love the nation and love each other, lest they hate God in light of all the cruelties that had appeared in society. Ultimately, his depiction of the political violence draws out an image of concluded struggle, the aftermath of which is a secular temporality (the birth of the nation) during which citizens could recognise the moral transformation that had already been put into place.[53]

Diyana and *Dayn*: True Religion and Debt

Not coincidentally, the words *diyana* (religion), and *dayn* (debt), both echo the meanings of indebtedness, duty and obligation.[54] Bustani's proposition of a universal conception of religion as the sole ground for shared communal living was tightly wedded to a projected eternity of reproduction of guilt and debt: 'If these events have incurred further animosities and hatred in your heart, then be certain that God will add spiritual atrophy to temporal atrophy'.[55] If people choose to ask for atonement from God, he argued, then their losses would be lessened and spiritual blessings imparted to them. Regardless of this spiritual atonement, however, the temporal catastrophe would remain irredeemable.

Consequently, the political violence could only be redeemed through the constant reaffirmation of symbolic debt. By relegating all private losses – the loss of lives, property and security – to a ledger of social and collective guilt, Bustani's discourse universalised guilt. This consciousness of guilt characterises capitalist modernity, for it reaches to the collective cult not for atonement but only for the universalisation of guilt itself.[56]

In this light, it is important to look closely at Bustani's gesture of positing religion (*din*) versus sect (*ta'ifa*) in the *Nafir*. The path to national reconciliation has to go through the affirmation of 'religions that are living, vigilant, and educating their followers in tolerance'.[57] These different religions are portrayed as 'members of one family, its father the nation, its mother the land, and its creator God'.[58] Religious tolerance is thus based on understanding all religions as 'sectarian' variants of one monotheistic faith and on a humanistic conception of one spiritual essence of man.

Invoking a saying pertaining to Luqman al-Hakim Bustani described the human as a being defined by its essential organs, the tongue and the heart (*inaa al-insaan bi asgharayh*).[59] Religion (the heart) and politics (the tongue) must remain separate. If all humans are God's creations, their father the nation, and their mother the earth, then the reasons for their competition and rivalry should be 'science, piety, reason, virtue, and respect for the neighbour, as well as the rights of man, and not lineage or belonging to one partisan group or another'.[60] In order to neutralise religious difference for political concord, religion is relegated to a specific form of faith, one of the secondary traits of man – the superficial skin that, once shed, reveals the essence of humankind, that being God-given mind and spirit:

> As long as our people cannot understand that religion is a relation between the creator and his slaves, while *civitas*, *al-madaniyat*, is between the individual and his fellow countryman, or between the individual and his government; and as long as they don't realise that it is only on the basis of *civitas* that the social body and political forms are erected; and as long as they don't separate these two principles, religion and politics, in matters of behaviour and belief, they shall never succeed in either of them if not in both of them altogether.[61]

The equivalence that is established here between the relationship between citizen and their government, and citizen and citizen, respectively, reveals a strong shift in discourse in relation to sovereignty. Sovereignty, previously reserved for the body of the king, the Ottoman Porte and its representatives, has now been placed in the hand of the citizens, in their smallest body parts, the heart and the tongue. We can see here an utterly modernist shift, from the political theology of Ottoman sovereignty to the biopolitical pressures or psycho-theology of popular sovereignty, from the body of the king to the other body of the king, the body of citizens.

With this discourse, the logic of politics becomes elevated above confessional affiliations and practices yet remains to be sustained by theological values and concepts. Labouring flesh and bone, the subject matter of political economy, do not enter this form of reconciliatory worldview, and individual flesh and bone must be consistently sacrificed for the social good, *al-salih al-'umumiy*. The main condition for reconciliation is 'a system of contractual laws and just reforms' that would recognise subjects as equal citizens with equal 'civil, religious, and moral rights'.[62] For 'the citizens have duties towards their nation as the nation has duties towards its citizens'.[63] Rehearsing the classical liberal abstraction of individual rights, we can see Bustani reaffirms the practical abstractions of commercial society.

Furthermore, 'true religion' is intrinsically linked to the decree that 'all private losses are indeed public ones'.[64] In the *Nafir* pamphlets, the 'material losses' of property, labour and time that had been incurred through violence are calculated as losses of the nation, as public losses. *Diyana* and *dayn* (religion and debt), once read through Bustani's rendering of a guilt history in the *Nafir*, reveal that the positing of ecumenical religions versus sectarianism is far from being the solution to political violence, as some historians have argued.[65] For it is the very category of universal religion (*diyana*) that is employed by Bustani to promote a liberal understanding of subjectivity, one that is based on valuing socially productive labour as a means to pay off the symbolic debt incurred by the lapse into violence and 'barbarism'.[66]

Bustani's calculation of society's 'moral and material losses and gains' (*al-khasa'ir al-madiyya w-al adabiyya*) necessitated an understanding of religion as universal, for 'God cannot be abandoned because of the calamity of war'.[67] Rather, the events are themselves effects of God's direct intervention, of his will,[68] and they are a lesson taught by a merciful God.[69] This universal conception of religion was constructed through a guilt-and-debt nexus, or a guilt history from which the sons of the nation can never escape. Bustani's conception of a 'true religion' as an end in itself, versus 'false religion' as a means to end, is intrinsically linked to his argument for the 'love of nation as an act of faith', a phrase that is said to have been in the *hadith* – no doubt adding to the symbolic value of nationalist sentiment in this historical moment.

The Liberal Fantasy of a Puritan Nation

The argument for universal religion was coincidental with the call for the division of labour as the only natural means for the satisfaction of needs in society. This position was elaborated on in the translation of the story of Robinson Crusoe, which was proposed as a motto of instruction for the nation.[70] Bustani claimed that he translated *Robinson Crusoe* 'within a span of five months of hard work' because the story was of 'utmost importance for society'.[71] The story of Robinson Crusoe, the man who was of no good to anyone but himself and thus had to be punished with a solitary, guilt-ridden existence, the lone body on an island emaciated by endless labour, has been analysed as the story of liberal political economy.[72] Crusoe speaks to the images of solitary figures that Bustani had painted into the natural landscape of the nation; like Bustani's nation, Crusoe was born anew only after his shipwreck on an island. The link between Crusoe and Bustani's larger political project is further affirmed by his use of the same Arabic stanza in the introductions to both the Crusoe and the *Nafi ir* pamphlets: 'he who is of no use to another has a useless existence altogether'.[73]

Bustani's appeal to piety, to 'the love of the nation as an act of faith',[74] and his call to return to labour and employment, can be read as attempts to renew the social foundations of a liberal polity, instilled by the Ottoman *tanzimat* reforms in an age when political power was less bound to property qualifications.[75] In the direct aftermath of 1860, Bustani called for the necessity of labour for society; a labour that had to be expended to pay off symbolic debt and beyond which individual and moral worth were deemed valueless. In pamphlet after pamphlet, the nation is warned of leaving both land and human labour power to waste, for this waste or excess itself would translate into material debt. Even the national ledger that Bustani drew up of national losses calculated 'wasted labour time' next to 'uncultivated land'.[76] Not coincidentally, this argument was concomitant with the establishment of money as the universal regulator of all values in the empire.[77] In a revealing moment in the text, Bustani calculated the monetary equivalent of potential labourers killed in the violence: '600 million Francs at the least'.

Crusoe's lesson was that shipwreck is the fate of any attempt to break the social contract normatively assumed by liberal thought. His shipwreck on an island that led him to live a brutish isolated life sets the stage for a conversion into both Christianity and civil society. *Robinson Crusoe* is, in fact, the story of the 'anticipation of civil society';[78] it depicts the social state of humans as being based on relations of exchange as the ideal of social relations. Crusoe's story naturalises the transformation of uncultivated resources into private property through the expenditure of labour: i.e. the island presents him with a state of existence for which he has tools in another *time*, in the time of civilisation or industrial society. The state of nature for both Crusoe's and Bustani's war-ridden societies is the source of the laws of nature, on which the social contract is based. In his introduction to the translation of Defoe's novel, Bustani writes:

> Read the story of *Robinson Crusoe* and you will see how much he suffered to find sustenance on the island on which he was destined to isolation. Then it will become clear to you that the individual necessarily needs others to aid him in fulfilling his needs and that this necessity is what made human society in the first place. One person cannot simultaneously be farmer, weaver, tailor, builder, carpenter, student, teacher, king, sheikh, and priest at the same time.[79]

This national imaginary posited the violence as a rupture from a pre-existing uniform and linear history of an imaginary nation, a natural history of the nation, defined primarily in terms of socially-determined individual production. By calling unto the 'sons of the nation' to return to labour and production and to learn from the 'true story of Crusoe',[80] Bustani made it seem as though the labouring individual born out of the ruptures of the tax-farming system was in fact an ideal that was to be projected onto the past. Like the Robinsonade tales of the Enlightenment, the individual subject to whom Bustani addressed his pamphlets is made to seem the point of departure of history rather than the conclusion of specific historical forces. Bustani warned his readers that if society did not go back to socially necessitated production – which is presumed to have always been in existence before the breakdown of the feudal system – to the abstract and normative ethics of labour, it would collapse. The story of Crusoe, the man who was of no good to anyone but himself, speaks to the isolated individual who is of no utility, of no contract of exchange with others. He is a figure who is not only outside the nation, but also outside the definition of humanity that Bustani adopted. Crusoe is a lesson to be learned from, a modern Cain, with no one in his pursuit, left to recognise the laws of God and nature in seclusion.

This argument cannot but remind us of Adam Smith's description of isolated man in comparison to productive individuals in civil society. Bustani, like Smith, posits the division of labour and socially necessitated labour time as the natural conditions of social existence for individuals. The story of Crusoe allowed Bustani to formulate an abstract, yet concrete, conception of time, one that is equivocated with the flesh and bone of the labour force: 'While for the European, time is worth gold, for us now time is worth life itself'.[81] Political violence had somehow reset the historical time of society back to a state of nature in which time is worth life itself. It is not only in such a state of nature that a pound of flesh is offered as payment of debt, but also within the temporality of the nation in which labour and toil provide the sole means of paying the debt. When Crusoe first arrived at the island it was as though he had arrived anew into the world as a whole, guilt-ridden, fearful of the punishment that he would face. This guilt, very much like the guilt called forth in the *Nafir* series, made Crusoe work to establish his own puritan monarchy, his own puritan nation on the island. Defoe's *Crusoe* provides the national subject with an image of man destined to create his own social bonds in liberal forms. In the novel, Crusoe's isolation gradually makes him resort to the same ways of civilisation: he takes for himself a private property on the island, farms a plot of land, makes straw baskets, takes on a slave he names Friday and teaches him language. On the island alone he creates for himself a labour schedule about which he writes in his diary until his 'ink runs out'.[82] By the time Crusoe left the island, it would be ready to be turned into a productive colony.

The national subject post-1860 was in a similar state to that of Crusoe: banished outside society, 'wretched and alone'; and like Crusoe it ought to think only of production and labour. Translating *Robinson Crusoe* and presenting it as a 'true story', Bustani made a necessary connection between a natural condition of mankind and a social one; in both Crusoe and the *Nafir*, the state of nature is the ground from which civil society would emerge. This epistemological move (of naturalising liberal political economy) inscribes the natural history of the nation: i.e. the opposition created between a state of nature and state of society constructs a natural state to which a specific form of society owes its existence.

The positive outcomes of the political violence that were deemed in the *Nafir* to be the 'gains of the nation', are that they had induced the people of society to convert into citizens of a nation. As in any other act of conversion, the key to its immanence is its irreversibility and its reliance on the omnipotence of God. Bustani establishes an analogy between the convert who places all aspirations in God and the citizen who places all aspirations in the nation.[83] If, after the violence, they accept the nation as their only refuge, it in turn promises them the avowal of guilt for what has 'happened' as well as escaping punishment for crimes that they did not commit.[84] The nation, born out of the pangs of 'civil war', comes to embody the fantasy of reconciliation and liberal subjectivity.

The nation in this sense functions as a regulative entity that will always come in a future time as a solution for the contradictions in the present. It is this nation that beseeches a distinct universal religious sentiment through invoking moral guilt as the binding force for national subjects. Guilt becomes the reason for lack of society: the source of its torments that binds the subject in a guilt history, in relations of debt that in turn structure social relations; every individual action is linked directly to God, who is vigilantly watching over the national subjects. Every stance and action were assigned a rating in the salvation economy drawn out by Bustani; his logic, however, does not offer atonement, but only functions by accruing guilt.

Sentiments of Exchange: Reciprocity and Guilt History

In the wake of 1860 there was an urgent need to 'return to labour, exchange, trade, and commerce' and 'to return to a state of harmony and fraternity'[85] that had been shattered by the political violence. A call upon nationality (*wataniya*) as a sentiment of reciprocity – as love (*mahaba*), fraternity (*'ukhuwwa*), neighbourliness (*al-jira*) and familiarity (*'ulfa*) – was a call for recognising certain forms of exchange as sentiments as against others that weren't.[86] These sentiment exchanges were to be based on an obligation to reciprocate and indebtedness to both the internal Other in the nation and its external one (those who had survived the violence and those who had sent humanitarian aid from the 'civilised world').

The calamity of 1860, according to Bustani, was that it was a 'temporal catastrophe' (*kharab zamaniy*),[87] which had caused society to lose time, in comparison to progressive productive time, and had placed it in a position of indebtedness to human civilisation as a whole.[91] This view of time is characteristic of the modern view of history as a progressive sequence of time, one that moves from past, present, to future. Guilt history is this fateful movement of time, the generative process by which guilt is incurred and which blocks history proper; it categorically excludes the possibility of leaving the chain of events.[92] If the political violence was deemed a source of guilt from which there would be no atonement except by labour and dutiful existence, then every individual activity in society had to be undertaken with regard to an economic index of productivity: both sensuous and intellectual activity had to be essentially productive, working to pay off the debt incurred by 'civil war'.

The people of the nation in the analogies drawn in the *Nafir* are like Cain and the Israelites: in perpetual exile with literally no one to help them, in a twist of faith they had been left to their own will. Even God, whom Bustani deemed to have predestined 1860 by a strike of his hand, is not absolved of the guilt: the only answer is to embrace the guilt, to remain chained to the debt through acts of faith, and it is in fact only the state of debt that will enrich the people of the nation.[88] Bustani equated the 'gains of the nation' that had been procured from these events with 'moral gains'.[89] The civil war had rendered society unproductive and thereby in a state of crisis that could only be amended through a return to production, to labour, to moral uprightness and to duty; thus the public debt, debt to the 'civilised world',[90] is translated into moral gain. Characteristic of the 'metamorphosis from secular economic credit into the sacramental credo',[91] this logic equates blasphemy with not remaining faithful to the public debt, the debt of the nation. The theogony of value to be incurred from debt is similar to God, who creates guilty images of him in the world: paying off God, paying off the creditors of the nation, does not seal the debt but rather transforms it into gain. That is the structure of this national fantasy: the citizen must sacrifice himself for the love of the nation and in turn the nation will sacrifice them for more credit. Bustani's rendering of the guilt into the moral domain is an attempt at averting the logic of material debt by dividing the gains and losses into both material and moral ones: the king could easily redeem the material losses, although in the form of a debt that the citizens of the nation must pay back, while the moral losses would be projected as eternal debt to God.[92] The material losses were calculated by adding up the estimated values of the number of houses and farms and the harvest burned, in addition to the number of unemployed workers and the labour force (both potential and actual) killed in the violence. Meanwhile the moral losses – broken families, loss of dignity, honesty, well-being, solidarity, communal bonds and fraternity – are losses that 'only God has the restitution for, and not the King'.[93]

Although morality is often seen as unrelated to exchange values, Nietzsche, Marx and Weber – each differently – show us that in fact it is related to the economic structure. Guilt emerges from debt: it also emerges in relations of reciprocity. Advocating the first-ever American and European humanitarian aid to Mount Lebanon in 1860, Bustani calculated the national debt as twice the value of the aid at least: 'blessed be the one who gives more than one who takes'.[94] The one who gives is, thus, less guilty than the one who takes; however, the relation of debt can only emerge out of this form of reciprocity in which a bystander is saved from the guilt of being a beneficiary by anguishing over the victims.

Thus, Bustani saw the rule of law and a reformed state as the sole refuge from human atrocity and argued that the only way to make sense of the violence was for the nation to accept its guilt: society had been placed on a path of predestination that bound it to guilt and obligation. In this sense, the violence of 1860 was read as the nation's formative original sin. Social relations, based on utility and exchange value, were tightly wedded to a religious ethos: because true religion is devoid of utilitarian interest (*al-diyana al-haqaqiyya al-khaliya min al-gharad*),[95] and it is antithetical to 'sectarian belonging' (*al-'intima' ila .ta'ifa aw ila fi'a*). Bustani's ledger of the nation's gains and losses, and his call for a return to relations of labour, were an essential component of this theological worldview. Ultimately, the nation was born into debt, symptomatic of the onset of a cash economy and fiscal integration into the European banking and finance system, as well as the first recorded humanitarian aid bestowed on Syria and Mount Lebanon by both the Ottomans and Europeans. The nation was in debt *ex nihilo*.[96] What irked Bustani was, however, the moral debt, the guilt and shame caused by the political violence: 'while the nation may be relieved in the future from the material debts incurred on it by the calamities, it will forever be indebted morally to the nations of the world'.[97] This focus on morality in Bustani's works is born out of the growing distance between politics and economy in late nineteenth-century liberal thought, whereby morality takes precedence over politics.[98]

Thereby the perception of nationalism as an 'act of faith', as a relation that one accepts *as if* the nation were already there, required a leap of faith. Thus, nationalism in this context was not essentially normative: it is not there because the nation already exists, but precisely because it doesn't. The citizen's relationship with the nation has to be sacrificial and based on faith: 'belonging to the nation is an obligation in this world and a promise in another'.[99] In other words, nationalism emerged as a sentiment that lives in borrowed time. This borrowed time, or the time of nationalism, becomes the only liveable time. The gap between political struggle and economic struggle is irreducible to either position, as the *Nafir* pamphlets reveal, and it is from this gap that Bustani constructed a discourse on guilt and morality: the guilt cannot be atoned for and morality is the only response to the violence of politics and the blindness of economy. In recognition of the perpetual life of this economy of guilt, Bustani exclaimed, 'the future can only be dark and foreboding'.[100]

Although the nation emerges as an ideal form in comparison with existing material conditions, as it does in our case here, its materiality is consolidated in its articulation in concrete relations of exchange as well as of production. As a sentiment of exchange, a guiltful nationalism introduces a measure into the community, by which every individual assumes a position in the world of relations of exchange in the social world.

However, this is only a zero-sum equation from the perspective of the nation form, and debt is not the only remaining surplus of capitalist modernity: sectarianism itself projects out of the unidirectional stream of history as a perpetually unresolved antagonism.

In Bustani's words, sectarianism forever remains as both a 'satanic haunting' and a result of God's direct intervention into history, a lesson to be learned from; while it is God's mercy alone that has saved the innocent citizens of the nation, and to which they are all eternally indebted: 'we lament our age for these flaws, while we are the source of them; indeed, we are this age's sole flaw'.[101] The most valuable 'moral gain' of the nation is 'repentance to God',[102] for 'salvation will only be possible if you refrain from sacrificing the goods of the spirit on the altars of bodily goods'.[103]

In the spectral presence of sectarianism's Other, a nation forged under the tenets of universal religion, society is to be organised around relations of exchange that perpetuate sentiments of guilt. Bustani's political theology, however, leaves little room for questions pertaining to immediate justice. Indeed, his political theology rereads the historical rupture in terms of a periodic crisis: one that can be overcome *with* time and not *in* time. The past will always be unjust – recall all the images in the *Nafir*: Cain and Abel, the Exodus, the Fall – and the possibility of exterminating the neighbour and the brother is always around the corner.

Necromancy and the Logic of Sacrifice

The discourse of rights formulated via the diagnosis of the violence as a fratricidal civil war lends itself to a repetition compulsion: the nation always arises victorious from violent crisis, from the sacrifice of the innocent who in turn are essential for the structural renewal of the nation as a historical form. Indeed, the nation portrayed in the *Nafir* is characterised by necromancy: an indebtedness to the dead in this world and the promise of the dead in the other – 'beyond the grave', as Bustani had put it. It can in fact be argued that the 1860 events institute a historical structure of repetition in a manner similar to Louis Napoleon's coup of 1799. In both instances there was a social struggle led primarily by a peasant class against an absolutist monarchy, and in both instances we have the emergence of the nation form as the proposed cure.[104] The nation is posited as the antidote to the violent events and all that remains in memory from the social struggle is the extreme violence of the events. However, historical repetition is never a repetition of similar events, but of historical forms and structures that return in the present. What is this return of the repressed if not the return of the banished monarch under the guise of a representative state?

The *Nafir* pamphlets present us with a formulation of the social contract as being based on:

> the exchange of rights and duties, the drafting of just and liberal laws that would respect the multiplicity of religious faiths, the appointment of decision-making 'sovereigns' (*hukaam*), as representatives of the people (*ahali*), and an adherence to the universal rights of man.[105]

In a comparable manner to the coup of Bonaparte, the 1860 events were watersheds for the eradication (and simultaneous repetition) of absolutist monarchy and its replacement by the logic of the modern nation-state. What emerges as an essential element of the latter is of course the crisis of representation: how should a divided society be represented? How to fill the stark gap or hole left by the receding body of the king, or Sultan in our case? If the events of Mount Lebanon, as other similar events in the Balkans, Greece and other sites of the empire, signalled the pangs of Ottoman integration into capitalism, then Bustani's *Nafir* urged the coming of the new in the guise of the old: the social contract to replace absolute sovereignty.

Bustani's response to the breakdown of the social order began by disavowing the political violence as a peasant struggle, and reading it in familial fraternal terms. Thus, political enmity in its fratricidal form must be countered by a love for the enemy on the one hand,[106] and by faith in the nation on the other.[107] The underlying premise of the *Nafir* is a call for the national community to convene on holy ground because the death of 'the innocent' (*al-abriya'*) is the scapegoat that is necessary for mutual agreement and collective sentiment (*'ulfa*) to be re-established. This national sentiment replaces the body of the Sultan with a community held accountable to codified law (*ahkamsarima*), firm laws (*shari 'a mutafiqa*) and consistent laws (*tandhimat 'adila ghayr mumtazija bil shara' i*')[108] – just reforms that are clearly separate from religious credo, as well as being responsible directly to God's mercy and grace (*shafaqa wa rahma*).[109]

The Arabic word *nafir* is used to designate the last two days of pilgrimage, specifically the days that follow the sacrifice (*al-nahr*).[110] It is certainly not a coincidence that Bustani chose this word as the title for his eleven public addresses. Some scholars have suggested the English word 'clarion' as a translation of *nafir*: a call to alarm, a golden horn, a trumpet declaring the urgent and holy need for congregation.[111] But if we trace the Arabic etymology of the word, we cannot ignore its specific post-sacrificial connotations. If the political violence of 1860 is to be read as a founding sacrifice for a national community – in the form of fratricide, as Bustani tells us – then his *Nafir* beckons a holy congregation, and it seeks to seal the covenant of blood with which Girard has called the 'mimetic desire underlying the scapegoating mechanism at the origin of all violence'.[112] It would of course be easy to analyse Bustani's gesture in terms of this Girardian schema: in which his *Nafir* speaks for the desire to identify with the innocent, with Abel but not Cain, with the Israelites but not with exile. In these Girardian terms, Bustani's discourse accepts a certain benefit from victimhood, a renewed faith in the nation, as long as the violence is not repeated right away. Describing the events as 'a strike from the hand of God', Bustani left open the possibility of the recurrence of violence at any time. Indeed, it can be argued that this sacrificial logic extends and intensifies the enmity, for it doesn't distinguish between being sacrificed and being used.[113] What I mean by this is, the violence was not originally senseless but only became sensible for the national imaginary by being read as a form of sacrificial violence.

Girard explains the origins of cultural and religious systems through the mechanism of sacrificial victimhood. This mechanism is driven by a mimetic impulse: 'there is nothing, next to nothing, in human behaviour that is not learned, and all learning is based on imitation'.[114] Girard's Aristotelian schema, which Bustani captures, proposes that mimesis and rivalry are the constituting basis of all sociality: 'because the victim is sacred, it is criminal to kill him – but the victim is sacred only because he is to be killed'.[115] The group can only be erected by the passage from mimetic disorder, rivalry and desire, to a sacrificial order. However, Bustani's call to the citizens to turn to nature (to mimic industrious ants and bees) for a reaffirmation of social bonds keeps open the prospect of the return of violence at any moment. Although the sacrificial logic of national sentiment aims at suppressing intercommunal rivalry and vengeance, it in fact eternalises the conditions of enmity. In other words, reading the violence as a sacrifice of the innocent does not wash away the foundational guilt because a relation is ultimately established between sacrifice and God's mercy, and the mercy of God remains forever an unrequitable debt: 'If you obey me and guard my commandments, the Lord says, you shall have the bounties of the land, and if you do not obey me, you shall be punished by the sword'.[116]

Bringing religious law into his address, Bustani linked the saving of his fellow countryman to God's law, and how in order to be saved they must have knowledge of what is to be believed, of what is to be desired and of what is to be done. The explication very much follows in line with the classical understanding of the fourfold nature of the law as laid down by Aquinas. Bustani acknowledged two impediments to knowledge of what is to be believed: the Devil had sown in man the disobedience to reason – 'desire has overcome reason'[117] – and the devil had interfered through inciting 'blind partisan interests' (*al-gharad al-a'ma*): 'No doubt the site of the calamity is frightening and distressing; what are its reasons, who are the ones who aided the Devil in causing so much moral and natural tragedy?'[118] The withdrawal into sin is, thus, a withdrawal into barbarism and savagery, a withdrawal that can only be cured by true religion and civilisation.[119] A homeostatic political economy of the passions was required to counter this evil and structured along these lines: in order to motivate the return to God's grace, Bustani employed the element of fear; the citizens of the nation must fear not only what has happened but also its possible recurrence by the will of God. As the pamphlets unfolded, the trope of love was introduced to counter that of fear alone, and divine love was equated with the commandment to love thy enemy read through the love of the nation as an act of faith. The nation was consequently understood both as a social contract of duties and rights, and as a nation of faith in God:

> We warn you with regard to an important matter: man has no real nation in this world, the only true nation is to be found beyond the grave ... The reasons for dying are many but death is one; we can only prepare for that day to come and that nation.[120]

In conclusion, it is clear that the national community embodies a vexing demand for identification, one that faces the subject directly with immanent death. And despite its retroactive projection of a sacrificial origin, and its binding of the citizen subject into debt in this world and the other (to the creditor, philanthropist, kings of the world and humanity at large), the nation appears to only be attainable in God and outside 'us'. On the other hand, the excessive flesh that the citizen has to carry, whatever is accrued over the heart and the tongue, must be managed through sentiments of exchange, through morality and symbolic debt. What waits to emerge from the endgames of this political theology of the hereafter, of this guilt-history, is a politics of the now.

Conclusion: The Abstractions of *Homo Economicus*: Now a Stomach, Now an Anus

All life long the same questions, the same answers!
— Samuel Beckett, *Endgame*

Hamlet is in our bowels.
— Henry Miller, *Hamlet Letters*

The modern impasse hails for the Arabic reading subject a crisis in symbolic identification: there is a retreat of the discourse of the master, a crisis in the symbolic and the relationship between language and law comes to fore. The nineteenth century in particular is marked by the emergence of a neurotic subject (Bustani) obsessed with questions of origins (original sin, origins of language, origins of society and habit, origins of culture) and a hysteric subject (Shidyaq) that asks: what do you want of me? The problem of origins does not cease to repeat itself in the corpus of texts from the time, it takes the shape of a compulsive reposing of the questions of beginnings and ends: where does taste come from (inclination, disposition, acquired)? What is the origin of sociality? How does habit originate? What is the origin of language? How to write a history of culture? When and how does culture originate? How does one become a woman? Bustani's encyclopaedic and lexicographic texts were largely an attempt to answer this problem of origins. He begins his treatise on culture, *Khutba fi adab al-'arab* (1869), by repudiating apologetics who claim a golden age of Arabic culture in the past: 'don't tell stories of origins and inheritance, the only origin is that which is actual in the present' (*la taqul asli wa fasli abadan inama asl al fata ma qad hasal*).[1] The actuality of culture (*ma qad hasal*) is not discerned from the past (its essence) but from its existence in the present: the essence of culture is nothing but that which manifests itself in the present. Culture in this understanding is the measure of the failures or successes of a society in the present: i.e. culture has a validity but not a value-in-itself. Bustani maintains that culture is a result of a process of self-reflection that goes against the principle of inheritance. Culture in this sense is similar to science:

> the sciences grow and develop organically like animals and plants. They cannot be the result of one individual mind but of the result of sociality (*ijtima'*) ... Sciences cannot be inherited like money and property, but they require individual effort and dedication. They are like guests that don't stay unless well hosted.[2]

Like science, culture cannot be left to spontaneous and spurious reproduction; it must be submitted to strict rules of judgement. Thus, Bustani undertakes the task of writing an encyclopaedic account of culture for which the schematic history of culture's evolution over time – that he presents in his essay – serves to organise (but not define) its major characteristics. This 'rationalisation of culture' is necessary for 'hosting' science and knowledge, which are perceived as universal endeavours that cannot be reduced to past inheritance. Bustani's encyclopaedic account of culture aimed to single out what culture ought to be rather than what it has been. His position somehow already presumes a category of progress: it does not posit time (*al-zaman*) as an unfolding of a final destiny but rather avows that it is no longer possible to experience time as a state of static remaining; there is an anticipation, an anxiety that underlies civilisation.

The problem of origins betrays the impossibility of staticity; the awareness of time as being subject to disappearance is the essence of a modern idea of progress as Bustani articulated it.[3] Not only does modernity bring with it the necessity of transformation, but it also introduces a mode of retrospection. Formal time is eternal (*al-waqt*); in it the future like the past is eternal, unpredictable, and can only be discerned through ages (*al-zaman*), which are nothing but a 'small measurement of time'.[4] In contradistinction, modern history introduces a real shift, a cut, because it is a history that carries within it the measure of 'truthfulness' and 'necessity of rational judgement'. While *al-waqt* and *al-zaman* are left to the poetic dimension and are transcendentally normative, history is then conceived as the reconfiguration of the relationship between the past, present and future. Bustani's rewriting of the history of culture is characterised by *prolepsis* and retroaction. An overwhelming anxiety characterises the modern condition, one that is generated from the absolutism of reality in the face of which culture and language are summoned to stave off these anxieties.[5]

The nineteenth century is 'an age like no other',[6] for it brought the promise of dispelling myth and superstition with the advances of science and the promise of progress: 'the age of knowledge and Enlightenment (*al-ma'rifa w-al-nur*), the age of inventions and discoveries, the age of literature and science, the age of industry and art!'[7] These words are spoken by an author who translated *Robinson Crusoe*, one of the formative myths of the modern age, comparable to *Faust* and *Don Quixote* (the latter Shidyaq's own favourite).[8] The modern myth of Crusoe, as we know, was written by Defoe, who perceived literature as the art of writing that allowed 'men to escape from the most corrupting, multiplying usage of tradition'.[9] Defoe's distaste for the 'writings of the ancients' and the fallacious reports of oral histories implies that writing is meant to be a process of both erasure and introducing new truths. Bustani himself claimed that Crusoe was the 'true story of civilisation',[10] that Crusoe was a sign of modernity, his island the wish-fulfilment of humanity and his trials the burdens of man for all posterity. There is nothing, however, that is particularly romantic about Crusoe – or about Fariyaq for that matter. Crusoe is not a 'beautiful soul' in Hegelian parlance; he is not a moral self-consciousness combined with grace; his morality does not come from the heart but is experienced as an external pressure, an exertion from the outside, against which Crusoe responds with stolid self-sufficiency: Crusoe's story is neither a tragedy nor a comedy; it is unlikely to make readers either laugh or cry.[11] It is the story of a busy state of alienation. And estrangement, Crusoe tells us, can only be mitigated through economic activity, production and more production. Alienation only begets more alienation through labouring activity. On his island, Crusoe keeps very busy, constantly producing in the anticipation of society: weaving baskets, farming, hunting, building. It is the compulsive story of the pursuit of self-interest, which turns work into a second nature, a habit, and a compulsion.

Under the definition of *human* (*insan*) in Bustani's encyclopaedia, *Da'irat al-Ma'arif*, the emphasis is placed on an Aristotelian view of the human as a social being.¹² While animals behave according to habits acquired by nature, the human is a sentient being who has to 'tame' his habits; society is but his second nature. The encyclopaedic entry adopts St Augustine's definition of the human as 'a rational soul that functions through earthly ephemeral organs'.¹³ The human is thus defined by rational and creative capacities that can only be cultivated in a social setting: 'If it had not been for society, the human would be the weakest and feeblest of creatures'.¹⁴ As such, the human can only exist for and in society – that is the universal trait of being human for Bustani: 'Society shapes the human the most, it is the source that provides him with ideas, principles, and habits'.¹⁵ These, according to the encyclopaedia entry, are the factors responsible for the emergence of different and specific types of human beings (*ajnas*)¹⁶: 'It is in this way that individual existence (*al-'isha al-khususiya*), and public existence (*al-'isha al-ummumiya*), are intrinsically linked and inseparable from each other'.¹⁷

Indeed, Bustani posits this connection between sociality and habit in his *Khutbah fi 'al-hay'a al-ijtima'iya* (A Speech on the Social Formation), where he defines the social order (*al-hay'a al-ijtima'iya*) as originating from 'the fulfilment of the needs of individuals as well as the abetting of their fears'.¹⁸ Social life is defined by the pursuit of satisfaction of human needs. This satisfaction can only proceed from the division of labour for which Bustani provides an extensive Smithian analysis.¹⁹ The prescriptive logic of this analysis shows how the political and economic transformations of modern society (which are historically determinate) reify human relations into an exchange determined by an abstract conception of needs. These relations of need are more 'progressive' than those of tribal and 'savage' societies, more 'progressive' than humans closer to an animal. The latter, according to Bustani, have fewer needs to satisfy, rendering their mutual relations weak and their societies lacking in unity and civilisation. Thus, it is the production of new needs and means to satisfy them that determines the progress of civilisation. Although Bustani's argument appears to provide a historical genesis or anthropological historicism for the origins of human sociality, what it offers is a logic that is necessary for a retroactive understanding of capitalist sociality. 'One person cannot be a farmer, harvester, teacher, baker alone',²⁰ Bustani claims; even a simple loaf of bread requires many different kinds of labour to produce it.

Pertaining further to the origins of society and sociality as subsiding in the production and satisfaction of needs, Bustani also defines habit (*al-'ada*) as the product of need. Habits, for Bustani, are to be separated from universal taste and judgement: they can only be accounted for by the benefits or disadvantages they bear for those who possess them. To substantiate this point, he provides a comparison of the habits of the Arabs with those of the Europeans. The comparison ultimately espouses a concept of culture that relies on *neutralising* or negating particular habits (of food, drink, clothing, hair care, social conventions) that are only to be judged by a universal principle of need as the basis of society.

For Bustani, the assessment of habits and culture ought to entail questions like these: how do habits fit into the lifeworld of a particular society under capitalist subsumption? And do they advance or detract from the good of productivity? What then happens when a particular lifeworld under capitalist subsumption submits certain acquired habits to judgement and transforms them? By what criteria are habits then to be judged if they correspond to world-historical changes instantiated by capitalism? If the habits of the Europeans have instilled a set of 'civilised' social relations that the Arabs are necessarily made to covet, what conclusions can be reached with regards to the difference in habits between the two? It is here that we begin to see how culture begins to transform from a transhistorical limit on consciousness to a historical stage of consciousness. In other words, the comparison of habits is not simply the result of an encounter with another culture, but of the transformation of social practices instilled by the alienated social forms – of the commodity and wage-labour – introduced by the spread of capital. It is only in capitalist modernity that we witness the emergence of a universal history within which particular histories and cultures become concrete moments of the contradictions of global capitalism itself.

Bustani's comparison of habits, in a public speech given for the Syrian Science Society, speaks of what Lukács deems the antinomies of bourgeois thought. The discourse of that speech represents the self-consciousness of a burgeoning middle class in Beirut: its discussion of habit is a symptom of a bourgeois consciousness in the making. Bustani argues that the superficial adoption of European habits of eating, speaking, socialising, the mixing of the sexes, fashion and clothing is mere pretence, for it takes the form of modern sociality while not recognising its essence. But what is this core or essence that Bustani refers to? The essential function of need in modern society, as well as the relations of exchange necessary to satisfy them, is the particular trait of the human subject that is abstracted as a generality. The division of labour, and the transformation of labour into a commodity in modern political economy, appears as the inescapable fate of humankind, its un-transcendable horizon. The total estrangement of man, however, is historically determined by the separation of labour, capital and land and by the division of labour, competition and private property. Bustani's portrait of modern society, fashioned according to Crusoe's story and articulated in terms of needs and propriety, confirms the historical result of capital: man is unessential and cannot appropriate the objective world through free activity. Practical activity can only result in the reduction of man to a creature of needs, a creature of habit, and society can only affirm the abstraction of human activity into functions such as eating, drinking and procreating. The discourse on habit is meant to generate a criterion for judging habits based on their ability to benefit or advance a society's ability to satisfy the constant production of needs.

Bustani categorises needs into the following types: natural (food, clothes and shelter), mental (books, philosophical tools), social (interaction, bonding), moral (charity), religious (faith and practice of religion), political (the selection of a number of representatives to safeguard the order, wealth and lives of the population) and complementary (music, luxurious commodities, coffee and tobacco). The variety of needs, which exceed biological need, can only be satisfied by the law of supply and demand: the latter in turn requires a society founded upon the division of labour. The confusion of the historical and the logical in this mode of thinking, through which the human is reduced to a creature of habits and needs, is the direct result of the form of abstraction of human activity that takes place in capitalist society. Abstraction works by essentialising a particular aspect of the particular: 'Abstraction particularises the general essence of a particular thing ... by essentializing a particular aspect of its concrete particularity, which is why abstraction implies an essentializing particularization of the particular'.[21] Effectively, abstraction accentuates an aspect of the particular while neglecting what is universal in it; it is a reductive process of essentialising the human to the worker, while considering the worker nothing but the sum of his bodily functions. As we have seen in previous chapters, Shidyaq's own bodily ailments – his division into a gut, an anus and other orifices – rehearses the same process of abstraction at work in Bustani's works.

Robinson Crusoe is the generic worker in this regard, relegated to a state of nature where he can only validate his existence based on his bodily functions. There is no distinction between being and having for Crusoe: he is what he has, labour power. There is, however, fortitude to Defoe's plight: in his isolation he becomes the formative myth of political economy, the figure of *homo economicus*, who provides the individual example of the law of capitalist economy: labour in the abstract is a value-producing commodity. But what does the myth of *homo economicus* entail? Individual man in his isolation *anticipates* a society organised around commodity production, which in turn assumes that a relationship of direct slavery is ideal (Crusoe and Friday) when it is guided by benevolent and undemanding patronage; woman does not exist on the island and sex only interferes with the pursuit of self-interest (i.e. sex is an unnecessary distraction). Indeed, society *tout court* is a distraction from the real abstraction at work in commodity production. In other words, Crusoe's myth illustrates how capitalist economy relies on the separateness of the individual who can only be socialised via an atomisation of their labour: human solitude and alienation are at the core of liberal individualism.[22]

Bustani's proclamation of Crusoe as the 'true story of civilisation' for a post-war society is an outright confession of the ethos of liberal individualism: against 'sectarian communal belonging' everyone must avow the Crusoe within, acting as though they are doomed to solitude as a repentance against the attempt to kill the father, or the law that safeguards symbolic identification. Crusoe, Cain, and Abel, are interchangeable metaphors for modern personhood: they are direct incarnations of the plights of the liberal subject, always and forever haunted by their disavowed Other (the father, the brother, the mother).

On Crusoe's island, after the shipwreck, which is consequent to Crusoe's defiance of the law and of his father in particular, he is faced with an overwhelming anxiety. After the escape from the symbolic law of his society, which had threatened to engulf him and leave him with no individual I as a resort, Crusoe is petrified in his loneliness during his island isolation; he is consumed by the thought of cannibalistic Others, the anticipation of whom fulfils the task of the symbolic function from which he has escaped. His practical activity, his labour, is expended to quell the anxiety that emerges in the absence of a concept of culture.

The imaginary resolution that culture procures in terms of providing the grounds for meaningful activity in the world is experienced by Crusoe as an unbearable burden, a weight of needs pressing down on him, making him labour compulsively in response to the demand from an Other.[23] Crusoe's allegory exposes the cut between the social man, the man of culture who has an 'ego' commanded by society, and the natural man, who is an absolute whole that refers solely to his own needs. It is only through being cut off from society – deformed as a linguistic being, isolated with no one to speak to – that culture emerges to reproduce and remake society: i.e. only through the dependency on nature can a denatured nature emerge. Crusoe then poses the question: where is the boundary, the dividing line between nature and culture? The task of the man of culture is the mastery of nature, however he is a master who must work for the survival of a second nature: he is not the master who gives the sign or signifier for which others must slave and labour. It is in this sense that Robinson Crusoe experiences the trials of labour to the utmost. He acquires his inner nature, a subjectivity, by shaping the objectivity of nature. Work is what keeps desire in check; there is a negativity that Crusoe must endure as a process of *bildung*. However, this negativity does not realise itself in the supersession of the objective world: Crusoe does not come to self-consciousness as an inward relation, a 'self-reflexive turn to itself', but he is stuck in an attachment to an object he cannot get rid of. From the island to Bengal, China, Japan and Russia, to Mount Lebanon and Beirut, the escape of death at every juncture only affirms Crusoe's attachment to an object he cannot identify but for which he is a slave.

Crusoe's 'Oedipal complex', his rebellion against the demands of his father for an obedient son, generates a dis-identification with the father (the escape) and leads eventually through the trials on the island to a feminine submission to the father – read through Crusoe's collapse and prayer for God's repentance, his conversion and offering of himself to God.

CONCLUSION | 169

In Bustani's translation, Chapter 38 is of particular importance; this is where Crusoe, in conversation with a Mr Will Watkins, refers literally to the 'killing of his father':

> Crusoe: say, did you really kill your father with your own hands?
> Will: No sir, I did not slaughter him but I robbed him of his happiness and comfort. I have shortened his life span and broken his heart.[24]

The two men share a fraternal bond in light of their confession of a common sin. As Crusoe says,

> Every tree in this valley and on this island is a witness to my sins and my subversion of my loving, tender father who shares in the traits you describe your own father with. Behold I have as well killed my own father, my repentance however is less redeeming than yours.[25]

But what is the atrocious sin that Crusoe commits in his defiance of the law if not an incestuous desire to actually be possessed by the symbolic law, by the name-of-the father? The fear of the cannibals, which is persistent throughout the novel, can be read as Crusoe's projection of his own repressed desire to be engorged as an object of the Other's desire. The enigma of what the Other wants is answered by Crusoe's sacrificial offering of himself to the Other's desire, an offering that is maintained in a constant state of fear and anxiety. The labouring Crusoe is consumed by an attachment to objectified life, an attachment that he cannot get rid of.

His state of anxiety is accentuated to a paralysis with the sighting of a trace in the sand on the island after three years of isolation, a footstep that appears out of nowhere, and leads to breakdown, then a frantic fortification of his 'castle':[26]

> One afternoon, as I was walking towards my boat, I suddenly saw a trace of a human bare foot in the sand. I was awe-struck and stood there frozen as though struck by lightning, having just witnessed a phantom (or a jinn). I listened then frantically looked left and right, but there was no voice to be heard or anyone to be seen.[27]

The trace literally appears out of nowhere; like the signifier, it appears to represent Crusoe himself for something else, an Other for whom he must now be represented. Up until this episode, Crusoe had spent his time objectifying nature, mastering it, building a monarchy for the unique and totalising ego, but it is only now that he is faced with that which is unsymbolisable, a trace of a Real perhaps? The petrifying truth of the nonrelation that underlies all social relations, for what is the footstep a trace of if not another human being? The trace, this signifier, is experienced as a hallucination (*wahm aw khayal*), a rupture in the symbolic sphere of the island which is the site of labour, of the creation of habits and second natures out of the confrontation of man and nature. The trace in the sand disrupts Crusoe's egoic paradise; something loses its foothold with the sighting of the footstep: the ego is threatened by something from an elsewhere, its uniqueness put to the test. The trace inaugurates the shift in relation to that between two self-consciousnesses, Crusoe and Friday. The moment that Crusoe comes into the position of master in this relation, death presents itself as the ultimate risk to be subverted. Facing death and detaching from biological life, Crusoe must contend with an object of another kind that materialises: one that is signalled by an effusion of the affect of anxiety. The ego, which is ultimately Crusoe's symptom, cannot bind anxiety when faced with the possibility of a double, a specular image: there is always an excess in the doubling that the ego cannot account for, a footprint that dislodges its foothold.

The entire adventures of Crusoe take him from country to country in search of a fortification without a surplus, without an excess element that threatens subjectivity from within. In a sense, the lone Crusoe is himself a trace of that which was not there before, a modern myth and a symptom that serves the purpose of instituting retroactively the story of capitalist sociality. Marx called the story of Crusoe an 'unimaginative conceit', for it provides an image of a pure ego, isolated with its own *imagos* (cannibals and savages), outside society producing *as if* and in anticipation of a society structured around commodity production. For Marx, this depiction is 'as much an absurdity as is the [conception of] the development of language without individuals living *together* and talking to each other'.[28]

A Trace of Nothing that was There Before

Anxiety is an affect that is particular to the formation of subjectivity: it inflicts the dialectics of identification (the relation between subject and

Other) and always emerges as a surplus element to the dialectic of recognition. Anxiety is generated as a remainder of acknowledging the self in a specular image at the cost of the self's *aphanisis*; it is an unconscious affect that takes hold of the subject and reveals that desire is essentially based on an absence of a concept. It is an affect that emerges from a fear of loss, from facing death. The mirror image in which the subject witnesses a narcissistic doubling of the self contains a component of loss, which the subject experiences simultaneous with the image of fullness. This object (*objet a* for Lacan) cannot be seen in the mirror; it is a 'nonspecular' part of the subject, 'which has no mirror reflection'.[29] The moment of imaginary identification coincides with the Real, and this is when anxiety is provoked:

> When I recognize myself in the mirror it is already too late. There is a split: I cannot recognize myself and at the same time be one with myself. With the recognition I have already lost what one could call 'self-being', the immediate coincidence with myself in my being and *jouissance*. The rejoicing in the mirror image, the pleasure and the self indulgence, has already been paid for. The mirror double immediately introduces the dimension of castration – the doubling itself already, even in its minimal form, implies castration. So the doubling, in the simplest way, entails the loss of that uniqueness that one could enjoy in one's self-being, but only at the price of being neither an ego nor a subject. The doubling cuts one off from a part, the most valuable part, of one's being, the immediate self-being of *jouissance*. The mirror in the most elementary way already implies the split between the imaginary and the real: one can only have access to imaginary reality, to the world one can recognize oneself in and familiarize oneself with, on the condition of the loss, the 'falling out', of the *object a*. It is this loss of the object a that opens 'objective' reality, the possibility of subject-object relations, but since its loss is the condition of any knowledge of 'objective' reality, it cannot itself become an object of knowledge.[30]

The object of anxiety is always substituted by other stand-ins or symbolisations of a missing signifier, which can only present itself in an imaginary object: a mother tongue, a pound of flesh, a phallus. Here, Lacan's account of anxiety is particularly different from Freud's. While for Freud anxiety signals a loss of something, for Lacan it is the anxiety of gaining something too much, of a too-close presence of the object, a lack of lack. What one loses with anxiety is precisely the loss – the loss that made it possible to deal with a coherent reality. 'Anxiety is the lack of the support of the lack', writes Lacan; 'the lack lacks, and this brings about the uncanny'.[31] The footstep in the sand can be seen as this uncanny element: it defamiliarises all that is familiar; even the landscape of the island becomes spectral as Crusoe escapes to his burrow.

Anxiety emerges when all of a sudden the truth of symbolic functions is exposed to the subject; it is the state of existence on Crusoe' island and in Bustani's post-war society. Namely all symbolic identification is premised on the subject's need for recognition in the desire of the Other. This Other however, is not an opposing self-consciousness, but an unconscious Other who invokes the subject's desire. The Other *does not know* that the desire of the subject is in the measure of a lack (in the Other). After all, the fantasy of the Other as a subject-supposed-to-know is always none other than the subject's own.

Anxiety in particular emerges when norms are lacking, and it signifies that there is something about norms that is correlative to the idea of a lack. The lack of norms translates into the *lack of a lack* that is experienced as an unbearable pressure on the subject, it does not come from within but from without, it is an objective condition. After the footsteps appear out of nowhere, Crusoe must now suspend agreement to habit, to the modus operandi, to what is routine. He can no longer be fooled by the image of himself as pure labour power, working to pay off the symbolic debt: he can no longer rely on speech to anchor himself in the world (the only speech he had was one directed at God and the voice of scripture which spoke to him in his loneliness). He was now faced with a scopic object, a remainder that could not be subsumed under the existing chain of signification.

Bustani's decision to translate William Defoe's *Pilgrim's Progress* and *The Adventures of Robinson Crusoe* – which he argued were pivotal civilisational texts – betrays the true obsessions of neurosis. Neurosis is foremost concerned with dead-ends: how to rediscover under the signifier the original sign, the desire of the Other and what the Other demands of the subject.³² In Bustani's Protestant politico-theological discourse, encountered in the previous chapter, we are constantly faced with the question: what does God want of me? How can I repay the symbolic debt of the Other? It is this particular logic that dictated subjective identification at the end of the nineteenth-century, by which citizens were interpolated into a liberal modernity. They must all become Robinson Crusoes.

In Bustani's texts on habit ('ada) and society, we find direct repercussions of the metaphor of Crusoe for the thinking of social action: 'we cannot allow ourselves to become slaves to habit, *'abidan lil 'ada*, rather we must make habit our slave, a slave that we can abandon whenever we please'.³³ The slave must be abjured for *tamaddun* (modernity) to be possible and the 'roughness of habit' (*khushunat al-'ada*) is 'softened' with the degree of progress in civilisation.³⁴ There is an opposition, then, between habit and freedom: habit is indeed mechanical, but it is also the means through which the subject elevates him/herself in 'higher' human activities. *Tahdhib* (refinement) is the particular word that Bustani uses here: habit is formed first by a reduplication of nature, which opens the way for further creativity. The metaphor that Bustani offers in thinking about habit is that of a circle: 'with habit it is as though they [in reference to Europeans here] travel around the circumference of a circle until they reach every time the first point of origin only to revolve again'.³⁵ There is a cycle of revolution in habit, one that takes stock of the past only to become a new point of origin. The human body, which is Bustani's focus throughout the discussion, becomes a means; it is transformed through habit, appropriated. The subject appropriates corporeality and turns it into something fluid and mobile. The differences between habits testify to this fluidity of the body.

For example, the European man's hair compares to the Arab's: the former went back to letting their hair grow in the nineteenth century, while the Arabs began shaving. Furthermore, amongst the Europeans themselves, there were stark differences in hairstyles: 'in their faces we can see all possible iterations imaginable, perhaps there is wisdom in this difference that cannot be easily discerned by the Eastern or Arabic mind'.³⁶ When Bustani compares the question of dress, however, things are further complicated:

'It is well known that the purpose of clothing is to protect the human body from heat and cold, and to conceal it from the other's gaze. Hence, every country has its particular type of clothing'.[37] The Europeans have tighter clothing, however, because it is befitting to the pace of their life: they have to be faster, more productive, because they value time, while the Arabs wear loose and baggy clothes that are (presumably) more fitting to their slow movement and general disregard for the value of time. Bustani argues that perhaps the Arabs value 'moral composure' (*al-razana al-adabiya*) over 'natural composure' (*al-razana al-tabi'iya*), hence they 'spend the majority of their lives languishing in the streets'.[38]

According to this logic, then, the second nature of Europeans, their 'natural composure', and their habits are attuned to a pace of production – that is, *closer to nature*. In contrast, Arabs are closer to a moral stoicism that recluses itself from the 'natural' pace of production. Furthermore, the Europeans have a knowledge of the sciences, which dictates their dispositions: for example, they tend to warm their hands and feet while leaving their heads bare, contrary to the Arabs, who expose their hands and feet and take great pains to adorn their heads. The reason for this difference – according to Bustani – is that the Europeans have scientific knowledge of blood circulation that is far for more advanced. The same goes for eating habits: the Europeans have diets well-suited for health benefits, their meals are simple and advantageous; while the Arabs seek pleasure from food, their meals complex and hard on the gut. Europeans prefer to eat in solitude, while Arabs wish to create social ties and strengthen them in sharing food. Europeans consume food based on need, while Arabs consider the abundance of food and sharing communal meals to be signs of love and fraternity. Europeans are parsimonious and moderate, Arabs are frivolous, indulgent. The former choose words economically and wisely, the latter coddle in small talk, unnecessary niceties and exchanges. Europeans pen their letters with modest respect; Arabs insist on unnecessary praise and panegyrics. Europeans have a 'simple language', 'clarified and clean from ambiguity'; Arabs always speak in metaphor and allegory.[39]

So, the Europeans are somehow closer in their habits to appropriating nature, if nature is understood through the metaphor of production, labour and utilitarian ethics; while the Arabs are farthest from nature, stuck in mindless habits geared towards enjoyment, idleness and waste. The Europeans are adaptable, keen on changing their habits and exchanging the old for the new, but always according to clear laws and principles; while the Arabs hold steadfast to habits as traditions, despite knowing that 'the world is advancing while they stagnate'.[40] Bustani's speech concludes with a call 'to prepare for burial the caskets of our old and weary habits, because I see the army of European habits preparing its onslaught . . . they are armed with patriotism, industriousness and craftiness, machines, and wealth'.[41]

As we have seen, the European habits praised are nothing but the incarnation of a capitalist ethic that perceives production as a natural function: labour, productivity and time are valued; wealth is the measure of commodities, and so on. Against all this, the resigned Arabs are fated to lose. The goal is not simply the adoption of Western cultural ways, a false *mimesis* of progress, it is also to acknowledge the universal relationship between consciousness (of habit) and unconsciousness (habit becoming a disposition) in the progress of civilisation. If habits are necessary for the functioning of consciousness, they need to be economised, harnessed for the future. Habit is like property: it is about having a potential for future purposes; after all, 'The tree of civilisation is only temporarily adorned with western fruit'.[42] Bustani's advice is yet again the poetry verse he introduces in his preface to the Crusoe translation and in the *Nafir* pamphlets: 'he who is of no good to an other has a useless existence altogether'.

The conclusion is that there is no permanent substance to or essence of being Arab (or European for that matter), but there needs to be a recognition of the way in which contingent external forces (climate, location, geography) shape habit internally while giving habit a universality – elevating it to a subjective disposition, as though it had always-already been there from the beginning, a trace of that which was not there before. There is an obliteration of origin when it comes to habit; thus, a self-reflexive relationship to habit works on that which had become a disposition accidentally. The change of habit, which Bustani calls for, is a change of disposition, a change in the mode through which the subject apprehends change. What is being called for is therefore a change in an unconscious mode of production. Shidyaq would even state 'what is the use of observing the history of civilisations if one's habits are allowed to overcome their reason?'[43] Surely then habit cannot be reformed without challenging the unity of the subject, or if we take Fariyaq's plights seriously, we could even say that habit can only be reformed once the ego recognises there is an other element at work in the subject, an unconscious mechanism. Shidyaq's language is in itself a site of practice of the dilemma of habit: for what is more habitual than language itself? What we have seen in Shidyaq's explosions of *lalangue* is a gradual emptying out of language itself. Fariyaq's idiotic memorisation and recital of endless lists of words serves to empty them out of meaning, the words become empty shells that can then be reinvested with a new meaning. Is there not a parallel in this process to the subject's relationship to habit?

The Old Ego Dies Hard: Anxiety and Habit

> Life is a habit. Or rather, life is a succession of habits.
>
> *Samuel Beckett, Proust*

The problem of habit emerges as Beckett once noted, when the 'boredom of living' is replaced with the 'suffering of being'.[44] Suddenly, the security offered by the old ego is faced with a phenomenon that cannot be reduced into a familiar concept, and there is a disruption to the frame of fantasy through which reality is experienced. In the place of this old ego now appears a menacing reality: Crusoe's island and Fariyaq's twisted tongues.

The purgatory of post-war society as Bustani depicted it consists of affirming the very conditions that engender civil war; thus, the only attributes to be affirmed for society are wage labour and commodity production: the wealth of society is now to be measured by its commodities while its 'moral composure' is rendered anachronistic. Crusoe's hell is thereby expanded to include the fate of all of humanity. Shidyaq's answer to the purgatory of modern capitalist society was different from Bustani's and has more of a Quixotic nature: the enemy is everywhere disguised in the windmills, in the trees, even in words themselves.[45] Fariyaq is a Quixotic character in many ways, waving his tongue like a sword in every direction, attacking with no inhibition. *Leg Over Leg* is an incitement to literature: there is an extravagance that is characteristic of the novel, an excessive attempt at establishing some form of artistic autonomy outside the strictures of the modern condition. Cervantes's *Don Quixote* is known for being an 'agent provocateur'[46] in literature; it instils literature as a mode of carrying out an originary act.

Adorno, Lukács and Foucault amongst others have singled out *Don Quixote* as the inauguration of modern literature, as the site of battle between identity and difference, interiority and exteriority. The novel begins in a time of the crumbling of authority, both in society and in relation to the written word, and it carries out a 'systematic undermining and de-mystification, the "secular de-coding", of those pre-existing inherited traditional or sacred narrative paradigms which are its initial givens'.[47] Foucault discusses *Quixote* as an exemplary text of modern literature. Modern literature, according to Foucault, is characterised by making up for the signifying function of language.

There is a threat to thinking that is faced by the retreat into fiction and literature, into literary tropes, in an attempt to assert an authorship in the face of the real abstractions of modern capitalism. With Shidyaq we have seen an attempt to escape into the beauty of language, which is experienced as a terrifying force that overtakes the subject, penetrates their body, and renders them more incapable of symbolising beyond metaphors. Family, birth, lineage and the body cannot be adequately symbolised, so there is an explosion of *lalangue*: all that is familiar appears as unfamiliar. We can only think back to Shidyaq's wordplays, his persistent slips of tongue that keep striking against the problem of sex. Am I man or woman? Can I procreate? Who can stop me? Who can place a limit to my linguisteria, who can make me whole again after my explosion into fragments of words, signifiers and symbols? Bustani, on the other hand, poses the question of subjectivity's own self-haunting, expressing an anxiety over habit: habit becomes a strange sign that signifies the fact that it signifies nothing, the problem of habit posing the question of universality as simultaneously impossible and necessary.

In the wake of this discovery, of what we could call the nominal insubstantiality of the subject, we can discern the dialectic of real abstractions that characterises modern capitalist society:

> Capitalism is a system of Real abstractions . . . generated through social practices. Where the unity of thought abstractions defies spatiotemporal localization because it is that of transcendent generality, the unity of real abstractions defies localization because it is spread out across space and time. Real abstractions are immanent without being particular, abstract without being transcendent.[48]

The category of society is a misrepresentation of a contradictory totality as a concrete whole: 'society' emerges in modernity as a representation of the abstractions that determine relations (exchange, value, commodity). *Al-hay'a al-ijtima'iya*, which becomes Bustani's preoccupation, is precisely the problem of the emergence of a concrete representation, that is society, at a moment when the particular determinations are diluted and can no longer present themselves as a local instantiation. That is, particular habits become a problem in the process through which a 'transcendent generalisation' of society occurs: localisation can no longer present itself outside the world-historical order of capitalist society, and it cannot as well present itself as singular, having its own immanent logic.

Under the conditions of real abstraction, the general essence of a particular thing is particularised: the moustache, the mode of dress, even labour power itself emerge as biological things, physiological attributes. What presents itself at this moment, a moment in the dialectic of real abstraction, is a pervasive anxiety. Why is there anxiety at this particular juncture? Why is there an anxiety under real subsumption? Furthermore, is there a way to not lend this anxiety to exploitation? In other words, can the struggle for autonomy ever not be infected by the virus of anxiety? Bustani reminded his readers that it had been God's will to destroy the Tower of Babel for speaking in tongues, and it was God's will again that had struck Mount Lebanon and Damascus in the year 1860 with the 'plague of civil war'. In 1861 and in the aftermath of civil war, he declared that his nation 'shall not become the Babel of languages as it is of religions'.[49] A Babel of tongues is surely inflicted by the curse of anxiety, the inability to place the self and Other in language, perhaps an absence of *lalangue*?

In the Babel of tongues, Bustani was concerned with putting language in order. He expressed an obsessive impulse for hoarding and ordering words in dictionaries and encyclopaedias: making sure that every word corresponded to a direct meaning and that 'useless' word were eliminated.[50] The anxiety generated by the desire for the unification of *lugha* expressed a fantasy structure in which Bustani thought of the 'Arabs' as a people who dwell in language: dwelling in language, however, appears to have been an uneasy task. In a commentary on the state of Arabic, he depicted the onset of modernisation as a direct assassination of the mother-tongue: its speakers had opted for *ifranja* languages, and 'the foreigners' spread the influence of their own languages gradually through a matricide, a 'killing [of] the mother language'.[51] It was a linguistic battle to death.

In the same manner, cultural habits had to be assassinated, rendering the image of this 'Arab self' uncanny: '*Ifranja* dress does not suit the Arabs', Bustani argued, 'nor does *ifranja* language'.[52] His solution to this dressing of bodies and words is striking and invokes a narcotic intoxication: what concerned Arabs must do, Bustani argued, is, on the one hand, to 'numb' the use of foreign words – like 'commission' and 'excuse me' and '*afandim*' – by giving them (the words) enough 'opium to put them to eternal sleep'; and, on the other hand, 'to awaken the Arab words using smelling salts from their deep sleep'; 'using this method, the corruption that has overtaken Arabic language and Arab taste will be eliminated'.[53] This suggested pharmaceutical cure for the ailments of an imaginary nation that has suffered a matricide is surely not coincidental to Bustani's taxonomic drive[54] and the *aporia* that underlies it: for how could the ailment and the cure (language) be one and the same thing?

The subject that emerges from these works is one who must awaken from a pre-reflexive, non-thinking existence in which the fusion between interiority and exteriority goes uninterrogated. This awakening, the realisation of the self in objective reality, becomes the very content of subjectivity. Universalism emerges haunted by its inescapable anxieties for it asks: how can the subject, the form, become its own content?.

This sense of self-awareness that overtook Arabic thought in the nineteenth century is an example of the rise of universality from a particular lifeworld. This universality depended upon a splitting of the self, for how could habit be the ailment and the cure at the same time? How could the self dwell in particular sites, yet beseech a universal subjectivity? The focus on bodily habits or their objects (on food, clothing, hair, gestures, mannerisms) in *nahda* works is indeed fetishistic – similar in some ways to recent twentieth-century ethical projects that focus on the face – yet it signals the abyssal nature of the subject: it signals the anxiety about what is concealed behind the object-body.

Rather than read the discourse on habits only as a reflection of the desire for a modernity that is understood as Western modernity, my argument here is that it is an expression of the anxiety underlying modern subjectivity: one in which the subject comes to misrecognise itself. Anxiety arises from a threat to the unity of the subject, from a lack of a unifying fantasy to suture society. Once seen in this light, the invocations of mirrors (language as a mirror) in nineteenth-century Arab thought, serving as an attempt to unify the self, cease to be curious metaphors and become instead explanatory devices.

Shidyaq argued that the motto for sociality should not be 'do unto others as you would have them do unto you' but rather ' know thyself'.[55] To be truly modern, one must recognise one's own limited knowledge: to 'know thyself' rather than to 'think for oneself'. The aim of knowing oneself shifts inwards the criticism of authority that is directed outwards. The questioning of certain habits (polygamy, consumerism, imitating European ways, attitudes towards women, indolence and unproductivity, the gluttony of aristocrats, ornate language that lacks real meaning) goes hand in hand with knowing oneself. Self-knowledge assumes that one can reflect upon the very subject doing the reflecting. Shidyaq and Bustani's work on Arabic assumes that the subject could somehow step outside language to confirm that it could indeed express a truth about the world in which it exists. The irony is that the critique of habit and tradition, as well as language, is only made possible by the exit from them.

The implications of this conception of habit for the thinking of subjectivity and the meaning of political action are significant: when individual habit is shaped by accommodation to external forces, as an internal feature it becomes elevated into a disposition, the defining trait of an inner essence. Thus, habits that are mandated by the external world become internal faculties that define individuals: subjectivity emerges from its own disappearance. Moreover, habits have the power to conceal the source of their origin and appear as natural traits. The Arab's moustache appears as a natural trait for the Arab, just as the European's hairless face is natural to the European. The difference in habits (here the reference is to hair grooming) was natural only insofar as it was cultural: 'things in themselves cannot carry contradictory features; contradiction and difference are the results of forces of habits and differences in tastes'.[56] The 'essence' of the human is therefore a social one – universal nature is always a second nature, while particular social habits are the originary essence of humankind. But this is precisely where the problem is located: how to overcome particular habits without a descent into madness, into a state that confuses symbolic identifications with the real of language, and exposes – as Shidyaq does – the problems of the sexual non-relation through grammar? Is it finally a choice between madness and habit?

The transformation of habits is a transformation of dispositions. In Hegel's dialectical process of the Spirit's emergence, the transformation of habit is the only way for rational faculties to evolve. The path to being human is the recognition of habit as an inhuman, mechanical disposition, and its transformation. Habit in this sense is not an 'external necessity of constraint, but a necessity of attraction and desire . . . a law of the limbs which follows from the freedom of spirit'.[57] Relatedly, Bustani's encyclopaedia definition of *freedom* claims that freedom perceived as the release from restrictions on action and desires is non-existent in the world: 'there is no true liberty in this world'.[58] Habit impresses unto the corporeal body and shapes it, forms it.

As we have seen, underneath the harmonious appearance of the subject as a creature of habit is a mechanism for the splitting or erasure of subjectivity. The internal world is essentially constructed on the outside, made to predict and to be instantiated by the external world. Action in the world that is guided by habit does not make individuals consider their plurality, but seeks rather to reinforce an image of the individual as a self-identical subject. This sociological determinism is both recognised and reckoned with through anxiety, for one cannot easily will away a habit by reasoning.

Shidyaq and Bustani expose the limitations of economism for society, and the limits of living a life in service to the desire for commodities. The contradictory ethics of political economy – acquisition, work and thriftiness, on one hand, and good conscience and virtue, on the other – did not escape their scrutiny. In fact, we can read the focus on habit in their texts as an expression of the tensions generated by this universal contradiction. There is recognition of the contradictory core of liberal politics at its onset. For how can one be free and good at the same time? How can good conscience be commensurate with life under the formal freedom of exchange? In response to this contradiction, Bustani seeks the guarantees of the Other by redefining the foundations of a social formation in an egoic principle of self-interest: for him (bourgeois) society can only be established by distinguishing between a productive and non-productive act. While Shidyaq remains recalcitrant, he is a spirit of negativity, bound to the actuality that is determining the social conditions of his time and that is determining his acts beyond the functions of an ego. He is against the bourgeois law of property: there is no propriety over his discourse, and there cannot be.

*

We are left with Fariyaq, an insomniac creature of habit, and a habit however, that is of no use-value: he is an Arabic writer and poet. Finally, he is at rest, cornered in his room in Paris, where he pens his 'Room Poems'. He is a blacksmith who forges 'verses and [has] a workshop for prevarication'.[59] His room smells of his notebooks and tobacco, which render his visitors 'senseless'. They are forewarned of his dangerous unwelcoming Mecca, for they are fellow-travellers like Fariyaq, fellows who cannot practice their trade, they are 'bankrupt', 'luckless', and 'debt-dodgers'. They must travel up many stairs to his 'cell . . . methinks I've been climbing to cry out, muezzin-like, "God is the Greatest!"'[60] Fariyaq is now the host, but no visitor is worthy, no visitor can penetrate his tower of Babel, as it shrinks and shrinks, his things, his body, and his house, 'each is exiguate, exiguate, exiguate'.[61] As he shrinks to a minimal thingly creature of letters and smoke, Fariyaq is belligerent: he can only get off on the letter and no other can follow suit.

none visit me but the depraved and the bawdy.
   So Abandon modesty, all ye who enter my place!
Modesty is hypocrisy's brother, and no two friends can relax.
   Without some breathing space.
And
Vistor, watch your head –
   From the Onslaught of grammar!
This Apartment of mine
   Hosts no bonesetter.[62]

He is weary but sharp, no broken bones, but restlessly sinking into a haze of tobacco:

> between me and my tobacco there's a friendship firm – when I sleep it does; when I don't, it takes no ease, and if anyone comes to see me, its smoke covers my eyes. For it reckons the sight of men is a disease.[63]

He is debauched and in rags, a 'king of creation', living in a state of constant commotion, with no company but that of letters. He is alone with the signifier:

> In my dreams I see myself fall,
> So exhausted am I, into the like of a cave,
> Then wake in my bed, with no strength left.
> No need for a seer – it must be my grave.[64]

Notes

Introduction

1. Safouan, Mustapha, *Why Are the Arabs Not Free? The Politics of Writing* (Oxford and Malden, MA: Blackwell Publishing, 2007), p. 83.
2. Ibid. p. 91.
3. Ibid. p. 93.
4. The contrast here is between Hegelian speculative actuality, wherein the gap between actual and possible is filled in, and Kant's semantic conditioning of actual experience.
5. I refer here to Gillian Rose's discussion of culture in *Hegel Contra Sociology* (London: Athlone, 1981) and Rebecca Comay's discussion of experience in Hegel's phenomenology as an *anti-bildungsroman* in *Mourning Sickness: Hegel and the French Revolution* (Stanford: Stanford University Press, 2011).
6. There have been numerous studies of Bustani within the field of Arabic and Middle Eastern Studies that must be acknowledged: Stephen Sheehi's *Foundations of Modern Arab Identity* (Gainesville, FL: University Press of Florida, 2004) remains seminal in its theoretical contribution, which is largely Hegelian. Sheehi's interest in modernism is maintained as well in his following articles: 'Inscribing the Arab Self: Butrus al-Bustani and Paradigms of Subjective Reform', *British Journal of Middle Eastern Studies* 27 (1) (2000): 7–24, p.7 and pp. 72–8; 'Modernism, Anxiety and the Ideology of Arab Vision' in *Discourse.* 28(1) (Bloomington: Winter 2006). I would also refer

to Jeffrey Sacks's deconstructionist engagement with Bustani in *Iterations of Loss* which I discuss in the coming chapter, note 37. For an earlier account of Bustani's thought (within the context of the Ottoman Empire and the rise of a proto-nationalist sentiment) refer to Butrus Abu-Manneh, 'The Christians between Ottomanism and Syrian Nationalism: the Ideas of Butrus al-Bustani', *International Journal of Middle East Studies* 11 (3) (May, 1980): 287–304. Further sources would be Jens Hanssen's *Fin de Siècle Beirut: The Making of an Ottoman Provincial Capital* (Oxford: Oxford University Press, 2005). More recently Hanssen and Hisham Safieddine have translated and published Bustani's *The Clarion of Syria: A Patriot's Call Against Civil War in 1860* (Oakland: University of California Press, 2019). It has to be noted that the analysis of the same text in this book takes on a rather different trajectory, I also would disagree with the translation of *nafir* as 'Clarion'. Refer to Chapter 4 where I analyse Bustani's liberal nationalism and his commitment to a burgeoning capitalist ideology at the time, and I show how his ideology is accompanied by a distinct political theology that justifies the socialisation of labour as a commodity. The translations I use of the text throughout are entirely mine.

7. Refer to the lists of words that Shidyaq created through *ishtiqaq* and *Naht* in Mohamad Ali al Zarkan's *Al-jawanib al llughawiya 'ind Ahmad Faris al-Shidyaq, A Study of the Linguistic Aspects of Ahmad Faris al-Shidyaq* (Damascus: Dar al Fikr, 1988).

8. Lacan, Jacques, *Écrits: The First Complete Edition in English*, trans. Bruce Fink, in collaboration with Héloïse Fink and Russell Grigg (New York: W. W. Norton, 2006), p. 78.

9. Ibrahim al-Yaziji, '*Al-mara'y*' (Mirrors), *Al-tabib* (Beirut: Dar Sader, n.d.) pp. 273–4.

10. The image of Yaziji's self-portrait is inserted at the beginning of an edited collection by Nadthir Abud of al-Yaziji's articles published in 1984. The articles were first published in *al-diya'* journal as a series on *Islah al-fasid fi llughat al-jara'id* (*Corrections of Corrupt Language Use in Newspapers and Journals*), and were re-titled *Llughat al-jara'd (The Language of Journalism)* (Beirut: *Dar Sader*, 1984). The first compilation of these articles was published in 1925 by an Arabic literature teacher at the teacher's college in Damascus, Muhammad Salim al-Jundi (Damascus: Matba'at al-Taraqi). The subscript of the image describes Yaziji wearing a 'Lebanese Costume'.

11. Lacan, *Écrits*, p. 78.

12. Lacan, Jacques, *Anxiety: The Seminar of Jacques Lacan, Book X*, ed. Jacques Alain Miller (Cambridge: Polity Press, 2016), p. 28.
13. Robert Young, 'Rereading the Symptomatic Reading', in *The Concept in Crisis*, ed. Nick Nesbitt (Durham, NC: Duke University Press, 2017), pp. 35–48. See also Macherey, Pierre, *The Object of Literature* (Cambridge: Cambridge University Press, 1990).
14. Rancière, Jacques, 'Dissenting Words: A Conversation with Jacques Rancière', *Diacritics* 30(2) (2000): 114.
15. Macherey, Pierre, *A Theory of Literary Production* (London: Routledge Classics, 2006), p. 6.
16. Ibid. p. 8.
17. I use the category 'modern-subject' to denote particularly a post-Cartesian subject of modernity: a modern subject who is characterised by being out of joint in the world, and not as the highest in the chain of the order of things. The Cartesian-subject or the modern subject of science is distinctly modern because it breaks away from everyday spontaneous experience to recognise that the thinking I is not identical to the I that is. The subject is born out of the cognisance of a fundamental split between the speaking subject and the spoken: I exist only when I am thinking. The unconscious is the flip side, the obverse side of the subject of reason: I only recognise myself when I am outside the given order of experience.
18. Shidyaq, *Sirr al-layal fi al-qalb w-al-ibdal* (Istanbul: Matba'at al-Jawa'ib, 1867): 2.
19. Ibid.
20. See Nobus, Dany, 'Annotations to "*Lituraterre*"', *Continental Philosophy Review* 46(2) (2013): 335–47.
21. This summation is presented in the most recent volume on *nahda* thought by Jens Hanssen and Max Weiss, *Arabic Thought Beyond the Liberal Age: Towards an Intellectual History of the Nahda* (Cambridge: Cambridge University Press, 2016).
22. Ibid. p. 16. In Fredric Jameson's 'Third World Literature in the Era of Multinational Capitalism' (*Social Text* 15 (1986): 65–88), Jameson diagnoses the postmodern obsession with 'third-world' literature as an obstacle to conceiving of world literature in the context of the global capitalist system. 'Third-world literature' is a category that emerges from disavowing an engagement with capitalist modernisation as a world-historical force: 'The radical split between the public and private, which characterizes modernity,

between the poetic and the political, between what we have come to think of as the domain of sexuality and the unconscious and that of the public world of classes, of the economic, and of secular political power: in other words, Freud versus Marx. Our numerous theoretical attempts to overcome this great split only reconfirm its existence and its shaping power over our individual and collective lives' (p. 69). Jameson therefore insists on reading third-world literatures not as poetic national allegories or psychological and libidinal subaltern states, but as part of an 'objective spirit' determined by the political and economic realities of capitalism.

23. See Peter Hallward's seminal book, *Absolutely Post-colonial: Writing Between the Singular and the Specific* (Manchester: Manchester University Press, 2001).
24. Jameson, 'Third-World Literature', p. 80.
25. See Fredric Jameson's discussion of this point in *The Prison House of Language: A Critical Account of Structuralism and Russian Formalism* (Princeton, NJ: Princeton University Press, 1972), p. 5.
26. Badiou, Alain, *Logics of Worlds*, trans. Alberto Toscano (London and New York: Continuum 2009), pp. 2–3.
27. Badiou, Alain, 'Eight Theses on the Universal', in *Theoretical Writings*, ed. Ray Brassier and Alberto Toscano (London and New York: Continuum, 2004), p. 151.
28. Alberto Toscano, 'The Open Secret of Real Abstraction', *Rethinking Marxism* 20: 2 (2008): 276.
29. For relevant sources on the integration of the Ottoman Empire into the capitalist world economy, refer to Chevallier, Dominique, *La société du Mont Liban a l'époque de la revolution industrielle en Europe* (Paris: Librairie Orientaliste Paul Geuthner, 1982); Pamuk, Sevket, *The Ottoman Empire and European Capitalism* (Cambridge: Cambridge University Press, 1987); Scholch, Alexander, William C. Young, and Michael C. Gerrity, *Palestine in Transformation, 1856–1882: Studies in Social, Economic and Political Development* (Washington, DC: Institute of Palestine Studies, 1993); Doumani, Beshara, *Rediscovering Palestine: Merchants and Peasants*, in *Jabal Nablus, 1700–1900* (Berkeley: University of California Press, 1995); A. Kais Firro, 'Silk and Agrarian Changes in Lebanon, 1860–1914', *International Journal of Middle East Studies* 22(2) (1990): 151–69; Waddah Sharara, *On the Origins of Sectarian Lebanon, Fi Usul Lubnan al-ta'ify: Khat al-yamin al-jamahiri* (Beirut: 2011); Hanssen, Jens, *Fin de Siècle*

Beirut: T*he Making of an Ottoman Provincial Capital* (Oxford: Oxford University Press, 2005); Fouad Khater, Akram, *Inventing Home: Emigration, Gender, and the Middle Class in Lebanon 1870–1920* (Berkeley: University of California Press, 2001). For discussions of the peasant revolts, refer to Makidisi, Ussama, 'Corrupting the Sublime Sultanate: The Revolt of Tanyus Shahin in Nineteenth-Century Ottoman Lebanon', *Comparative Studies in Society and History* 42(1) (2000): 180–208. Earlier analyses of the Kisrawan revolt can be found in Porath, Yehoshua, 'The Peasant Revolt of 1858–1861', *Asian and African Studies* 2 (1966): 77–157; and Eliav Freas, Erik, 'Ottoman Reform, Islam, and Palestine's Peasantry', *Arab Studies Journal* 18(1) (2010): 196–231.

30. *Nafir Surriya* are a series of eleven nationalist pamphlets that Bustani published anonymously between 1860 and 1861, in the wake of the sectarian violence of Mount Lebanon and Damascus. The original manuscripts are held in the American University of Beirut, Archives and Special Collections Department, and have been reprinted in the book volume *Al-Mu'allim Butrus al-Bustani, Nafir Surriya* (Beirut, 1990).

31. Marx, Karl, *Capital: Volume 1*, trans. Ben Fowkes (Harmondsworth: Penguin, 1990), p. 280. 'Freedom, because both buyer and seller of a commodity, say of labour-power, are constrained only by their own free will. They contract as free agents, and the agreement they come to, is but the form in which they give legal expression to their common will. Equality, because each enters into relation with the other, as with a simple owner of commodities, and they exchange equivalent for equivalent. Property, because each disposes only of what is his own. And Bentham, because each looks only to himself'.

32. Sartori, Andrew, *Bengal in Global Concept History: Culturalism in the Age of Capital* (Chicago: University of Chicago Press, 2009): 51.

33. Lukács, Georg, 'The Old Culture and the New', *Telos* 5 (Spring 1970): 21–30.

34. Lukács's analysis of culture in 'The Old Culture and the New' (p. 26) is relevant here. However, I do not adopt a Lukácsian reading of culture, *per se*, because Lukács maintains an attachment to the 'beauty of old culture', which is seen to have a validity in itself, as an autonomous subjective experience, as a unity between subject and object. The concept of reification, which Lukács puts to use in the analysis of culture, remains abstract for it assumes that labour is a synthesising activity that constitutes the objectivity of all possible experience. This mode of analysis assumes there is an unknowability to the

social, political and historical determinants of knowledge and action. Refer here to Gilian Rose's poignant critique in *Hegel Contra Sociology*.
35. This is a story that Bustani translated into Arabic during the wars of 1860. He refers to the plight of Crusoe, who is shipwrecked and isolated, when discussing post-war society in the *Nafir Suriyya* (*The Clarion of Syria*) pamphlets (1860–1), as well as in his speech on society in 1849.
36. Lacan maintained, *contra* a moralistic understanding of offering oneself to the other, that this is a classic fantasy of obsessional neurotics: 'everything for the Other, my *semblable*'. The oblativity of the subject is the premise of this fantasy.
37. On the ego as modern symptom, see Rabaté, Jean-Michel, *James Joyce and the Politics of Egoism* (Cambridge: Cambridge University Press, 2004).

Chapter 1

1. De Man, Paul, 'Literary History and Literary Modernity', in *Blindness and Insight* (London: Routledge, 1996), p. 385. Jeffrey Sacks's engagement with Arabic literature is indebted, as he himself states, to de Man's theory of the aesthetic, refer to *Iterations of Loss: Mutilation and Aesthetic Form from al-Shidyaq to Darwish* (New York: Fordham University Press, 2016). Jens Hanssen and Max Weiss in their recent edited volume in *Arabic Thought Beyond the Liberal Age: Towards an Intellectual History of the Nahda* (Cambridge: Cambridge University Press, 2016) also adopt the view that modern Arabic thought has only been properly engaged with after the literary turn, i.e. after the post-colonial and deconstructionist readings provided by figures like Tarek El-Ariss, Jeffrey Sacks and Joseph Massad. It would not be an overstatement to say that the post-Saidian field of Middle East Studies is largely influenced by deconstruction, hermeneutics and phenomenology. It thus becomes here a necessity to engage with the De Man's understanding of a 'literary modernity' in order to lay out why it is not an approach I choose to adopt here. Notwithstanding the increasing focus on translation studies in the field of Arabic and Middle East studies that are largely influenced by a Derridean framework.
2. Ibid. p. 385.
3. This opposition that de Man assumes is a rather specific formulation, which opposes the dialectical understanding of history as a modern category. In fact, de Man's formulation is specifically Heideggerian in so far as it rejects the dialectical understanding of history pertaining to Enlightenment

modernity. For Hegel and Marx, the central figures of radical Enlightenment, to think of history philosophically is to think from within the historical moment with the aim of institutionalising the concept of freedom as a universal norm. Marx takes Hegel's account of human history as arguing that although human history has been driven by a constant striving for freedom it has also consistently produced the conditions for the oppression of freedom; hence Marx's claim that 'the history of all hitherto existing societies is the history of class struggle'. In Marx's account, history is nothing but the playing out of the contradiction in which human emancipation takes the form of human subjection. See Sartori, Andrew, 'Hegel, Marx, and World History' in *A Companion to Global Historical Thought*, ed. Prasanjit Duara, Viren Murthy and Andrew Sartori (London: Wiley-Blackwell, 2014), pp. 197–213.
4. Ibid. p. 399.
5. Ibid. p. 400.
6. Ibid. p. 398.
7. See Heidegger, Martin, *Being and Time*, trans. John Macquarrie and Edward Robinson (New York: Harper Perennial Modern Thought, 2008).
8. Ibid. p. 389.
9. Ibid. p. 390.
10. Ibid. p. 390.
11. Ibid. p. 391.Lin
12. Ibid. p. 392.
13. Ibid. p. 402.
14. Ibid. p. 402.
15. Lacan, Jacques, *Le Sinthome: The Seminar of Jacques Lacan, Book XXIII*, trans. Adrian Price, ed. Jacques-Alain Miller (Cambridge: Polity Press, 2016), p. 74.
16. Ibid. p. 74.
17. See Lewis, Michael, *Derrida and Lacan: Another Writing* (Edinburgh: Edinburgh University Press: 2008), pp. 28–32.
18. See Mladen Dolar's discussion of this point in Dolar, Mladen, 'Which Repetition?', unpublished text.
19. Zupančič, Alenka, *Why Psychoanalysis?* (New York: NSU Press, 2008), p. 16.
20. Ibid. p.17.
21. Ibid. p. 17.

22. Freud, Sigmund, *The Interpretation of Dreams and On Dreams*, Standard Edition vol. 5, trans. James Strachey (London: Hogarth Press, 1981), p. 506.
23. Ibid. p. 177.
24. The notions of archaic language and primitive horde in Freud have recently been criticised by Wendy Brown as a theory of liberal individualism. I address Brown's critique later in this chapter.
25. See Slavoj Žižek's distinction between historicism and historicity in Slavoj Žižek, Judith Butler and Ernest Laclau (eds), *Contingency, Hegemony, and Universality* (London: Verso: 2000), pp. 110–13.
26. The written for Lacan is not equivalent to literature but is reserved for the formalistic language of science that he resorts to for describing the topology of the unconscious. However, it is notable that in his particular analysis of Joyce, Lacan claims that literature in its function as a disruption of the symbolic comes close to the status of science in modernity.
27. Lacan, Jacques, '*Liturattere*', *Continental Philosophy Review* 46 (2013): 327–34.
28. Lacan, Jacques, 'Létourdit', *Scilicet* 4 (1972): 15.
29. Chiesa, Lorenzo, *Subjectivity and Otherness: A Philosophical Reading of Lacan* (Cambridge, MA: MIT Press, 2007), p. 190, n. 287.
30. Lacan, *Le Sinthome*, Wednesday, 18 November 1975.
31. Lacan, *Le Sinthome*, Wednesday, 13 January 1976.
32. Ibid.
33. Dolar reads the master/slave dialectic through Lacan as one which involves a theft of enjoyment: what the master takes from the slave is surplus enjoyment; and what the slave works to recuperate is a pure enjoyment, which fetishises the master as a subject-supposed-to-enjoy. See Dolar, Mladen, 'Hegel as the Other Side of Psychoanalysis', in *Jacques Lacan and the Other Side of Psychoanalysis: Reflections on Seminar XVII*, ed. Justin Clemens and Russell Grigg (Durham, NC: Duke University Press, 2006), pp. 129–55.
34. Lacan, *Écrits*, p. 733.
35. 'Defile' here is used as a noun and not a verb: it means 'definition', to be understood in the sense of a narrow doorway. Lacan, *Écrits*, p. 727.
36. Nobus, Daniel, 'Illiterature', in *Re-Inventing the Symptom*, ed. Luke Thurston (New York: Other Press, 2002), p. 30.
37. Lacan, '*Liturattere*', p. 328.
38. Lacan, '*Liturattere*', p. 331.

39. Lacan, *Le Sinthome*, Wednesday, 18 November 1975.
40. Lacan, '*Liturattere*', p. 331.
41. Lacan, *The Sinthome: The Seminar of Jacques Lacan, Book XXIII*, trans. Adrian Price, ed. Jacques-Alain Miller (Polity Press 2016) pp. 141–8.
42. Daniel Nobus, 'Illiterature', p. 30.
43. Dolar, 'Which Repetition?'.
44. Lacan, *Écrit*, p. 35.
45. Lacan, *Écrits*, p. 54.
46. Dolar, 'Which Repetition?' p. 14.
47. Lacan, *Écrits*, p. 53.
48. Lacan, *Écrits*, p. 431.
49. It is perhaps here that we can consider Lacan's notion of repetition *contra* Charles Peirce's understanding of signification as infinite semiosis.
50. Lacan, *Le Sinthome*, Wednesday, 18 November 1975.
51. Lacan, *Le Sinthome*, Wednesday, 18 November 1975.
52. Dolar, *A Voice and Nothing More* (Cambridge, MA: MIT Press, 2006) p. 37.
53. Lacan, *Le Sinthome*, Wednesday, 13 January 1976.
54. Rabaté, Jean-Michel, *James Joyce and the Politics of Egoism* (Cambridge: Cambridge University Press, 2004), p. 40. Rabaté's discussion is important because it brings forth the centrality of egoism in the modernist movement, in which he places Joyce.
55. Mladen Dolar makes a distinction between Joyce's omniscient additions and Beckett's subtractive impotence in 'The Voice and the Stone, from Hegel to Beckett' (unpublished paper).
56. For Lacan, the subject of science, the Cartesian *cogito*, is constituted in a rejection of all knowledge: which does not simply anchor the subject in being, but introduces the subject as split or crack in being itself. Refer to Lacan, 'Science and Truth', in *Écrits*, p. 727.
57. Even the modern scientific revolution for Lacan with Copernicus maintained this position of saving the truth, since revolution is about a constant return to an origin, while psychoanalysis is concerned with a constant work of decentring and through which a worldview can never be formulated.
58. Lacan, Jacques, *Encore: The Seminar of Jacques Lacan, Book XX*, trans. Bruce Fink, ed. Jacques Alain Miller (New York: W. W. Norton, 1995), p. 28.
59. Lacan, *Encore*, 33. A better translation, as suggested in the footnote by Bruce Fink, is 'the reading of what one hears qua signifier'.
60. Lacan, *Encore*, 37.

61. Cf. Nadia Al Baghdadi, 'The Cultural Function of Fiction: From the Bible to Libertine Literature. Historical Criticism and Social Critique in Aḥmad Fāris al-Šidyāq', *Arabica*, T. 46, Fasc. 3, *Vers de Nouvelles Lectures de la Littérature Arabe/Towards New Approaches of Arabic Literature* (1999), pp. 375–401.
62. The close similarity to Schreber's paranoid delusions is notable here. In his analysis of Schreber, Eric Santner notes that there is a historical moment of institutional crisis in symbolic identification in late enlightenment Germany which is essential for understanding Schreber's case; a conflicting legacy that manifests in knowledge and techniques of discipline between the *liberties* and the *disciplines*: 'One might say that the entire 'plot' of the *Memoirs* revolves around Schreber's attempt to integrate these two fathers, to find a way to reconcile the 'outlaw' or extralegal paternal presence – this 'surplus father' – with the father identified with the Order of the World and the law of proper distances'. Santner, Eric, *My Own Private Germany, Daniel Paul Schreber's Secret History of Modernity* (Princeton, NJ: Princeton University Press, 1996), p. 62.
63. Dolar, Mladen, 'Subject Supposed to Enjoy', in Alain Grosrichard's *The Sultan's Court: European Fantasies of the East* (London: Verso, 1998).
64. Ibid. p. xi.
65. Ibid. p. 63.
66. Ibid. p. 64.
67. Ibid. p. 66.
68. Ibid. p. 66.
69. Ibid. p. 24.
70. Ibid. p. 24.
71. Ibid. p. 24.
72. Kantorowicz, Ernst H., *The King's Two Bodies: A Study in Medieval Political Theology* (Princeton, NJ: Princeton University Press, 1957), p. 506. This body-politic is one that Foucault and Agamben argue has never died but rather is an already undead kingly authority with an 'afterlife' that is carried on into modernity, in the concept of bio-power.
73. Santner, Eric. *The Royal Remains, The People's Two Bodies and the Endgames of Sovereignty* (Chicago: University of Chicago Press, 2011), p. xii.
74. Santner, *My Own Private Germany*, p. 23.
75. Ibid. p. 37.
76. Ibid. p. 37.

77. Ibid. p. 37.
78. Foucault, *Dits et Écrits: 1954–1988*, vol. 4 (Paris: Gallimard, 1994), p. 619.
79. Zupančič, Alenka, 'When Surplus Enjoyment Meets Surplus *Jouissance*', in *Reflections on Seminar XVII: Jacques Lacan and the Other Side of Psychoanalysis* edited by Justin Clemens and Russell Grigg (Durham, NC: Duke University Press, 2006), p. 173.
80. Ibid. p. 173.
81. Safouan, Mustapha, *Al-'ubudiya al-mukhtara* (Cairo: Dar al-Ahali, 1990). This is Safouan's translation of La Boétie's Voluntary Servitude.
82. Žižek, Slavoj, *For They Know Not What They Do: Enjoyment as a Political Factor* (London: Verso, 1991), p. 201.
83. Tomšič, Samo, 'Lacan's Second Return to Freud via Saussure' in *The Capitalist Unconscious: Marx and Lacan* (London: Verso, 2013).
84. Freud, Sigmund, *An Outline of Psychoanalysis* (New York: W. W. Norton; The Standard Edition, 1989), p. 65.
85. Zupančič, *Why Psychoanalysis*, p. 2.
86. Ibid.
87. Wendy Brown's recent critique of Freud as a liberal thinker is perplexing given this fundamental understanding of the unconscious. I respond to Brown's critique later in this chapter.
88. 'Language is not univocity but equivocity, not a relation but the paradigmatic example of non-relation. And because there is no such thing as metalanguage, there is no language either. The linguistic and the economic system form an open set. Consequently, the inexistence of a metalanguage (the Other of the Other) and the inexistence of the Other are one and the same'. Tomšič, Samo, *The Capitalist Unconscious*, p. 15.
89. Tomšič, *Capitalist Unconscious*, p. 17.
90. Ibid. p. 17.
91. Cf. Dolar, Mladen, 'Beyond Interpellation', *Qui Parle* 6(2) (Spring/Summer 1993): 77.
92. Ibid. p. 77.
93. Ibid. p. 77.
94. Ibid. p. 80.
95. Lorenzo Chiesa, *Subjectivity and Otherness* (Cambridge, MA: MIT Press, 2007), pp. 14–19.
96. Jacques Lacan, Seminar XI. p. 278 .

97. Freud, Sigmund, 'Negation', *Standard Edition* 19 (1925), pp. 235–9.
98. Ibid.
99. Lacan, *Écrits*, p. 207.
100. Lacan, *Écrits*, p. 214.
101. Jacques Lacan, Jacques-Alain Miller, James Hulbert, 'Desire and the Interpretation of Desire in Hamlet', *Yale French Studies, Literature and Psychoanalysis. The Question of Reading: Otherwise* 55/56 (1977):11–52.
102. Lacan, *Écrits*, p. 225
103. Keneth Reinhard, *After Oedipus*, p. 166.
104. Samo Tomšič, *The Capitalist Unconscious*, pp. 69–70
105. Cf. Slavoj Žižek's discussion of this in *The Sublime Object of Ideology* (New York: Verso, 1989), pp. 24–7.
106. Cf. Alfonso Maurizio Iacono, *The History and Theory of Fetishism*, trans. Viktoria Tchernichova and Monica Boria, with the collaboration of Elizabeth MacDonald (Basingstoke: Palgrave Macmillan, 2016).
107. Ibid. p. 117.
108. Tomšič, *Capitalist Unconscious*, pp. 168–92.
109. Ibid.
110. See Dominico Losurdo's *Liberalism: A Counter-History*, trans. Gregory Elliot (New York:Verso, 2011).
111. Cf. Sartori's discussion of this point in *Bengal in Global Concept History*, p. 27.
112. Sartori, *Bengal in Global Concept History*, p. 47.
113. Ibid. p.47.
114. Ibid. p. 51.
115. Brown, Wendy, 'Subjects of Tolerance: Why We Are Civilized and They Are the Barbarians', in *Political Theologies: Public Religions in a Post-secular World*, ed. Hent de Vreis and Laurence E. Sullivan (New York: Fordham University Press, 2006), p. 299.
116. Ibid. p. 300.
117. Ibid. p. 300.
118. Cf. Oliver Feltham 'Enjoy Your Stay: Structural Change in Seminar XVII' in Justin Clemens *Lacan and The Other Side of Psychoanalysis* (Durham, NC: Duke University Press, 2006), p. 184
119. Slavoj Žižek, *Cogito and the Unconscious* (Durham, NC: Duke University Press, 1998), pp. 2–4.

120. Ibid. p. 19.
121. See first Mladen Dolar's 'Cogito as the Subject of the Unconscious', in Slavoj Žižeks' *Cogito and the Unconscious*.
122. Brown, 'Subjects of Tolerance', p. 301.
123. See, first and foremost, Zupančič, Alenka, *Ethics of the Real: Kant and Lacan* (London and New York: Verso, 2000).
124. Brown, p. 301.
125. Ibid.
126. See Ruda, Frank, *Abolishing Freedom* (Lincoln, NE: University of Nebraska Press, 2016).
127. See Ruda, Frank, 'Marx in the Cave', in *Reading Marx*, ed. Agon Hamza, Frank Ruda and Slavoj Žižek (Cambridge: Polity Press, 2018), p. 78.
128. Ruda, 'Marx in the Cave', p. 92.
129. Ibid. p. 94.
130. Brown, p. 302.
131. Ibid. pp. 302–3.
132. Ibid. p. 303.
133. This distinction which Brown first makes in *States of Injury* is symptomatic of the neoliberal culturalisation of politics from which the discourse of tolerance emerges as a fundamentally exclusionary logic: those who are had by culture and those who have culture.
134. Ibid. p. 303.
135. Ibid. p. 304.
136. Ibid. p. 304. This is also Brown's reading of Hegel in *Regulating Aversion*: the category of liberal individuality is read as a Hegelian *a priori* 'ontologically true yet historically achieved. And the more developed and rewarded this individual is *as* an individual, the more the collective identity is eroded or undercut by individualism and especially individual ego strength, and the greater the prospects for a tolerant world' (p. 185).
137. Ibid. p. 305.
138. In his last days Freud jotted down this memorandum with a note for it to be included in *Moses and Monotheism*. Sigmund Freud, *Findings, Ideas, Problems. The Standard Edition of the Complete Psychological Works of Sigmund Freud, Volume XXIII (1937–1939): Moses and Monotheism, An Outline of Psycho-Analysis and Other Works* (London: The Hogarth Press and the Institute of Psychoanalysis, 1938), pp. 299–300.
139. *Letters of Sigmund Freud*, p. 375.

140. See Dolar, Mladen, 'Of Drives and Culture', *Problemi International* 1(1) (2017): 55–79.
141. Ibid. p. 9.
142. Ibid. p. 11.
143. Ibid. p. 11.
144. Brown, *Subjects of Tolerance*, p. 308.
145. Ibid. p. 309.
146. Ibid. p. 309.
147. Ibid. p. 307.
148. Ibid. p. 307.
149. Ibid. p. 309.
150. See first Mladen Dolar's analysis of this in *Beyond Interpellation*, 81
151. Ibid. p. 83.
152. Brown: 'slavish devotion to something external to it, and if such devotion incites the naturally egoistic subject to give up a significant part of its individuality, then Freud has succeeded in defining group belonging as the inherent sacrifice of individual freedom (rooted in deliberation, self-direction, and conscience) on the altar of love for that which dominates it. Strong social bonds arise only and always as an effect of domination and as a sign of dangerous regression to a de-individuated and hence derepressed state', p. 309.
153. Brown, *Subjects of Tolerance*, p. 311.
154. Ibid. p. 303.
155. Ibid. p. 304.
156. Ibid. p. 303.
157. Ibid.
158. We can only recall here the importance of Freud's analysis of Daniel Schreber and his delusional paranoia, Schreber as we know saw himself as an un-manned feminised wandering Jew.
159. Zupančič, *Why Psychoanalysis?*, p. 39.
160. Freud, *An Outline of Psychoanalysis*, p. 147.
161. Ibid. p. 170.
162. Tomšič, *The Capitalist Unconscious*.
163. We can recall here Lacan's statement about a 'certain academic obscenity, which calls itself hermeneutics [that] has buttered its bread from psychoanalysis' in 'The Mistaking of Subject Supposed to Know', published in *Silicet* 1, pp. 31–41. Republished in *Autres écrits* (Paris: Éditions du Seuil, 2001), pp. 329–39.

164. Santner, *My Own Private Germany: Daniel Paul Schreber's Secret History of Modernity* (Princeton, NJ: Princeton University Press, 1996), p. 106.
165. Toscano, Alberto, 'Beyond Abstraction: Marx and the Critique of Religion', *Historical Materialism* 18 (2010): 3–29.
166. Ibid. p. 428.
167. Brown, *Subjects of Tolerance*, p. 317.
168. Ibid. p. 317.
169. I have in mind here Eric Santner's useful distinction between global and universal consciousness in *The Royal Remains*.
170. Dolar, Mladen, 'Cutting of the King's Head', in *Lacan Contra Foucault: Subjectivity, Sex, and Politics* edited by Nadia Bou Ali and Rohit Goel (London: Bloomsbury Academic, 2018) pp. 37–55.
171. I am indebted here to Rabaté's analysis of James Joyce in *James Joyce and the Politics of Egoism*.
172. Yusif Qazma al-Khuri ed, 'hub al-watan min al-iman, al-ghira 'ala al-watan', [Love of the Nation as an Act of Faith, and Patriotism] *Mukhtarat min Athar* Ahmad Faris al-Shidyaq [Selections from the Works of Ahmad Faris al-Shidyaq] (Beirut: al-Mu'asasa al-Sharqiya lil Tiba'a w al-Nashr, 2001) pp. 212–15.

Chapter 2

1. I am referring here to Abu l- 'Aswad ad-du'ali's, who died in the year AD 668. Refer to Keeth Versteegh's discussion of this in *The Arabic Linguistic Tradition* (London: Routledge, 1997), p. 3.
2. Ibid. p. 59.
3. This reading is indebted to Jean-Claude Milner's interpretation of linguistics, which relies on Alexandre Koyre's claim that the epistemic break of modern science relies on the mathematisation of the empirical. Refer to *Oeuvre Claire, Le Periple Structurale, For the Love of Language*, and the special edition on Milner, 'Cahier Jean Claude Milner', ed. Justin Clemens and Sigi Jottkand, *S: Journal of the Circle of Lacanian Ideology Critique* 3 (2010).
4. Banfield, Ann, 'What do Linguists Want? The Age of Linguistics', in 'Cahier Jean-Claude Milner', *S: Journal of the Circle for Lacanian Ideology Critique 3* (2010): 100.
5. Refer to Samo Tomšič's discussion of the miser and the hoarder in *The Capitalist Unconscious*, p. 69.

6. Bustani, Butrus, *Muhit al-Muhit* (Beirut: Maktabat Lubnan, 1998), p. 819.
7. Ibid. p. 819.
8. Shidyaq, Ahmad Faris, *Al-Saq 'ala al-Saq fi ma huwa al-Fariyaq aw ayyam wa ashuhur was a'wam fi 'ajam al-'arab wa al-a'jam* (Beirut: Dar Maktabat al-hayat, 1885), p. 164.
9. The debate on whether this text is to be considered a modern novel form or a hybrid mix of novel and *maqama* is not relevant to the discussion here. If the minimal definition of the novel is that it is a form of narrative fiction, a conjunction between narration and consciousness, then we can assume that this book is novelistic in nature.
10. Shidyaq, Ahmad Faris, *Sirr al-layal fi al-qalb w-al-ibdal* (Istanbul: *Matba 'at al-Jawa'ib*, 1867), p. 2.
11. Cf. Jacques Alain Miller, *For the Love of Language*, p. 60.
12. Ibid. p. 60.
13. Refer to Shidyaq's introduction to *Sirr al-Layal fi al-Qalb wa al-Ibdal*, p. 2, and Mohamad Sawaie's discussion of this in *Fursan al-Lugha al-Arabiya*, pp. 53–64
14. Ibid. p. 59.
15. Refer to Mohamad Sawaie's study of Shidyaq's linguistic neologies in 'al-Ḥadathah wa-muṣṭalaḥāt al-nahḍa al-'Arabiyah fi al-qarn al-tasi''ashar: dirāsah fī mufradāt Aḥmad Fāris al-Shidyāq fī jarīdat (al-Jawā'ib)' (Beirut: al-Mu'asasa al-'arabiya li al-tiba'a w al-nashr, 2013).
16. Pierce, Charles Sanders, *Collected Papers*, eds. Charles Hartshorne and Paul Weiss, vol. 2 (Cambridge, MA: Harvard University Press, 1932): 'A sign, or representamen, is something which stands to somebody for something in some respect or capacity. It addresses somebody, that is, creates in the mind of that person an equivalent sign, or perhaps a more developed sign. That sign which it creates I call the interpretant of the first sign. The sign stands for something, its object. It stands for that object, not in all respects, but in reference to a sort of idea, which I have sometimes called the ground of the representamen' (p. 228). Pierce continues here to describe the Idea in a 'sort of Platonic sense', as a continuation of a thought process, a repetition of thinking about the same idea, an 'interval of the same idea'.
17. The relationship between Pierce and Lacan on the one hand, and Lacan and Frege on the other is a complex matter for which I cannot devote a lengthy discussion here, suffice to say that Lacan had been influenced by Pierce's realism and his insistence on a category of the Real that is irreducible to the

duality of ego and non-ego, as well as his critique of Aristotle's logic (in the essay 'Quadrangle'). For further discussions of this relationship refer to Michel, Mathias, 'Pierce's Reception in France: Just a Beginning', *European Journal of Pragmatism and American Philosophy* 1 (2014):15–23; Balat, Michel, 'Peirce C. S., Des fondements sémiotiques de la psychanalyse: Peirce après Freud et Lacan suivi de la trad. de 'Logique des mathématiques' de C. S . Peirce préf. de Gérard Deledalle (Paris: l'Harmattan, 2000); and Silverman, Kaja, *The Subject of Semiotics* (Oxford: Oxford University Press, 2000).

18. Refer to Tomšič's discussion of this in the *Capitalist Unconscious*.
19. Pierce, *Collected Works*. 'A sign stands for something to the idea which it produces, or modifies. Or, it is a vehicle conveying into the mind something from without. That for which it stands is called its object; that which it conveys, its meaning; and the idea to which it gives rise, its interpretant. The object of representation can be nothing but a representation of which the first representation is the interpretant. But an endless series of representations, each representing the one behind it, may be conceived to have an absolute object at its limit. The meaning of a representation can be nothing but a representation. In fact, it is nothing but the representation itself conceived as stripped of irrelevant clothing. But this clothing never can be completely stripped off; it is only changed for something more diaphanous. So there is an infinite regression here. Finally, the interpretant is nothing but another representation to which the torch of truth is handed along; and as representation, it has its interpretant again'. (Vol. 1, p. 339).
20. Lacan, *Écrits*, p. 47.
21. Chiesa, *Subjectivity and Otherness*, p. 34.
22. Ibid., p. 47.
23. Miller, *For the Love of Language*, p. 59.
24. Lacan, *Écrits*, p. 186.
25. Lacan, *The Language of the Self: the Function of Language in Psychoanalysis*, trans. Anthony Wilden (Baltimore and London: The Johns Hopkins University Press, 1986) pp. 9–27.
26. Lacan, Book III, *The Psychoses*, ed. by Jacques Alain Miller, trans. Russell Grigg (New York: W. W. Norton, 1997) p. 54.
27. This split subject for Lacan is none other than the Cartesian subject: 'I think where I am not, therefore I am were I do not think'. Refer to Chiesa on this and Mladen Dolar's extended reading.

28. 'Within the meaning, and the real, which is discourse that has actually taken place in a diachronic dimension'. Lacan, Book III, *The Psychoses*, p. 63.
29. Ibid. p. 167.
30. Ibid. p. 167.
31. Refer to Tomšič's discussion of this in *Capitalist Unconscious*, pp. 15–18.
32. Lacan, *Écrits*, p. 434.
33. Lacan, Book III, *The Psychoses*, p. 260.
34. Cf, Jean-Michel Rabaté, *The Ghosts of Modernity* (Gainesville, FL: University Press of Florida, 2010).
35. Refer to T.S. Eliot's review of Joyce 'Ulysses, Order, and Myth', in *The Dial* 65(5) (November 1923).
36. I am employing here Rabaté's reading of modernism in *The Ghosts of Modernity*, p. 3.
37. Ibrahim al-Yaziji, 'Amaly al-llughawiya' (My Ambitions for Language), *Al-Tabib* (The Doctor) (15 April, 1884), 49 in the published collection of the journal's full editions from 1884 to 1885.
38. Sandor Ferenczi, 'On the Symbolism of the Head of Medusa', in *Further Contributions to the Theory and Technique of Psychoanalysis* (New York: Boni and Liveright Publishers, 2013), p. 360; Sigmund Freud, 'Medusa's Head', in *Writings on Art and Literature*, ed. Werner Hamacher and David E. Wellbery (Stanford: Stanford University Press, 1997), 264–6. Freud also discusses Ferenczi's account in 'The Infantile Genital Organization' of 1923.
39. This lack effects the masculine and feminine differently, however: on the level of symbolisation there is no sign for woman's sex (woman symbolised as not-all in relation to phallus); the absence of this symbolisation is substituted for by the imaginary, while for man there is a highly prevalent symbol. However, despite the centrality of phallic signification, the sexual difference between man and woman is an imaginary bipolarity of a two that can never become one, or rather of a One that doesn't exist in the first place, splitting into two. The phallic signifier for both cases of the feminine and masculine brings with it a collateral register of the Real, one that is not exhaustible with symbolic identification. As Zupanic recently puts it, 'Sex is real because it marks an irreducible limit (contradiction) of the signifying order (and not something beyond or outside this order' (2017, p. 46). This is why the question of sex for Lacan is summed up in 'there is no sexual relation': there is no relation because the feminine and masculine are both

inherently unstable, indifferent and have no substantial content. Hence their relation proves to be a logical problem, a problem pertaining to the logic of signification. Refer also to Chiesa, Lorenzo, *Not Two: On God and Logic in Lacan* (Cambridge, MA: MIT Press, 2016).

40. At least not in the first Oedipal stage. Refer to Lorenzo Chiesa's elaboration of this distinction in Lacan's rereading of the castration complex in the two registers of symbolic and imaginary: *Subjectivity and Otherness*, pp. 79–84.
41. Castration and not instinct: i.e. imaginary identification and symbolic law.
42. Freud, Sigmund, 'Medusa's Head'; and cf. Hertz, Neil 'Medusa's Head: Male Hysteria under Political Pressure' *Representations'* 4 (Autumn 1983): 27–54.
43. Refer to Reinhard Lupton, Julia and Kenneth Reinhard, *After Oedipus: Shakespeare in Psychoanalysis* (USA: The Davies Group Publishers, 2009).
44. Refer to *Sexuation*, ed. Renata Salecl (Durham, NC and London: Duke University Press, 2000), especially Verheage's discussion of the problems of the Oedipal question in Freud.
45. Lacan, *Écrits*, 723.
46. Ibid. p. 579. 'For the phallus is a signifier, a signifier whose function . . . the signifier conditions them by its presence as signifier. For it is the signifier that is destined to designate meaning effects as a whole. Let us thus examine the effects of this presence. They include, first, a deviation of man's needs due to the fact that he speaks: to the extent that his needs are subjected to demand, they come back to him in an alienated form. This is not the effect of his real dependence . . . but rather of their being put into signifying form as such and of the fact that it is from the Other's locus that his message is emitted'.
47. Alenka Zupančič's recent formulation in *What is Sex?* (Cambridge, MA: MIT Press, 2017) is particularly instructive: 'what Freud calls the sexual is not that which makes us human . . . rather it is what makes us subjects, [the sexual] is coextensive with the emergence of the subject', p. 7.
48. I use the Cormac Gallagher translation here of Seminar X, http://www.lacaninireland.com/web/translations/seminars/, p.48, which corresponds to p. 53 in Jacques Lacan *Seminar X: Anxiety*, ed. Jacques Alain Miller (New York: Polity Press, 2014).
49. Refer to Eric Santner's analysis of this for the case of Schreber *My Own Private Germany*, 'The surprise offered by the analysis of paranoia – which, as shall become clear, bears important structural relations to hysteria, the

proliferation of which in *fin-de-siècle* Europe has been much researched – is that an 'investiture crisis' has the potential to generate not only feelings of extreme alienation, anomie, and profound emptiness, anxieties associated with absence ; one of the central theoretical lessons of the Schreber case is precisely that a generalized attenuation of symbolic power and authority can be experienced as the collapse of social space and the rites of institution into the most intimate core of one's being. The feelings generated thereby are, as we shall see, anxieties not of absence and loss but of overproximity, loss of distance to some obscene and malevolent presence that appears to have a direct hold on one's inner parts. It is, I think, only by way of understanding the nature of this unexpected, historical form of anxiety that one has a chance at understanding the libidinal economy of Nazism, and perhaps of modern and postmodern forms of totalitarian rule more generally', p. xii.
50. This will be discussed in the following chapter.
51. Bustani, Butrus, *Muhit al-muhit* (Beirut: Maktabat Lubnān, 1988). First published in Beirut 1870, the original print is available at the Archive Collection of the American University of Beirut. The references hereafter are to the reprinted version of 1988. This dictionary is in an abridged and reordered version based on Fairūzābādī's *Qamus al-muḥıṭ* but with an alphabetised ordering of the words, a novel method in the history of Arab lexicons, and with the addition of word meanings that are of relevance to Bustani's time.
52. Ibid.
53. Bustani, *Khutbah fi adab al arab*, p. 19. This is a recurring theme in Bustani's work and it is evident in his *Muhit al Muhit* dictionary.
54. Bustani uses this definition both in the *Khutbah* and in the introduction to the *Da'ira* encyclopaedia.
55. Bustani, 'Introduction', *Da'irat al Ma'arif*, p. 1.
56. Bustani, 'History', '*al Tarikh*', *Da'irat al Ma'arif*, vol. 6, p. 10.
57. Bustani, 'Introduction', *Da'irat al Ma'arif*, p. 1.
58. Bustani, '*Muqadimah*' (Introduction), *Da'irat al Ma'arif*, vol. 1, p. 7.
59. Bustani, '*Tiba'a*, Printing', *Da'irat al Ma'arif*, vol. 11, p. 202.
60. Bustani, *Da'irat al-Ma'arif*, vol. 1, p. 1.
61. Ibid. p. 1.
62. Chad Wellmon, 'Touching Books: Diderot, Novalis, and the Encyclopaedia of the Future', *Representations*, 114(1) (Spring 2011): 72.
63. Ibid.

64. James Creech, '"Chasing After Advances": Diderot's Article "Encyclopaedia"', *Yale French Studies* 63 (The Pedagogical Imperative: Teaching as a Literary Genre, 1982), p. 187.
65. Michel Foucault, *The Order of Things* (New York: Random House, 1970), p. 206.
66. James Creech, 'Chasing After Advances', p. 186.
67. Ibid. p. 188.
68. Creech, 'Chasing', p. 194.
69. Bustani, 'Introduction', *Da'irat*, p. 4.
70. Ibid. p. 4.
71. Creech, 'Chasing', p. 193.
72. Wellmon, 'Touching Books', p. 77
73. James Creech, 'Chasing After Advances', p. 195
74. Bustani, *Da'ira*, vol. 8, p. 591.
75. Bustani, 'Introduction', *Da'irat* vol.1, p. 4.
76. Ibid. p. 4.
77. 'How can we not all sense that the words on which we depend, are in a way imposed on us? This indeed is why what is called a sick person sometimes goes further than what is called a healthy man. The question is rather one of knowing why a normal man, one described as normal, is not aware that the word is a parasite? That the word is something applied. That the word is a form of cancer with which the human being is afflicted. How is it that there are some who go as far as feeling it?' Lacan, *Le Sinthome*, p. 128.
78. Shidyaq, *Sirr al-Layal fi al-qalb w al-ibdal*, p. 1.
79. Refer to Shidyaq's discussion of this in the introduction to Sirr, pp. 1–27 with a focus on pp. 2–7.
80. That Shidyaq also dedicates his *Muntaha al-'ajab al-'ajab fi khas'is lughat al-'arab*, which is often cited by him, but is a missing publication to date.
81. Shidyaq, *Sirr al-Layal fi al-qalb w al-ibdal*, p. 2.
82. Ibid. p. 2.
83. Bustani argued, in *Khutba fi adab al-arab* [American University of Beirut, Archives and Special Collections Department, NBMAS Mic-A:548: Master: c.1] in 1859, that 'God established the first civilization (*al-tamaddun al-awwal*) from which all of humanity originates, savage, barbaric, and civilized'. Language is God's gift to Adam, he added; 'language, the jewel of reason, is possible because of human freedom. And through it, the mind

is educated, thought is trained, and inventions are possible, thus the spread of civilization and culture [tamaddun and adab]', p. 32.
84. Shidyaq, *Mukhtarat min athar Ahmad Faris al-Shidyaq*, p. 391.
85. Shidyaq, *Leg Over Leg*, vol. 1, p. 165.
86. Ibid. p. 165.
87. Ibid. p. 165.
88. Ibid. p. 165.
89. Ibid. p. 165.
90. Ibid. p. 165.
91. Ibid. p. 165.
92. Ibid. p. 169.
93. C.f. Eric Santner, *The Weight of All Flesh: On the Subject-Matter of Political Economy* (Oxford: Oxford University Press, 2016).
94. In *Civilization and Its Discontents*, Freud had claimed that the progress of civilisation is tethered to a prosthetic drive that is to be conceived in topological terms at the points of transition between the inside and outside of the body, the anal and oral drives. The tools of civilisation (science, technology, and so forth) are the means through which humanity advances as a 'prosthetic God. When he puts on all his auxiliary organs he is truly magnificent; but those organs have grown on to him and they still give him much trouble at times'. The source of man's divinity is the prosthetic nature of progress, which is acquired through extending the body via tools. Freud's model for culture relies on its function as a discharge and damming up of energetic flows, culture is the result of the relation between two drives, Thanatos and Eros. Freud's theory of drives goes against the theory of instincts because the drives are not simply about a satisfaction of instinctual needs. The satisfaction of needs always has a surplus element to it that splits it from within, produces a new need that self-perpetuates and reproduces itself. In other words, there are no pure natural needs that can be satisfied.
95. Michelle Arrive's formulation is relevant here: 'And how could one forget that the very meaning of the word 'letter' brings out the fact that the notion is anchored in the body? For it is not for nothing that we can speak *literally* [à la etter], of the *body of the letter* of its *head* and of its *eye*. And especially of its *foot:* it is by taking words literally that one gets off on the letter'. *Linguistics and Psychoanalysis* trans. James Leader (Amsterdam: Johan Benjamin's Publishing Company, 1992) p. 53.

96. Shidyaq, *Leg Over Leg*, vol. 1, p. 170.
97. Ibid. p. 171.
98. Shidyaq, *Leg Over Leg*, vol. 1, p. 171.
99. Ibid. p. 169.
100. Jacques Lacan, *Le séminaire, Livre III, Les psychoses, 1955–56* (Paris: Éditions du Seuil, 1981), p. 13.
101. Ibid. p. 173.
102. Cf. Miller, Jacques-Alain, *For the Love of Language*, pp. 64–73.
103. Dolar, *A Voice and Nothing More*, p. 144.

Chapter 3

1. Shidyaq, p. 163.
2. Shidyaq, p. 49. *Al-surr* does not come from sex but is more like pleasure as *jouissance*.
3. Ibid. p. 49.
4. Shidyaq, *Leg Over Leg*, vol. 3, p. 199.
5. Ibid. p. 199.
6. Shidyaq, *Leg Over Leg*, vol. 1, p. 51.
7. Shidyaq, *Leg Over Leg*, vol. 3, p. 61.
8. Ibid., p. 141.
9. Ibid., p. 107.
10. Shidyaq, *Leg Over Leg*, vol. 1, p. 249.
11. Ibid., Chapters 5 to 17.
12. Shidyaq, *Leg Over Leg*, vol. 3, p. 141.
13. Ibid. p. 141.
14. Ibid. p. 141.
15. Ibid. p. 145.
16. Ibid. p. 145.
17. Ibid. p. 157.
18. Cf. Rabaté's analysis of James Joyce and the relationship between Hospitality and Sodomy.
19. Shidyaq, *al-Saq*, vol. 3, p. 145.
20. The symbolic in psychoanalysis, following Lacan's elaboration on Freud's metapsychology (Beyond the Pleasure Principle after the 1920s) is not reducible to nature or culture but is a transcendental function that is 'present in absence and absence in presence' (Lacan, Seminar II, 38). The 'function' of the symbolic is to introduce a certain asymmetry into imaginary

egoic identifications, it has an autonomy and is universal because it is can be formalised in mathematical language. The symbolic in Lacan's account is formal because it establishes structural relations or the law.

21. Shidyaq, *Leg Over Leg*, vol. 3, p. 347.
22. Ibid. p. 347.
23. Cf Milner, Jean-Claude, 'Pleasure's Treble', *S: Journal for the Circle of Lacanian Ideology Critique* 3 (2010): 61.
24. Ibid. p. 42.
25. A philological digression here is necessary. The Arabic word for 'guest' is *dayf* and is the root for the adjective 'hospitality' (*al-diyafa*) and carries the meaning of addition. It is also a term used in grammar to denote genitive construction, in which one definite noun is annexed to another indefinite noun to generate a phrase. Al-Razi defines it in the *Suhah* as the annexation or addition of a noun to another in a manner that affirms a distinction. *Idafa* works according to the principle of sameness, as a noun is annexed to another to identify that which is in the other noun as distinct; it is an affirmation of identity through difference: 'if one thing had complete self-knowledge it would not require an additional noun to define it'. Imam Mohammed Ibn Abi Bakr Ar-Razi, *Mukhtar us-Sihah* (Beirut: Librarie du Liban, 1993), p. 162.
26. Given the numerological significance of the number 13, I cannot but think of Lacan's *Seminar 13*, 'On the Names of the Father', as the seminar in which he challenges Freud – the father of psychoanalysis – on his reading of Moses and monotheism. In it Lacan introduces the figure of the Ram in Abraham's sacrifice to argue that in Judeo-Christianity there is a distinct separation between God's *jouissance* and his desire: the aim of the sacrifice is to 'diminish biological lineage' and the Ram signifies the impossible Real, an excess object that emerges in the place of the problem of origins.
27. Shidyaq, *Leg Over Leg*, vol. 2, p. 175.
28. Shidyaq, *Leg Over Leg*, vol. 4, p. 191.
29. Shidyaq, *Leg Over Leg*, vol. 2, p. 185.
30. Shidyaq, *Leg Over Leg*, vol. 1, p. 193.
31. Ibid. p. 193.
32. Ibid. p. 193.
33. Ibid. p. 193.
34. Ibid. p. 195
35. Ibid. p. 195.

36. Ibid. p. 199.
37. Ibid. p. 199.
38. Ibid. p. 201.
39. Ibid. p. 201.
40. Dolar, *A Voice and Nothing More*, p. 148.
41. Ibid. p. 147.
42. Ibid. p. 147.
43. Shidyaq, *Leg Over Leg*, vol. 1, p. 199.
44. For Lacan 'subject supposed to know' is the first supposition of analysis, it allows for transference to occur only for that transference (the love relation that emerges in analysis) to be overcome, to reveal that the Other does not have the knowledge the subject seeks, that the knowledge lies in the impasse of the subject's enjoyment and hence leading the subject to their 'subjective destitution'. What I am suggesting here is that we can perhaps see Fariyaq as the Other that fulfils Shidyaq's desire for a master, a subject supposed to know, only for Shidyaq to be struck again by the blindness of his own enjoyment.
45. Shidyaq, *Leg Over Leg*, vol. 1, p. 204.
46. Ibid. p. 204.
47. Ibid. p. 204.
48. Ibid. p. 207.
49. Cf. Eric Santner's discussion of this in the context of Daniel Schreber in *My Own Private Germany*; Chapter 1 in particular is relevant here. Freud's reading of Schreber's delusions through the frame of the father complex focus on the means through which symbolic power is transmitted through names. Santner's critical reading of Freud's 'reduction' of Schreber's problem to the question of a repressed homosexuality is particularly enlightening. Santner illuminates the problem of sexuation and symbolic identification *tout court* in bourgeois society: 'Schreber tends to characterize the maddening fact that agencies and institutions entrusted with the care of individual and social well-being exert a sexualizing pressure in the language that dominated cultural analyses of late nineteenth-century bourgeois society' (p. 51). In Santner's reading, Schreber was unable to keep a distance from the symptoms of bourgeois decadence and his neuro-theological delusions are 'inseparable from his "perverse" capacity for identifying with, acting out, and, so to speak, enjoying these symptoms' (p. 52).
50. Dolar, *Beyond Interpellation*, p. 88.

51. Shidyaq, *Leg Over Leg*, vol. 1, p. 253.
52. Ibid. p. 242.
53. Ibid. p. 273.
54. Ibid. p. 273.
55. Refer to Ussama Makdisi's works on this.
56. A notion as we know put forth by John Locke, the father of modern liberalism, who argued against the principle of inheritance for property replacing the fraternal with the paternal model.
57. Shidyaq, *Leg Over Leg*, vol. 1, p. 275.
58. Ibid. p. 275.
59. Ibid. p. 276.
60. Marx, Karl, *Capital*, vol. 1 (New York: Penguin Classics, 1990), p. 874.
61. Shidyaq, *Leg Over Leg*, vol. 1, p. 287.
62. Ibid. p. 279.
63. Ibid. p. 275.
64. Kojin Karatani's analysis of the miser's desire as capitalist drive in *Transcritique: Kant and Marx* (Cambridge, MA: MIT Press, 2003) is very relevant here: 'The desire for money or the right to exchange is different from the desire for commodities themselves. I would call this "drive [Trieb]" in the Freudian sense, to distinguish it from "desire". To put it another way, the drive of a miser is not to own an object, but to stand in the position of equivalent form, even at the expense of the object. The drive is metaphysical in nature; the misers' goal is to "accumulate riches in heaven", as it were'. p. 7.
65. Marx, Karl, *Capital*, vol. 1 (New York: Penguin Classics, 1990), p. 254.
66. Ibid. p. 254.
67. Shidyaq, *Leg Over Leg*, vol. 1, p. 279.
68. The word for taste is *dthawq* and in Shidyaq's understanding taste is the result of forces of habit and custom: 'taste cannot be delimited or specified by any boundaries beyond those of habit and custom, refer to Shidyaq, *Fi al-dthawq: al-ʿada w al-ʿulfa*'(On Taste: Habit and Custom) in *Mukhtarat Ahmad Faris al-Shidyaq*, pp. 167–70.
69. Shidyaq, *Leg Over Leg*, vol. 1, p. 283.
70. Ibid. p. 283.
71. Ibid. p. 285.
72. Ibid. p. 285.
73. Ibid. p. 285.

74. I use my own translation here rather than Davis's 'surmise and assertion'.
75. Again, Davis translates *ra's al-mal* as 'stock-in-trade', I refer to it as Capital. Refer here to Fawaz Trabulsi's and Aziz al-Azmeh's list of Shidyaq's translations.
76. Shidyaq, *Leg Over Leg*, vol. 2, p. 15.
77. Ibid. p. 29.
78. Ibid. p. 29.
79. Ibid. p. 31.
80. Ibid. p. 35.
81. Ibid. p. 37.
82. Karatani, Kojin, *Transcritique*, p. 8.
83. Žižek, Slavoj, *The Sublime Object of Ideology* (London: Verso, 1989).
84. Zupančič, Alenka, *What is Sex?* p. 61.
85. Shidyaq, *Leg Over Leg*, vol. 1, p. 55.
86. Shidyaq, *Leg Over Leg*, vol. 3, p. 343.
87. Ibid. p. 343.
88. Ibid. p. 343.
89. Ibid. p. 343.
90. Ibid. p. 331.
91. Ibid. p. 331.
92. Ibid. p. 331.
93. Ibid. p. 333.
94. Ibid. p. 333.
95. Ibid. p. 333.
96. Ibid. p. 333. I intervened in the translation here.
97. Ibid. p. 333.
98. Ibid. p. 335.
99. Ibid. p. 337.
100. We cannot ignore here the wealth of material that Freud provides in his analysis of Daniel Schreiber's similar symptoms: for Freud Schreiber's feminisation fantasies are the symptoms of the onset of paranoia as a defense against an influx of homosexual libido. I would also refer the reader to Eric Santner's discussion of the Judge Schreber material here in *My Own Private Germany*: Schreber, Daniel Paul, *Secret History of Modernity* (Princeton, NJ: Princeton University Press, 1996). Santner suggests that Schreiber's fantasies of feminisation can be read as a 'crisis in symbolic investiture' (p. 32), which is a 'crisis pertaining to the *transfer* of symbolic power and

authority'. This crisis according to Santner, pushes the bounds of Freud's repressive hypothesis, and shows that rather than perceive the relation between law and desire as repressive, 'Schreber's experience of his body and mind as the site of violent and transgressive interventions and manipulations, produce, as a residue or waste product, a kind of surplus enjoyment' (p. 32). This surplus enjoyment goes to show that the law is experienced as an excessive demand (Schreber's breakdowns are linked after all to his appointment as a high juridical authority in the courts of Saxony), with a residual element of enjoyment that is maintained goes to show that authority exercises a from of power that always exceeds it symbolic pact (p. 37). Shidyaq here provides a similar case of comparison on the one hand but also challenges Santner's insistence on linking Freud's disavowal of his own Judaism and his reading of Schreber's repressed homosexuality as a source of feminisation. Santner maintains the discourse of psychoanalysis is itself a result of a crisis in symbolic investiture pertaining to the anti-Semitism surrounding Freud at the time.

101. Shidyaq, *Leg Over Leg*, vol. 3, p. 337.
102. This is the title of Chapter 18 of vol. 1 of *Leg Over Leg*.
103. Shidyaq, *Leg Over Leg*, vol. 1, p. 271.
104. Shidyaq, *Sirr al-layal*, p. 3.
105. Ibid. p. 3.
106. Rabaté, *James Joyce and the Politics of Egoism*, p. 57.
107. Shidyaq, *Leg Over Leg*, vol. 1, p. 61.
108. Shidyaq, *Leg Over Leg*, vol. 1, p. 36.
109. Shidyaq, *Leg Over Leg*, vol. 2, p. 8.
110. Shidyaq, *Leg Over Leg*, vol. 3, p. 8.
111. Shidyaq, *Leg Over Leg*, vol. 4, p. 11.
112. Shidyaq, *One Leg Over the Other*, vol. 1, p. 58.
113. I borrow this qualification from Rabaté's reading of Joyce, despite the lack of a direct literary comparison between Joyce and Shidyaq, one cannot but note the thematic similarities between *Ulysses* and *Leg Over Leg*: in both we find the problem of desire and law being interrogated as the socially constructed necessary elements for survival.
114. Rabaté, *James Joyce and the Politics of Egoism*, p. 57.
115. Ibid. p. 57.
116. Ibid. p. 57.
117. Pierre Macherey, *The Object of Literature*, p. 109.

118. Ibid. p. 109.
119. C.f Tareq El-Ariss's book *Trials of Arab Modernity: Literary Affects and the New Political* (New York: Fordham University Press, 2013).
120. Lacan's account of literature in his seminar on *Le Sinthome* is essential for this formulation. Refer to my discussion of this above.
121. Eric Santner's reading of Schreiber is important here.
122. Shidyaq, *Leg Over Leg*, vol. 1, p. 63.
123. Shidyaq, *Leg Over Leg*, vol. 3, p. 165.
124. Shidyaq, *Leg Over Leg*, vol. 1, p. 163.
125. Shidyaq, *Leg Over Leg*, vol. 3, p. 221.
126. Ibid. p. 227.
127. Ibid. pp. 227–8.
128. Conversation between Fariyaq and Fariyaqa in *Leg Over Leg*, vol. 3, p. 323.
129. Freud's reading, as Santner has shown, links the repressed homosexual impulse in nineteenth-century male paranoia to the specific form of homosocial desire, which was both compulsory (fraternal gentlemanly relations) and prohibited. Consider here the intense relations of enmity and praise between *nahda* male figures like Shidyaq, Bustani, Yaziji and others.
130. Shidyaq, *Leg Over Leg*, vol. 3, p. 228.
131. Ibid. p. 229.
132. Cf. Levinson, Micheal, *Modernism and the Fate of Individuality: Character and Novelistic Form from Conrad to Woolf* (Cambridge: Cambridge University Press, 1991).
133. Cf. Santner, *My Own Private Germany*; Schreber, *Secret History of Modernity*.
134. Shidyaq, *Leg Over Leg*, vol. 1, pp. 58–9.
135. Ibid., p. 55.
136. Ibid., p. 57.
137. Ibid., p. 59.
138. Ibid. p. 61.
139. Ibid. p. 61.
140. Grosrichard, *The Sultan's Court*, p. 29.
141. Shidyaq, *Leg Over Leg*, vol. 1, p. 141.
142. Ibid. p. 241.
143. Shidyaq, *Leg Over Leg*, vol. 1, p. 25.
144. Shidyaq, *Leg Over Leg*, vol. 3, pp. 313–15. In a conversion between the Fariyaq and Fariyaqa, they discuss the relation between man and woman

and the overtly patriarchal symbolic sphere of society, which excuses man's infidelities in marriage and blames women for them constantly. The accusations against the wife to justify man's unfaithfulness are listed by Fariyaqa as faults of these kinds; the woman is said to 'defecate while being fucked ... whining through her nostrils ... spraying water during intercourse and making a noise with her vulva, or of having a hernia and making a sound with her vagina, or of having a hole too small to admit the penis and being given to farting, or of being insatiable in intercourse and having a *mons veneris* that both squeaks and passes wind ... or having no flesh on her thighs and a bottomless tunnel, or of having smelly foreparts and a loose vagina, or of leaving her anus half-washed and stinking and having privates on which no hair grows ... or of coming as soon as man plays with her and having a tiny 'thing', or of menstruating through her anus ... of having not been circumcised and having a wide space between her anus and her vagina, or of having a flabby vagina, or having thighs so tightly pressed together there is no gap between them ... or having a rectum and vagina that form a single passage, or of having a long clitoris, or wide sexual organs, or being one who, having vagina and rectum as a single passage, loses control of her bowels during intercourse'.

145. Shidyaq, *Leg Over Leg*, vol. 3, p. 311.
146. Shidyaq, *Leg Over Leg*, vol. 1, p. 21.
147. Ibid. p. 21.
148. Shidyaq, *Leg Over Leg*, vol. 1, p. 23.
149. I am indebted to the distinction that Rabaté posits, in his reading of Joyce, between modernist egoism and egotism.
150. Shidyaq, *Leg Over Leg*, vol. 1, p. 245.
151. Ibid. p. 245.
152. Ibid. p. 245.
153. Ibid. p. 245.
154. Ibid. p. 245.
155. Ibid. p. 247.
156. Santner, *My Own Private Germany*, p. 139.
157. Ibid. p. 139.
158. Shidyaq, *Leg Over Leg*, vol. 1, p. 25.
159. Cf. Grosrichard, *The Sultan's Court*, pp. 7–16.
160. Shidyaq, *Leg Over Leg*, vol. 3, p. 249.
161. I have amended here the translation from Davis, from man to slave: *malik* and *mamluk*.

162. Shidyaq, *Leg Over Leg*, vol. 3, p. 249.
163. Shidyaq, *Leg Over Leg*, vol. 3, p. 81.
164. Ibid. p. 141.

Chapter 4

1. The transformation of relations of production in Mount Lebanon and Damascus had led to the gradual independence of the peasants from the *iltizam* land-tenure system and to the separation of labour skills from land property. In this context, and leading up to 1860, the Christian peasants of Keserwan in Mount Lebanon revolted against the Christian *Muqa'tiji* and the moneylenders in 1858 following a year of bad crops and the repercussions of the global economic financial crisis of 1857–8. Led by a farrier, Tanyus Shahin, the rebels stopped paying taxes, expelled the *muqat'ici* from their lands, and established a political structure with a representative body. The Europeans and Ottomans worked against the growing momentum of the peasant movement, which failed to garner alliances with the merchants and nobles, and it began to take on a sectarian character when Christian peasants rebelled against Druze feudal lords in search of the successes of the revolts in Keserwan. Although the Druze lords won the battles by orchestrating unprecedented large-scale massacres, the result was that the land-tenure system that they had headed lost to the forces of capitalism in the Lebanese mountains: in the aftermath of these as the main form of production, wage labour replaced tax-farming to a large extent, and family and gender relations were significantly transformed.
2. Bustani, *Nafir Surrıya* (The Clarion of Syria), American University Archives and Special Collections.
3. Bustani, *al-Tuhfa Bustiniya fi- al- asfar al- kuruziya* (Bustani's Masterpiece of Crusoe's Travels) (Beirut, 1860), American University of Beirut, Archives and Special Collections.
4. The 'nation form', as Étienne Balibar has defined it, emerges and persists as a global ideological form premised on the retroactive construction of national singularity. This nation form is tethered to the development of modern capitalism, within which it has diffused to almost all societies in the past centuries. The form determines a central process: the nationalisation of society and the production of a people as a *homo nationalis*. Thus, the tracing back of an origin for the nation form as an imaginary identification must take account not of its historical origin but of its formal structure and

the symbolic forms that determine it. This means that the nation cannot be solely traced to Creole nationalism, as Benedict Anderson argued in his attempts to debunk the Eurocentric appropriation of the nation. Indeed, if the nation did indeed emerge from the sociohistorical context and debates of the French Revolution, it is not because of some natural French essence that it did so, but because of the central position of France as a world empire within the world system then. The resurfacing of nationalism in different historical moments after the French Revolution is a worldwide phenomenon that has been linked to the intervals of crises of state–capital formations. In moments of crisis, the nation emerges to fill the gaps of state–capital's organisation of social life; however, the reaffirmation of the structural causality (of crisis and reorganisation of society through nationalism) exposes the historicity of that equation. This structure of repetition is not evential but formal; as Kojin Karatani has argued, the nation emerges as a representative structure to establish some form of class equilibrium where there is none. Complementing the analysis of the nation at the formal level, an adequate understanding of nationalism as a modern social form requires that it 'captures the dynamic interplay between sociohistorical processes and the embodied, constituting character of everyday practices and cultural categories of understanding', for the nation lies at the conjunction of the socially generated divide between subjectivity and objectivity in capitalist modernity. Refer to Sewell, William, 'The French Revolution and the Emergence of the Nation Form', in *Revolutionary Currents: Nation Building in the Transatlantic World*, ed. Michael A. Morrison (Chicago: University of Chicago Press, 2004), pp. 91–125; Karatani, Kojin, *The Structure of World History* (Durham, NC: Duke University Press, 2014); Goswami, Manu, 'Rethinking the Modular Nation Form: Toward a Sociohistorical Conception of Nationalism', *Comparative Studies in Society and History* 44(4) (2002): 770–99; and Balibar, Étienne, 'The Nation Form', in *Étienne Balibar and Immanuel Wallerstein, Race, Nation, Class: Ambiguous Identities* (London and New York: Verso, 1991), pp. 86–106.

5. I borrow the term 'psychotheology' from Santner, who employs it as an amendment to Freud's 'psychopathology of everyday life'. Santner, Eric, *On the Psychotheology of Everyday Life: Reflections on Freud and Rozenzweig* (Chicago: University of Chicago Press, 2001).

6. Hourani, Albert, *Arabic Thought in the Liberal Age* (Cambridge: Cambridge University Press, 1983). Makdisi, Ussama, 'After 1860: Debating Religion,

Reform, and Nationalism in the Ottoman Empire', *International Journal of Middle East Studies* 34(4) (2002): 601–17.
7. Makdisi, 'Corrupting the Sublime Sultanate', p. 194.
8. Ibid. p. 194.
9. Makdisi, in his reading of sectarianism and of Bustani's discourse, rehearses the classical secularist false dilemma, in which overcoming religion is perceived as essential for political emancipation. Marx's rebuttal of Bruno Bauer's radical secularism is instructive here. Marx argues that while religion indeed expresses a limit or a defect in human sociality, it is not the cause of that defect but indeed 'the manifestation of secular narrowness' (Tucker, Robert C., *The Marx/Engels Reader* [New York, 1978], p. 26). Liberal secularists argue that individuals can be emancipated from religion but not from the state and not from their particularities (religion, private property, etc.), while for Marx emancipation can only be carried out by overcoming these secular restrictions and particularities themselves. The universalism of the political state and its internal contradictions is oxymoronic for Marx, for how can freedom and equality be embedded in the realm of rights, as ends, while the concrete means for achieving them are absent?
10. Makdisi, 'After 1860', p. 613.
11. Jeffrey Sacks, *Iterations of Loss, Mutilation and Aesthetic Form: Al-Shidyaq to Darwish* (New York: Fordham University Press, 2015), 88.
12. Makdisi, 'After 1860', p. 613.
13. Ibid. p. 90
14. Bustani, *Nafir Surriya* (hereafter NS), Pamphlet 9, 14 January 1861.
15. Bustani, *NS*, Pamphlet 4.
16. Bustani, *NS*, Pamphlets 1, 5, 7, 8
17. Bustani, *NS*, Pamphlet 8.
18. Bustani, *NS*, Pamphlets 1, 5, 9.
19. Bustani, *NS*, Pamphlet 1.
20. Bustani, *NS*, Pamphlet 5. It should be noted here that *harb ahliya* is closer to the ancient Greek term of *stasis* rather than 'civil war'. Refer to Agamben's *Stasis: Civil War as a Political Paradigm* (*Homo Sacer II*) (Stanford: Stanford University Press, 2018) which signifies a civil war as the simultaneous politicisation of kin and a de-politicisation of the polis.
21. Bustani, *NS*, Pamphlet 5, 1 November 1860.
22. Bustani, *NS*, Pamphlet 7, 19 November 1860.
23. Bustani, *NS*, Pamphlet 3, 15 October 1860.

24. Bustani, *NS*, Pamphlet 6, 8 November 1860.
25. Ibid.
26. Bustani, *NS*, Pamphlet 2, 8 October 1860.
27. *Nafir Surriya, al-muʿalim* Butrus Bustani, editor unknown (Beirut, 1990).
28. Austin, J. L., *Philosophical Papers* (Oxford: Oxford University Press, 1979).
29. Refer to Honig, Bonnie, 'Declarations of Independence: Arendt and Derrida on the Problem of Founding a Republic', *American Political Science Review* 85(1) (1991): 97–113.
30. Hamacher, Werner, 'On the Right to Have Rights', *New Centennial Review* 14(2) (2014): 169–214.
31. Ibid.
32. Bustani, *NS*, Pamphlet 2, 8 October 1860.
33. Derrida, Jacques, 'Declarations of Independence', *New Political Science* 7(1) (1986): 7–15, at 11.
34. Bustani, *NS*, Pamphlet 4.
35. Al-Bustani, *NS*, Pamphlet 5.
36. Bustani, *NS*, Pamphlet 1, 29 September 1860.
37. Agamben argues that sovereign power is premised on the production and exclusion of bare human life for the purposes of justification of its legitimacy. Giorgio Agamben, *Homo Sacer: Sovereign Power and Bare Life*, trans. D. Heller-Roazen (Stanford: Stanford University Press, 1998).
38. Santner, *On the Pscyhotheology of Everyday Life*, p. 101.
39. Bustani, *NS*, Pamphlet 4.
40. Ibid.
41. Bustani, *NS*, Pamphlet 7
42. Bustani, *NS*, Pamphlet 6.
43. Bustani, *NS*, Pamphlet 3.
44. Ibid.
45. Ibid.
46. Bustani, *NS*, Pamphlet 3.
47. Pamphlets 6 through 9 were dedicated to drawing out a ledger for calculating the losses and gains for the nation.
48. Bustani, *NS*, Pamphlet 2.
49. Bustani, *NS*, Pamphlet 7.
50. Bustani, *NS*, Pamphlet 3.
51. Bustani, *NS*, Pamphlet 5.

52. Bustani's Speech on social organisation, *Khuṭba fi al-hay'a al-'ijtima'iyya* (1869), carries the same task forward by providing an anthropological description beholden to American Puritanism. In it Bustani draws out an understanding of society based on distinguishing social spheres from each other: the religious, the moral, the economic, and the political.
53. Rober Meister further argues in relation to this point: 'To believe that we are living after evil and before justice is the essence of what it means to live in a secular age. Secularity is always a secondary concept, defined by whatever element of the sacred is absent from it, and by how that element of sacredness would be conceived'. Meister, Robert, *After Evil: A Politics of Human Rights* (New York: Columbia University Press, 2011), p. 12.
54. In fact, in Bustani's dictionary (*Muhit al-muhit* [Beirut, 1998], p. 301), *diyana* and *dayn* are listed under one entry *danahu*. He defines *diyana* as 'a word for all the ways in which God is worshiped, *milla* and *madhab*, plural form diyanat'. And *al-dayn*: 'infinitive noun, meaning a postponed loan'.
55. Ibid.
56. Hamacher, Werner, 'Guilt History: Benjamin's Sketch "Capitalism as Religion"', *diacritics* 32(3–4) (2002): 81–106.
57. Bustani, *NS*, Pamphlet 7.
58. Ibid.
59. Ibid.
60. Ibid.
61. Bustani, *NS*, Pamphlet 9.
62. Refer to Santner, Eric, *The Royal Remains: The People's Two Bodies and the Endgames of Sovereignty*.
63. Bustani, *NS*, Pamphlet 4.
64. Bustani, *NS*, Pamphlet 1.
65. Makdisi, 'After 1860'.
66. Bustani, *NS*, Pamphlet 1
67. Bustani, *NS*, Pamphlet 2.
68. Bustani, *NS*, Pamphlet 7.
69. Ibid.
70. Bustani, *NS*, Pamphlet 2.
71. Bustani, *NS*, Pamphlet 7.
72. Marx, Karl, *The Grundrisse: Foundations of the Critique of Political Economy*, trans. Martin Nicolaus (London: Penguin, 1973), p. 86.

73. Bustani, 'Introduction', in *al-Tuhfa*; Bustani, *NS*, Pamphlet 11. Refer to the discussion of the Robinson Crusoe translation in Nadia Bou Ali, 'Butrus al-Bustani and the Shipwreck of the Nation', *Middle Eastern Literatures* 16/3 (2013), 266–81. Bustani , 'Introduction', in Bustani, *al-Tuḥfa Bustaniya fi al-asfār al-kurūziyya* (Bustani's Masterpiece of Crusoe's Travels) (Beirut, 1860).
74. Bustani, 'Hub al-watan min al-iman' (The Love of the Nation Is an Act of Faith), *al-Jinan* 1 (1871): 303–6, at p. 303.
75. The execution of the Khazen feudal family by the peasants was a pivotal moment during the violence as it provoked increased interference and interest from the Ottoman governors as well as local and foreign merchants. This family represented the tax-farming system: its execution at the hands of the peasants repositioned the Maronite Church and the Beiruti notables against the peasants.
76. Bustani, *NS*, Pamphlet 6.
77. Ibid.
78. Ibid.
79. Bustani, *Khuṭba fi al-hay'a al-'ijtimā'iyya*, 7.
80. Ibid.
81. Bustani, *NS*, Pamphlet 3.
82. Bustani, *NS*, Pamphlet 3.
83. Bustani, *NS*, Pamphlet 1, 2, 4.
84. Meister, *After Evil*, analyses the triad of perpetrator/beneficiary/victim in relation to national reconciliation projects post-1990. He also constructs parallels with postwar Lincolnian ideas on reconciliation in the late nineteenth century. The innocence of national subjects is made possible through projective identification with good victims that seek no retribution, as well as the repudiation of their status as beneficiaries through the avowal of collective guilt.
85. Bustani, *NS*, Pamphlet 3.
86. Karatani, *Structure of World History*, p. 213.
87. Bustani, *NS*, Pamphlet 11, 22 April 1861.
88. Bustani, *NS*, Pamphlet 9.
89. Ibid.
90. Ibid.
91. Hamacher, 'Guilt History', p. 93.
92. Bustani, *NS*, Pamphlet 6.

93. Bustani, *NS*, Pamphlets 6, 7, 8, 9.
94. Ibid.
95. Ibid.
96. The unification of monetary values had already been under way since the mid- nineteenth century; refer to P. L. Cottrell, Monika Pohl Fraser, and Ian Fraser, eds., *East Meets West: Banking, Commerce, and Investment in the Ottoman Empire* (London: Taylor and Francis, 2008); and Sevket Pamuk's *A Monetary History of the Ottoman Empire* (Cambridge: Cambridge University Press, 2000). Also, 1860 was the first moment of humanitarian intervention in the Levant – an international tribunal was convened comprising Prussian, French, Ottoman and British delegates. These proceedings were recently compiled and published in three volumes: Father Antoine Daw, ed., *Ḥawādith 1860 fi lubnan wa dimashq, lajnat bayrūt al-dawliya, al-maḥ ādir al-kamila* (The Events of 1860 in Lebanon and Damascus: The Beirut International Tribunal Complete Proceedings) (Beirut, 1996).
97. Bustani, *NS*, Pamphlet 6.
98. This has a similar structure to the late nineteenth-century intellectual arguments in the Muslim world that Faisal Devji describes in 'Apologetic Modernity', *Modern Intellectual History* 4(1) (2007): 61–76. Devji analyses the apologetic stance through which modernity was appropriated by Muslim intellectuals at the end of the nineteenth century, by which modernity was conceived in moral terms: 'Modernity was being conceived in the classical terms of a beautiful life rather than in those of citizenship, even though this art of living had now come to constitute the morality of a new kind of national community, which did not participate in the life of a state. Ethics, in other words, was not a kind of citizenship, and Islam was not a kind of state, but both might well have served as ciphers for the citizenship and state that were denied to colonial subjects in general and minority populations in particular. The Muslim community for which the Aligarhists spoke was in fact a nation in suspense, one that struggled to position itself in a non-demographic space to avoid a politics determined by categories of majority and minority'. Devji argues that the response to modernity was cultural and moral, and posited counter to the legal and political categories of the state.
99. Bustani, *NS*, Pamphlet 6.
100. Ibid.
101. Bustani, '*Hub al-watan min al-iman*', p. 303.

102. Bustani, *NS*, Pamphlet 6.
103. Ibid.
104. For discussion of the case of the French revolution refer to Sewell, 'The French Revolution and the Emergence of Nation Form'; and for a discussion of history and repetition in relation to the nation form refer to Kojin Karatani's *History and Repetition* (New York: Columbia University Press, 2011).
105. Bustani, *NS*, Pamphlet 7.
106. Bustani, *NS*, Pamphlet 3.
107. Ibid.
108. Bustani, *NS*, Pamphlet 7.
109. Ibid.
110. It is important to note that in Bustani's *Muhit* dictionary, *Nafīr Surrīya* is added to the entry under *al-nafar* and following the subentry *nafīr*: 'a trumpet or horn, Persian. The *Nafīr Surrīya* are hopes of ours that we had published during the events of AD 1860 in eleven pamphlets we called then the nationalist papers, *wataniyat*'.
111. Sheehi, Stephen, *Foundations of Modern Arab Identity* (Gainesville, FL: University Press of Florida, 2004).
112. Girard, René, *Violence and the Sacred* (London: W. W. Norton, 2005), p. 7.
113. Robert Meister's discussion of religious anthropology in *After Evil* is seminal here.
114. Girard, *Violence and the Sacred*, p. 7.
115. Ibid. p. 1.
116. Bustani, *NS*, Pamphlet 6.
117. Bustani, *NS*, Pamphlet 5.
118. Bustani, *NS*, Pamphlet 3.
119. Bustani, *NS*, Pamphlet 1.
120. Bustani, *NS*, Pamphlet 4.

Conclusion

1. Bustani, *Khutba*, p. 4.
2. Bustani, *Khutba*, p. 2.
3. Needless to point out, this is a properly Hegelian point. Hegel's understanding of progress in his philosophy of history is precisely directed at the thinking of origins as the impossibility of remaining. Historical origins are animated

by the restlessness and negativity of the universal. History is the movement of self-consciousness as it suffers violence at its own hands in its constant movement of going beyond itself: as the inability of Spirit to fully realise itself.

4. Butrus al-Bustani, *Da'irat al-Ma'arif* (Encyclopaedia of Knowledge), vol. 6, p. 244.
5. This absolute realism of capitalist society is diagnosed by a number of thinkers, such as Fredric Jameson, Mark Fisher and Slavoj Žižek.
6. Butrus al-Bustani, *Khutba fi Adab al-'Arab*, Jafet Library, American University of Beirut, NBMVA Mic-A:548, p. 39. 'The Nineteenth Century' has become a categorical expression that reflects both ways: for people who saw themselves as part of 'an age' or 'an era' – like Butrus al-Bustani, for instance (tradition leading up to Marx and Weber) – and for those who commit to the conception of modernity as a radically new age of humanity.
7. Ibid. p. 39.
8. Refer to Shidyaq's '*Fi 'uluhiyat don quixote*', in *Mukhtarat*, pp. 100–4.
9. Cf. Watt, Ian, 'Defoe And Richardson On Homer: A Study of the Relation of Novel and Epic in the Early Eighteenth Century', *The Review of English Studies* 3(12) (October 1952): 330.
10. The romanticist invocation of myth as a response to Enlightenment rationality, is always an attempt to claim that the reconciliation between reason/science and art/poetry has always been there to begin with. Of course romanticists do not cease to stumble on the horrors and uncanny elements in stories of origin, there is a terror to be also discovered in myth, there are sublime beauties that are also monstrous: Medusa in particular presents this incomprehensible difference between horror and beauty.
11. Cf. Watt, 'Robinson Crusoe as Myth', p. 117.
12. Butrus al-Bustani, *Da'irat al-Ma'arif*, vols. 1–11. (Beirut: Dār al-Ma'rifa, n.d.). The dictionary was compiled between 1867 and 1882, and ironically it remained incomplete at the last entry, Ottoman.
13. *Da'irat al-Ma'arif*, vol. 4, p. 466.
14. Ibid. p. 466.
15. Ibid., p. 466.
16. Ibid., p. 466.
17. Ibid., p. 466.
18. Butrus al-Bustani, *al-Hay'a al-ijtima'iya, w-al-muqabala bayn al-'awa'id al-'arabiya w-al-ifranjiya* (On Social Organisation and the Comparison

between Arab and European Cultures) 1849, American University of Beirut Archive and Special Collections.
19. Nadia Bou Ali, 'Butrus al-Bustani and the Shipwreck of the Nation, *Middle Eastern Literatures: Incorporating Edebiyat*' 16(3) (2013): 266–81.
20. Bustani, *Al-Hay'a al-'Ijitima'iya*, p. 17.
21. Refer to Frank Ruda's discussion of this in 'Marx in the Cave' (in *Reading Marx*, p. 75).
22. This does not imply that overcoming alienation is equivalent to the overcoming of alienation, but that there is a prior layer of alienation, which is constitutive of the human condition, but which comes to be mediated by the alienated social forms of capital such as the commodity and value.
23. Cf. Damisch, Hubert's two articles, 'Robinsonnades I: The Allegory' and 'Robinsonnades II: The Real Robinson', *October* 85 (Summer 1998), pp.19–40 and pp. 28–40.
24. Bustani, *al-Tuhfa al-Bustaniya fi al-asfar al kuruziya*, p. 98.
25. Ibid.
26. Bustani, *al-Tuhfa al-Bustaniya fi al-asfar al kuruziy*, p. 101.
27. Ibid. p. 161.
28. Marx, *Grundrisse*, p. 84
29. Dolar, 'I shall be with you on your wedding night', p. 13.
30. Ibid.
31. Ibid.
32. Cf. Lacan's elaborations on obsession in *Seminar X*.
33. Butrus al-Bustani, *Khutba fi al-hay'a al-ijtima'iya*, 1869, p. 18.
34. Ibid. p. 18.
35. Ibid. p. 20
36. Ibid. p. 21
37. Ibid. p. 22.
38. Ibid. p. 22.
39. Ibid. p. 32.
40. Ibid. p. 34.
41. Ibid. p. 39.
42. Ibid. p. 41.
43. Yusif Qazma al Khuri *Mukhtarat min ahmad faris al-shidyaq*, 'fi al'adat', p. 171.
44. Samuel Beckett, 'Proust' in *Proust and Three Dialogues with Georges Duthuit* (London: John Calder Publishers, 1999 [1931]) p. 19.

45. Shidyaq translates a selection from Quixote and deems the story as one of the best ever written, 'On the Divinity of Cervantes's Don Quixote', *Mukhtarat min ahmad faris al-shidyaq*, pp. 100–2.
46. Rasula, Jed, 'When the Exception is the Rule: *Don Quixote* as Incitement to Literature', *Comparative Literature* 51(2_ (Spring 1999): 125; 123–51.
47. Jameson, Fredric, *The Political Unconscious: Narrative as a Socially Symbolic Act* (Ithaca: Cornell University Press, 1981), p. 152.
48. Brassier, Raymond, 'Concrete-in-Thought, Concrete-in-Act: Marx, Materialism, and the Exchange Abstraction', *Crisis and Critique* 5(1): pp. 111–29.
49. *Nafir Suriya*, Pamphlet 10, 24 February 1861. Around the same time, Stratford Canning, the British ambassador to Constantinople, stated that 'Europe is at hand with its science, its labour, and its capital. The Koran, the harem, and Babel of languages are no doubt so many obstacles to advancement in a Western sense'. The Arabic tongues signified to Canning as they did to Eli Smith the missionary. In a speech for the Syrian Science Society in 1859, Smith told the audience the following: 'Your Arab race's [*jins*] literary corpus [*adab*] is a ring in the chain that connects the ancient world adorned with the sciences of the Romans and the Greeks to the modern world that is adorned with the sciences and civilisation of the Europeans [Europe the righteous inheritor of the Greeks] . . . Although your tongue is no longer deeply related to the past, it is related in terms of language kinship to ancient languages whose lexica has survived and in which we are presently involved in with intricate research . . . thus your tongue may shed some light on some of the mysterious phrases of these dead languages. And if I may add, an image of a ruin, or an inscription on a rock or a prologue to a book or a sentence in your many written texts that your people have rarely thought of might add to the treasures of knowledge sought after by scholars in European countries'.
50. The views on what defines 'useless' words varied. For example, Bustani, in his introduction to the dictionary *Da'irat* complained about redundant synonyms in Arabic dictionaries (the hundreds of synonyms for 'camel'), words that are defined by metaphoric meanings (*majaz*) prior to the 'real' meaning (*haqiqi*), and that these metaphoric meanings needed to be eliminated from the dictionary of Arabic.
51. Bustani, *Khutba fi Adab al-'Arab*, p. 19.
52. Ibid. p. 19.
53. Ibid. p. 19.

54. After all Bustani compiles the first modern Arabic dictionary *Muhit al-muhit: ay Qamus muṭawwal li al-lughat al-'Arabiya* [The Circumference of the Ocean: an expanded dictionary of the Arabic language], 1867–1870 (Beirut: Maktabat Lubnan, 1998 [1977]) as well as the first Arabic encyclopaedia, *Da'irat al-ma'arif*, vols. 1–11 (Beirut: Dar al-ma'rifa, n.d.).
55. Shidyāq, '*Fi usul al-siyasa*' (On the Principles of Politics), in *Mukhtarat*, p. 157.
56. Bustani, *al-Hay'a al-ijtima'iya*' (On the Social Organisation), p. 16.
57. Felix Ravaisson, *Of Habit* (London: Contiuum, 2008), p. 59.
58. Bustani, '*al-hurriya*' (Liberte'-y) in *Da'irat al-Ma'arif*, vol. 7, pp. 2–4
59. Shidyaq, *Leg Over Leg*, vol. 4, p. 389.
60. Ibid., p. 385.
61. Ibid., p. 375.
62. Ibid., p. 371.
63. Ibid., p. 379
64. Ibid., p. 379.

Index

'aada see habit
abstraction, 13, 166–7, 178
Adorno, Theodor, 177
agalma, 71–2
aggression, 56
alienation, 44–5, 47–8,
    163, 223n22
Althusser, Louis, 43
anxiety, 2, 3, 8, 14, 170–2
  and castration, 81–3
  and Crusoe, 167–8, 169
  and culture, 17
  and habit, 53–4, 177–82
  and language, 15–16
  and modernity, 163
  and Schreber, 202n49
  and Shidyaq, 39–40
aphanisis, 44, 76, 78, 83, 171
Arabic language, 1, 3, 6, 9–10
  and anxiety, 8–9
  and al-Bustani 5, 84–6, 179
  and community, 10–11
  and desire, 15–16
  and grammar, 70–1
  and misrecognition, 13–14
  and modernisation, 74
  and Shidyaq, 89–97, 124
  see also written language

Arabs, 173–5, 181, 224n49
Aristotle, 36, 39, 51, 53
As-Sirafi, 71
Augustine, St, 164
Austin, J. L., 142

Badiou, Alain, 11–12
Bag-men, 113–19
Banfield, Anne, 71
Baudelaire, Charles, 21
Beckett, Samuel, 176
Beirut, 14
Benveniste, Émile, 74
Bible, the, 4, 5
blasphemy, 113–15
body politics, 37
bourgeoisie, 165–6
Brown, Wendy, 51, 52–3
  and Freud, 54–5, 57–62, 65–6
  Subjects of Tolerance, 67–8
al-Bustani, Butrus, 3, 4–6, 9
  and anxiety, 83
  and Crusoe, 167–70
  and culture, 17–18
  Da'irat al ma'arif (*The Circumference
    of Knowledge*), 5, 85, 86, 88, 89,
    163–4
  and ego, 69

INDEX

and encyclopaedias, 84–9
and freedom, 181
and guilt, 153–5
and habit, 173–6, 177–8
Khutba fi adab al-'arab, 161–3
Khutbah fi 'al-hay'a al-ijtima'iya
   (A Speech on the Social Formation),
   164–7
and language, 178–9
and liberalism, 149–52
and *lugha*, 72
Nafir Surriya (*The Clarion of Syria*),
   137–8, 140–9, 152–61, 188n30
and nation, 14, 141–6, 158–60
and religion, 138–41, 146–9
and society, 182
and studies, 184n6

Canning, Stratford, 224n49
capitalism, 13, 16–17, 98, 115–19
   and abstraction, 178
   and al-Bustani, 164–7
   and desire, 209n64
   and fetishism, 46–7
   and Market-men, 113–20
   and modernity, 37–9
   and reciprocity, 152–6
   and Shidyaq, 176–7
   and universality, 49
Cartesian subject, 51, 53
castration, 80, 81–3
Chiesa, Lorenzo, 75–6
Christianity *see* Maronites; Protestantism
citizenship, 14
civil society, 142, 150–1
civil war, 14, 126, 137, 139, 140–6
civilisation, 55, 56, 61–2, 163, 205n94
   and language, 84–5, 92–3
   and neurosis, 22, 24, 172–3
class, 17, 165–6
cogito, 51–2
colonialism, 10, 48–9
commodities, 36, 46, 113–20, 176
community, 10–11, 62, 143–4
condensation (*Verdichtung*), 23–4, 25, 30
consciousness, 22, 175; *see also*
   unconsciousness

Creech, James, 87
Crusoe, Robinson *see* Robinson Crusoe
culture, 1, 2, 3, 11
   and al-Bustani 161–3, 165
   and Crusoe, 168
   and Freud, 56–8
   and liberalism, 16–18, 48–51, 53
   and Lukács, 188n34
   and politics, 67, 68

de Man, Paul, 19–21, 33, 189n3
death, 55–6
debt (*dayn*), 138, 146–9, 153–6
Defoe, Daniel
   Pilgrim's Progress, 172
   see also Robinson Crusoe
Derrida, Jacques, 143
Descartes, René, 32, 51
desire, 8, 15–16, 30, 45–6, 64
   and capitalism, 209n64
   and castration, 80–3
   and mothers, 90
   and sodomy, 102–3
despotism, 2, 35–6, 134–5
Devji, Faisal, 220n98
dictionaries, 5, 6, 10, 84, 85
Diderot, Denis, 87
discontent, 55–6
discourse community, 11
displacement (*Verscheibung*), 23–4, 25, 30
diyaana (religion), 146–9
Dolar, Mladen, 29, 32, 52, 56
Don Quixote (Cervantes), 177
dreamwork, 23–4, 25, 64
drive, 55–8, 62

ego, 44–5, 47–8, 52, 69
   and Freud, 54–5, 59–61
   and language, 76–7
   and Shidyaq, 79
emancipation, 48
encyclopaedia, 5, 10, 83–4, 85–9, 163–4
Engels, Friedrich, 125
Enlightenment, 35, 36, 40, 163
   and culture, 50, 51
   and encyclopaedias, 87, 88
enunciation, 32, 41, 52, 76, 77, 78, 79

equivocation, 72–4, 78, 91, 95
Europeans, 173–5, 181, 224n49

fantasy, 30–1, 34–41, 61, 127–8, 149–52
  and feminisation, 120–3, 132–3
Fariyaq/Fariyaqa, 18, 34–5, 69, 90, 108–13, 182–3
  and buttocks, 100–3
  and character, 125
  and fantasies, 120–1, 123
  and grammar, 95–6
  and literature, 103–4
  and marriage, 135–6
  and pleasure, 106–8
  and social order, 130–1
  and trade, 113–18
  and women, 128–30, 212n144
feminine, 18, 201n39
feminisation, 120–3
Ferenczi, Sandor, 80
fetishism, 36, 46–7
feudalism, 17
Foucault, Michel, 63, 68, 87, 104, 177
  History of Sexuality, 38–9
fratricide, 157–8
freedom, 2, 16, 52–3, 181; see also unfreedom
French Revolution, 214n4, 221n104
Freud, Sigmund, 63–4, 80, 171–2, 208n49, 210n100
  Beyond the Pleasure Principle, 29
  Civilisation and Its Discontents, 55–9, 61–2, 205n94
  and ego, 54–5, 125
  Group Psychology and the Analysis of the Ego, 59–61, 62–3, 65–6
  and homoeroticism, 102, 212n129
  Moses and Monotheism, 66–7
  and negation (*Die Verneinung*), 23–5, 44–5
  and unconscious, 41–2, 77

Girard, René, 158–9
grammar, 35, 70–2, 83–4, 92–7
Grosrichard, Alain, 35–6, 131
group formation, 55, 57–62, 65–6
guilt, 138, 152–6

habit (*'aada*), 6, 15, 40, 53–4
  and anxiety, 177–82
  and al-Bustani, 164, 165–6, 173–6
al-Hamadthani, 105
Hegel, Georg Wilhelm Friedrich, 32, 54, 181, 189n3, 196n136, 221n3
Heidegger, Martin, 19
  Being and Time, 20
history, 19–21, 24–5, 153, 162–3, 189n3, 221n3
  and al-Bustani 84, 85
homo economicus, 167
homoeroticism, 102, 116
hospitality, 102, 103, 104
Hourani, Albert
  Arabic Thought in the Liberal Age, 138
humanism, 138–40
humans, 163–4

Ibn Athir, 85
Ibn Hazm, Abu Rushd 'Brains'
  The Book of Balancing the Two States and Comparing the Two Straits (*Kitab Muwazanat al-halatayn wa-murazant al-alatayn*), 105–6
Ibn Rushd, 105
ifranja language, 179
ignorance, 99
imaginary, 7–8
inheritance, 113–19
instincts, 55
Islam, 4

Jameson, Fredric, 186n22
al-Janna (periodical), 5
al-Jawa'ib (newspaper), 3, 4
al-Jinan (journal), 5
jouissance, 25, 26–7, 28, 30–1, 33, 63, 66
  and pleasure, 103–8
  and satisfaction, 55–6, 57, 164–5
Joyce, James, 21–2, 25–7, 31–4, 211n113
Judaism, 66
al-Junayna (*The Garden*) (newspaper), 5

Kant, Immanuel, 52–3
Kantorowicz, Ernst H., 37
Karatani, Kojin, 209n64

INDEX

Kierkegaard, Søren, 29
knowledge, 85–9, 99, 163, 180, 208n44

La Boétie, Étienne de
  The Discourse of Voluntary Servitude, 2, 39
labour, 14, 17, 149–52
  and al-Bustani, 152, 155, 166–7
Lacan, Jacques, 7, 8, 23, 43–4, 51, 199n17
  and anxiety, 82, 171–2
  and ego, 52
  and *jouissance*, 66
  and Joyce, 21–2, 25, 26, 32–4
  and language, 76–7, 78
  and linguistics, 74
  and Marx, 46
  and mirror stage, 47–8
  and modernity, 38–9
  and psychoanalysis, 63
  Seminar on the Purloined Letter, 28–31
  Seminar XXIII, 27–8
  and unconscious, 42, 75–6
lack, 172
lalangue (language of the unconscious), 21–2, 72–3, 78–9, 92
language, 20–1, 174, 178–9
  and ego, 76–7
  and pleasure, 103–4, 108
  and unconscious, 43
  see also Arabic language; grammar; *lalangue*; linguistics; speech; written language
law, 158–60
Lebanese Civil War, 141–2
Lee, Samuel, 4
Leg Over Leg (*al-Saq 'ala al Saq*) (al-Shidyaq), 4, 72–3, 90, 124–6, 133–4
  and number 13, 104–5
  and women, 132–3
  see also Fariyaq/Fariyaqa
Lévi-Strauss, Claude, 74
liberalism, 16–18, 48–54, 67–8, 149–52
  and Freud, 54–5, 57–8, 59, 61–2
  see also neoliberalism
linguisteriks, 98, 108, 110–12
linguistics, 10–11, 41, 71, 73–5

literary mode, 19–22, 25–7
literature, 19–21, 27–8, 29–30, 33–4, 177, 186n22
lituratterre, 26, 27–8, 31–3
Locke, John, 209n56
logic, 70–1, 74
love, 59, 60, 159–60
lugha, 9–10, 15, 72–3, 124
Lukács, Georg, 165, 177, 188n34

Macherey, Pierre, 126
Makdisi, Usama, 138–9, 140
maqama, 104–5
Maronites, 3–4, 137
Marx, Karl, 16, 30, 36, 63, 154
  and capitalism, 115, 116–17
  Communist Manifesto, 125
  and fetishism, 36, 46
  and habit, 54
  and history, 189n3
  and liberalism, 48
  and secularism, 216n9
materialism, 11–12
mathematics, 71
Medusa, 80–3
metaphor, 30, 93, 95, 113–14
metathesis, 91–2
metonymy, 30
Milner, Jean-Claude, 104, 198n3
mirrors, 6–8, 44, 47–8, 80, 85, 171
modernity, 10, 11, 16, 186n17, 220n98
  and de Man, 19–21
  and desire, 45–6
  and fantasy, 34–41
  and Shidyaq, 79–80
  and spectres, 125–6
monarchy, 1–2, 156–7
Montesquieu, 35
  Persian Letters, 131
morality, 15, 120–1, 154
Mount Lebanon, 3–5, 14, 102, 137
  and humanitarian aid, 154, 155
multiculturalism, 51
myth, 163, 167, 222n10

nahda (intellectual movement), 3, 10, 138–9, 180

name-of-the-father, 2, 18, 26, 33, 81
   and Crusoe, 168–9
   and Freud, 66
   and al-Shidyaq, 123
Napoleon, Louis, 156–7
narcissism, 2, 7, 59
Nasser, Gamel Abdel, 2
nation, 14–15, 90, 156–9, 214n4
   and al-Bustani, 137–8, 140–2
   see also nationalism
national identity, 10, 11
nationalism, 140–6, 152–6
necromancy, 156–60
negation, 23–4, 44–5
neoliberalism, 63, 68
Nietzsche, Friedrich, 20, 21, 154
Nobus, Daniel, 27

objet a, 26–7, 28, 33, 45–6, 171–2
ontology, 87
Oriental despotism, 35–6
origins, 161, 162
Other, the, 7, 8, 29, 43–4
   and Crusoe, 168, 169–70
   and desire, 45–6, 82, 172–3
   and despotic power, 35, 36
   and language, 76–7
   and love, 60
   and psychoanalysis, 66
   and unconscious, 42–3
Ottoman Empire, 4, 6, 14, 34–7, 98–100, 147
   and *tanzimat* reforms, 137, 149
Ovid, 7

paraphrases, 91–2
parapraxis, 91–2
paternity, 1–2, 103, 110–11, 135–6,
   see also name-of-the-father
peasant uprisings, 14, 156–7, 214n1, 219n75
Peirce, Charles Sanders, 74, 75, 199n16–17
phallus, 80–1, 82–3, 202n46
phonology, 108
Plato, 104

pleasure *see jouissance*
politics, 37, 50, 62, 67, 68
   and God, 35, 143–5, 153–4, 178
   and religion, 138–41
   and violence, 145–6, 152–5
   God, 35, 143–5, 153–4, 178
poststructuralism, 63
power, 1, 35–6, 38–9, 134–5
prolepsis, 87, 88–9, 163
Protestantism, 3, 4–5, 113–14, 138
psychoanalysis, 21, 27–8, 64–5
   and culture, 50, 51
   and Joyce, 26–7, 31
   and language, 76
   see also Freud, Sigmund

Rabaté, Jean-Michel, 123, 125
race, 48
Real, the, 23, 25–6, 31–2
real abstraction, 13, 46, 67, 68–9, 167, 177–8
reason, 51
reflection, 80, 86
religion, 1, 66–8, 146–9, 138–41; *see also* Maronites; Protestantism
repetition, 21, 22–3, 25–6, 28–9
repression (*Verdangung*), 23–4, 25
   and Freud, 41–2, 56, 57–8, 61
Robinson Crusoe (Defoe), 17–18, 69, 83, 138
   and alienation, 163
   and anxiety, 172
   and al-Bustani, 149, 150–2, 167–70
   and liberalism, 149, 150–2
   and myth, 163
   and nationalism, 138

Sacks, Jeffrey, 140
Safouan, Mustapha, 2, 3
   Why Are the Arabs Not Free?, 1
Said, Edward, 1
Santner, Eric, 17, 37–8, 138, 193n62, 208n49
al-Saq 'ala al Saq see Leg Over Leg
Sartori, Andrew, 16
satisfaction, 55–6, 57, 164–5

Saussure, Ferdinand de, 74, 75
savoir-faire, 99
Schreber, Daniel, 37–8, 193n62, 208n49, 210n100
　Memoirs, 134
science, 163, 174
sectarianism, 14, 138–41, 143, 156
secularism, 67–8, 216n9
semiotics, 74–6
servitude, 1, 2, 8, 39, 46
sexuality, 18, 25, 100–4, 121–2
　and fantasy, 127–9
　and Freud, 56, 57
　and Joyce, 26–7
　see also castration
al-Shidyaq, Ahmad Farid, 3–4, 6
　and anxiety, 83
　and buttocks, 100–3
　and capitalism, 176–7
　and ego, 69
　al-Jasus 'ala al-qamus (*The Spy on the Dictionary*), 4, 74, 89
　Kashf al-mukhaba 'an tamaddun urupa wa-al-wasita fi ma'rifat ahwal malta (*The Unveiling of European Civilisation's Secrets and the Means of Knowing the Conditions of Malta*), 4
　and knowledge, 180
　and *lalangue*, 72, 79–80
　and language, 89–97
　and lineage, 111–12
　and linguistics, 74
　and literature, 103–4
　and *lugha*, 9–10
　and pleasure, 104–8
　and religion, 113–14
　and scribal work, 98–100
　Secrets of the Night in Metathesis and Substitution, The (*Sirr al-layali fi al-qalb w al-ibdal*), 89, 91
　and sexuality, 18
　and social conditions, 126–7, 182
　Spy on the Dictionary, The, 4, 74, 89
　and women, 121–3, 127–9
　see also Leg Over Leg

al-Shidyaq, Asa'd, 113
signifier, 15, 44, 74–5
　and autonomy, 41, 42, 43, 77–8
　and puns, 96
sinthome (writing as symptom), 21–2, 25–7, 28, 31–2
slips of the tongue, 38, 41, 65, 76, 78, 177
Smith, Adam, 151
Smith, Eli, 4, 5
society, 5, 14–15, 163–7; *see also* capitalism; civil society
sodomy, 100–3, 127–8
sorrow, 129–30
sovereignty, 36–8, 147
specular image, 7–8
speech, 1, 2, 11, 15, 76–7, 78–9; *see also lalangue*; *lugha*
subjectivity, 13–14, 41–4, 51–2, 208n44
substitution, 91–2
symbolic, 7, 8, 14, 17, 25–8, 29
　and fantasy, 30–1
　and gender, 201n39
　and Joyce, 22–4
　and psychoanalysis, 206n20
　and subject, 13, 15
　and textuality, 20
symptom *see sinthome*

tahdhib (refinement), 173
tolerance, 54–5, 61, 67–8
Tomšič, Samo, 46
Tower of Babel, 178–9
transference love, 60
truth, 12–13

umma, 80, 83, 86, 90
uncanny, 13, 14
unconscious, 21–2, 23–5, 31, 32–3
　and Freud, 41–2, 62–3
　and Lacan, 42–3, 75–6
　and language, 76–8
　and psychoanalysis, 64–5
　and subject, 51–2
undercapitalised parasites, 118–19
unfreedom, 1, 2
universality, 12–13, 14–15, 179–82

Van Dyck, Cornelius, 5
victimhood, 158–9
violence, 138–9, 143–6, 152–5, 156–9

al-watan see nation
Weber, Max, 154
Weltanschauung see worldview
women, 120–3, 127–9, 132–3, 201n39
World War I, 126

worldview (*Weltanschauung*), 48, 50, 63–5
written language, 1, 2, 3, 35, 98–100, 133–4; *see also* literary mode

al-Yaziji, Ibrahim, 7
al-Yaziji, Nasif, 5
Yunis, Abu Bishr Matta ibn, 71

Žižek, Slavoj, 39

EU representative:
Easy Access System Europe
Mustamäe tee 50, 10621 Tallinn, Estonia
Gpsr.requests@easproject.com

www.ingramcontent.com/pod-product-compliance
Lightning Source LLC
Chambersburg PA
CBHW070347240426
43671CB00013BA/2427